Eastern Phoenix

Wyggeston and Queen Eliza

Ple

EASTERN PHOENIX
Japan Since 1945

Mikiso Hane
KNOX COLLEGE

WestviewPress

A Division of HarperCollins*Publishers*

To my brothers and sisters

Copyright © 1996 by Westview Press, Inc., A Division of HarperCollins Publishers, Inc.
Published in 1996 in the United States of America by Westview Press, Inc., 5500 Central Avenue, Boulder, Colorado, 80301-2877, and in the United Kingdom by Westview Press, 12 Hid's Copse Road, Cumnor Hill, Oxford OX2 9JJ

Library of Congress Cataloging-in-Publication Data
Hane, Mikiso.
  Eastern phoenix : Japan since 1945 / by Mikiso Hane.
    p.   cm.
  Includes bibliographical references and index.
  ISBN 0-8133-1812-2 (hc).—ISBN 0-8133-1813-0 (pb)
  1. Japan—History—1945– I. Title.
DS889. H1986   1996
952.04—dc20

                                                              95–45849
                                                                  CIP

The paper used in this publication meets the requirements of the American National Standard for Permanence of Paper for Printed Library Materials Z39-1984.

10   9   8   7   6   5   4   3   2   1

Contents

+TRADE see 259

Preface and Acknowledgments

For many of us born years before 1945, reviewing developments since the end of World War II is like discussing current affairs. But if we consider the developments not in terms of years but in terms of the significant changes, Japan in the past half-century underwent far greater changes than in the century before 1945— that is, the century after the Meiji Restoration (1868)— or the half millennia before the Meiji Restoration.

In 1945 Japan was devastated by massive air attacks, and its people were traumatized by the atomic bombs and defeat in a war that their leaders had told them Japan was winning. Who could have imagined that from the ruined cities, where residents lived in tents and shacks, would in fifty years rise the second largest economic power in the world, a country with a respected place in the community of nations?

Following Japan's surrender to Allied powers on August 15, 1945, the U.S. occupation forces commanded by General Douglas MacArthur arrived and introduced revolutionary changes and reforms. The guiding principles of the Supreme Commander of the Allied Powers (SCAP) were freedom, democracy, equality, and justice. Japan was demilitarized; the emperor disclaimed his divinity, got off his white horse, and traveled about the land as a kindly old grandfather figure. A new constitution was adopted and democratic government instituted. Economic reforms were initiated: The elite conglomerates' stranglehold on the economy was loosened, and land reforms were put into effect. Education reforms were implemented, liberalizing the administrative system and the curriculum. And social reforms designed to foster equality were initiated. A bill of rights was introduced in the constitution providing for the political, civil, and social rights of all citizens. The status of women officially was made equal to that of men, and class distinctions were legally removed. The introduction of reforms, of course, did not mean the immediate realization of democracy, equality, freedom, and justice, but the process began and gradual improvements came about and continue to be made.

Unquestionably the area where the most spectacular developments occurred is the economic sector, with its burgeoning business enterprises and technological developments. The Japan that had been regarded as producer of cheap and shoddy goods began to produce high-quality automobiles, TVs, VCRs, and a whole host of high-tech electronic goods. Japanese name brands such as Sony, Toyota, Honda, Nikon, Seiko, and Yamaha gained recognition world-wide.

But all the dramatic outward changes that have unfolded in the past fifty years do not mean that Old Japan has disappeared forever. Many of the old traditions remain, especially in the social and psychological areas. Traditional attitudes, values, and behavior can still be found. The sense of Japanese uniqueness still persists. Western individualism has not replaced the strong attachment to the family and the community. Social conformity, social cooperation, and a sense of hierarchy are still strong in Japan. Traditional aesthetic values also have not disappeared, and creativity in the cultural arena remains vibrant. The island mind-set that prevailed in the prewar years has not vanished, but the voices of those who favor making the Japanese more internationally minded are getting stronger.

In the pages that follow, I have sought to survey the postwar developments and changes in all these areas. Japanese names have been presented in the traditional style, that is, surname first and given name second. The Hepburn system has been used for the transcription of Japanese names and terms.

I wish to thank my friends and colleagues at Knox College from whom I received much helpful advice, and my wife, Rose, and my daughters, Laurie and Jennifer, for their assistance and moral support. I also wish to express my appreciation to the readers who examined an early draft of the manuscript and made many helpful suggestions about the content, organization, and mode of elucidation. And I am especially grateful to the editorial staff of Westview Press, without whose assistance this history would not have been completed. Peter Kracht initiated and pushed forward this project, making many helpful suggestions. Michelle Asakawa oversaw the process to make certain that the manuscript was in publishable shape. And Michele Wynn meticulously scrutinized every word and sentence, striving to ensure that what I had written was logical, consistent, accurate, and clear. Needless to say, whatever errors and flaws that still remain are due to my carelessness and misperceptions.

Mikiso Hane

Introduction

August 6, 1945, the day the atomic bomb was dropped on Hiroshima, was a milestone in human history, marking the beginning of the atomic age. August 14, 1945, a landmark date in Japanese history, was the day on which the Japanese government admitted defeat in the war with the Allied powers and accepted the terms of the Potsdam Declaration and surrendered. On the 15th, the official date of surrender, the emperor publicly announced to the people his decision to end the war.

After the attack on Pearl Harbor on December 7, 1941, and following successful military campaigns in Southeast Asia and the Pacific islands, the Japanese leaders' dream of establishing the East Asia Coprosperity Sphere and forging a huge Japanese empire seemed to be on the verge of becoming reality. But the tide of the war turned as early as June 1942 when U.S. naval forces defeated the Japanese fleet in the Battle of Midway. By late 1942, U.S. marines had landed in Guadalcanal, and Japan was forced to shift to a defensive campaign. The Chinese, who had been subjected to Japanese aggression and the occupation of large sections of their country since the early 1930s, continued to resist the Japanese forces while the British were turning the tide against Japan on the Burma front. In 1943–1944, U.S. forces gained control of the Marshall and Mariana Islands in the Pacific and in late 1944 began launching massive air raids on Japanese cities from the air base in Saipan. The U.S. forces landed troops in Okinawa in April, 1945 and had subdued the Japanese forces there by June. By mid-1945, they had recaptured the Philippines. In August 1945, the final month of World War II, atomic bombs were dropped on Hiroshima and Nagasaki: the Soviet Union joined the war against Japan on August 8, and the end for Japan finally came on August 14.

Although August 14, 1945, marked a decisive turning point in Japanese history by designating the end of Japan's imperialistic dream and the beginning of peace, democracy, the rule of law, and the pursuit of economic gains, there were other defining points earlier in the course of Japanese history that had virtually transformed the nature of Japanese society, culture, and weltanschauung. A brief overview of these defining events follows.

The settlement of the Japanese islands by people from the Asian continent gave rise to the prehistoric Jomon (pre-250 B.C.) and Yayoi (ca. 250 B.C. to A.D. 250) cultures. The Jomon (cord markings) culture, which may have emerged as far back as 7,000 to 8,000 B.C., was named for its pottery, typically embedded with cords that made designs. The Jomon people were hunter-gatherers who lived in pit dwellings. The Yayoi culture was named for the area in Tokyo where the pots identified with their culture were discovered. The introduction of rice cultivation from the southern regions of the continent in the Yayoi period, around 100 B.C., was certainly a significant historical event because rice growing altered and molded the island dwellers' economic and social life.

The arrival of tribal groups from Korea, who vied with the chieftains in Japan for political control starting around the fourth century A.D., marks another important milestone in the political history of ancient Japan. Eventually one of the clan chieftains, whose descendants later claimed descent from the Sun Goddess, extended the clan's control from northern Kyushu to the central region of the main island, Honshu. The area of Honshu where Kyoto is located was known as Yamato, thus this era is referred to as the Yamato period (ca. A.D. 300 to 645).

From the cultural standpoint, a momentous development occurred with the introduction of Chinese civilization via Korea in the fifth century. This resulted not only in the adoption of the Chinese writing system but also in the infusion of Chinese literature, learning, and culture. The Chinese philosophy, Confucianism, and the Chinese religion, Buddhism, were also introduced by way of China and Korea and coexisted with the indigenous Shinto religion, an animistic, folk religion without any theological underpinnings.

Confucianism, with its focus on the precedence of family and group over the interests of individuals, came to define the social mores of Japan. Social principles such as harmony, social hierarchy (based on age, sex, and social status), proper human conduct, rectitude, decorum, and conformity were stressed. Buddhism soon spread from the aristocracy to the masses. Chinese civilization and Buddhism permanently altered Japanese culture, introducing a variety of art forms, ideas, and inventions—the fine arts, architecture, poetry, history, the calendar, the zodiac—as well as many other cultural features, ranging from chopsticks to tea, apparel, medicine, arts and crafts, new farming techniques, and principles of commerce.

Other Chinese practices, particularly legal, administrative, taxation, and land-holding methods, came to be adopted as the ruling class sought to establish its hegemony over the land. The Chinese practice of establishing a capital city was adopted, first at Nara in the year 710, then at Kyoto (known as Heian-kyo) in 794. The imperial court in Heian-kyo was be patterned after the Chinese court, with the emperor claiming to be the heavenly ruler. Chinese culture was first adopted, then adapted and Japanized. As a result, during the Heian period (794–1185), Japanese culture and literature flourished, producing the golden age of Japanese literature. For example, the classic *Tale of Genji* was written during this era by Lady Murasaki, a lady-in-waiting at the imperial court in the early eleventh century.

While the urban court aristocracy was wallowing in high culture, in the countryside a rival group was emerging, composed of military warriors, later known as the samurai, or *bushi*, who had developed their own chivalric code of conduct, called Bushido. These regional military clans were supported by loyal samurai vassals and steadily increased their holdings of tax-free estates. Eventually, they challenged the Heian court rulers.

The leader of the Minamoto clan, Yoritomo, defeated his opponents and gained political ascendancy. He established his power base in Kamakura and was appointed shogun by the imperial court in 1192. The imperial court remained in Heian-kyo, but power was now held by the shogunate, or *bakufu*. This period, therefore, marks the beginning of "feudal" Japan, insofar as the shogunate was founded on the lord-vassal relationship. This system of warrior rule lasted until 1867, with the shogunate periodically falling under the control of different warrior clans. Following more than one century of civil strife, as warlords called daimyo contended for power, finally peace and order was established under Tokugawa Ieyasu. He was appointed shogun in 1603 and laid the foundation for over two and one-half centuries of Tokugawa hegemony.

Japan was first exposed to the West in the sixteenth century when Portuguese traders arrived, with firearms; they were followed by Jesuit missionaries. To ensure their political control, the Tokugawa shoguns banned Christianity, in effect sealing the land off from the outside world (allowing limited access to only the Dutch, Chinese, and Koreans). In addition, they established a stringent system of control over the daimyo, who then numbered between 250 and 270, allowing them to govern their own land but making them pay homage to the shogun and abide by certain restrictions.

The Tokugawa shogunate, with its control over the land for over two and one-half centuries, virtually froze the social, economic, and political order, thereby exerting tremendous influence over the Japanese mode of thinking and way of life. Closing the country to the outside world contributed to congealing the ethnocentric island mentality. A rigid class system of samurai, peasants, craftsmen, and merchants was maintained, with the samurai class keeping the lower classes in place by virtue of the sword edge. The peasants were bound to the soil and were required to work the land to support the needs of the ruling class. During this time period, Confucianism was imposed as the official ideology, and only a minimal level of external influence was tolerated.

Even though the economy was based on agriculture, domestic commerce developed, and urban centers, like Tokyo (known then as Edo), and Osaka, and Kyoto, as well as daimyo castle towns, grew in size and flourished. The urban class of merchants and craftsmen developed a distinctive way of life and culture. Prose fiction, puppet and Kabuki (highly stylized plays) theater, wood-block printing, haiku (seventeen-syllable poems), and arts and crafts flourished among the townspeople.

The Tokugawa shogunate began to be confronted with an increasingly disenchanted populace—the result of growing economic difficulties and the emergence of proimperial ideology, Shinto nationalism, and the influence of Dutch learning. Peasant uprisings began to break out with greater frequency during the latter half of the Tokugawa era, and the samurai class as well as the shogunate and the daimyo began to experience acute financial difficulties. Then the coup de grâce was inflicted on the Tokugawa *bakufu* by the West with the arrival of the American Commodore Matthew Perry in 1853. Japan was then forced to open its doors to the West. This provided the opposition forces with an opportunity to challenge the shogunate and push for the restoration of imperial rule. In 1868, the imperial court, backed by the domains of Choshu (western Honshu) and Satsuma (southern Kyushu) reclaimed political authority, and Japan entered a new era with the young Meiji emperor placed on the throne. The sudden cultural, political, economic, social, and intellectual incursions from the West had an impact on the society that was as great, or even more dramatic, as the importation of Chinese culture had been in the past.

The restoration of the imperial court to power—referred to as the Meiji Restoration—set Japan on the path of an economic and military buildup (the slogan adopted by the Meiji government was "rich country, strong military"). The *bakufu* and daimyo domains were abolished, and the entire country was placed under the jurisdiction of the Meiji government. Then, certain aspects of Western political and legal institutions were adopted. The feudal class system was abolished, replaced by the institution of private ownership of land. Western industries and technology were imported, and the government set out to foster industry and trade. A modern army and navy, with universal military conscription, was built.

Further, a system of universal education was introduced, and emulation of Western art, literature, and culture followed. However, the Western liberal ideals of freedom, democracy, people's rights, and equality were not adopted, despite the initial push for "enlightenment and civilization" by a small circle of westernizers. In the mid-1880s, the educational system was transformed from the earlier liberal approach to a highly centralized system designed to indoctrinate students in a Shintoistic imperial credo upholding the myth of the imperial descent from the Sun Goddess. Thus, the notion of the "cult of the emperor" was instilled in all Japanese subjects to foster nationalistic sentiments. Traditional Confucian ideals were also stressed in the schools, through instruction on proper conduct and the importance of "knowing one's proper place."

In these ways, a new Japan with a government possessing centralized authority was established. In 1889, a constitution that lodged sovereignty in the emperor was adopted. A parliament, with limited male franchise, called the Diet, was established. It consisted of two houses, the House of Peers, which was composed of members from the newly established system of nobility, and the House of Representatives. But real power was held by a clique of court advisers, an oligarchy that came to be known as the genro (the elder statesmen).

The economy developed steadily during the Meiji years, and by the turn of the twentieth century, Japan had become a modern industrial nation. The most rapid increase in production occurred in the textile industry, with Japan becoming one of the world's major producers of silk. In addition, mining, the iron industry, shipbuilding and other strategic industries were promoted by the government. Commercial, financial, and industrial enterprises became concentrated in the holdings of a handful of major companies, and conglomerates known as *zaibatsu* (financial cliques) eventually dominated the economy. The Mitsui and Mitsubishi companies acquired monopolistic control over key sectors of the economy. Workers, however, remained subject to low wages, long hours, and adverse working conditions. The government, supporting the big-business industrial firms, kept any move to organize strong labor unions under strict control.

Although the process of industrialization was ongoing, the country still remained predominantly agrarian, and the peasants remained impoverished, with the percentage of tenant farmers continuously rising. In the early Meiji period, 20 percent of the land was farmed by tenant farmers. This figure rose to 45 percent by 1910. By the mid-1940s, 70 percent of the farmers were tenant farmers or were renting part of their farmland. Poverty compelled many poor workers and farmers to sell their daughters to houses of prostitution, whose existence was legal in prewar Japan.

Although Western-style legal systems were adopted, the concept of equality was not instituted. The Civil Code adopted in 1898 denied women equal rights with men, and social discrimination against women remained common at home and in the public domain. Also, despite abolition of the Tokugawa class system, class distinctions were retained, and people were classified into *kazoku* (nobles or peers), *shizoku* (the former samurai class), and *heimin* (commoners). People who had been categorized as "outcaste" members were labeled *shin-heimin* (new commoners).

In international relations, the new leaders of Japan emulated Western imperialism and set out to dominate their weaker neighbors. The move to extend Japanese influence into Korea resulted in clashes with China and war in 1894–1895. After defeating China, which was beset by internal divisions and Western imperialism, Japan went to war with Russia in 1904–1905 as a result of conflicts over the two nations' interests in Korea and Manchuria. After its victory over Russia, Japan annexed Korea in 1910.

In 1912, Emperor Meiji died and was succeeded by Emperor Taisho, who remained on the throne from 1912 to 1926. By participating in World War I on the side of the Western powers, when Germany lost Japan gained access to the German holdings in the Qingdao Peninsula and the Pacific. The victory of the democratic nations in this world conflict provided the proponents of democracy with an opportunity to push for democracy under Emperor Taisho. In 1925, a system of universal manhood suffrage was adopted, and during the 1920s, the practice of allowing the majority party in the lower house of the Diet to form the government was followed. Reform movements among workers, women, and the outcaste groups gained momentum in the Taisho years.

In the realm of foreign affairs, government leaders generally pursued a policy of international cooperation, taking part in international conferences like the 1921 Washington Conference that led to a naval arms limitation agreement by the United States, Great Britain, France, Italy, and Japan. But the move toward democracy and international cooperation foundered with the advent of the Great Depression, political crisis in Japan, and Japan's move to solve its economic difficulties by expanding on the continent.

These events resulted in the rise of ultranationalism and militarism, which meant a turn toward imperialism and totalitarianism, accompanied by the suppression of liberal, democratic elements. In March 1928 and April 1929, the Japanese government conducted mass arrests of Socialists and Communists and persecuted harborers of "dangerous thought." Among those arrested were Tokuda Kyuichi, who spent eighteen years in prison until he was released by the U.S. occupation forces in 1945. The rising militancy of right-wing nationalists, including civilians and young military officers, led to assassinations of political and business leaders of whom they disapproved. In 1931, army officers instigated an incident in Manchuria, where Japan had acquired mining and railroad rights following the Russo-Japanese War of 1904–1905. In the military campaign of 1931–1932 Japan conquered Manchuria and established a puppet government there.

This set the nation on the path of militarism and imperialism. The events in Manchuria fanned right-wing, ultranationalist extremism. In May 1932, a group of extremists, including young naval officers, assassinated Prime Minister Inukai Tsuyoshi, the head of a major political party called Seiyukai, thus bringing an end to party government. From this point on until its defeat in the Pacific War, Japan plunged into a state of fascism at home and imperialistic expansion abroad.

Domestically, right-wing extremists began to blame all the ills at home and abroad on "evil court advisers," corrupt politicians, and *zaibatsu* leaders. The army leadership split roughly into two factions. One was the Imperial Way Faction (Kodo-ha), whose members favored direct action to eliminate "evil" misguided leaders and to strengthen the imperial order. The other faction, called the Control Faction (Tosei-ha), was composed of army officers who believed that the necessary changes could be brought about without violence by using legitimate means under the leadership of the army central headquarters. The Imperial Way Faction was impatient with this approach and attempted to stage a coup d'état on February 26, 1936. The group assassinated a number of high-ranking officials, but the Emperor Showa (who had succeeded his father, Emperor Taisho, in 1926) took a hard stand and quashed the coup attempt.

This event resulted in the decline of the Imperial Way Faction, and the Control Faction gained ascendancy in the political arena. The group screened and chose the heads of government, thereby guiding the policy of imperialism. Among those who had gained the army leaders' approval and who were willing to cooperate with them was Prince Konoe Fumimaro, who played a key political role as Prime Minister just prior to the attack on Pearl Harbor and the consequent war with the United States.

Having abandoned the policy of working with the democratic nations, Japan turned to alliance with Germany and Italy. Pursuing an anti-Soviet policy, Japan signed the Anti-Comintern Pact with Germany in 1936. Italy joined the pact the following year. In 1940, Japan, Germany, and Italy concluded a military alliance, the Tripartite Pact, also referred to as the Axis Alliance. The clash of interests between Japan and the Soviet Union erupted in Russo-Japanese military conflicts between the two countries along the borders of Korea and Outer Mongolia.

The Japanese military action that ultimately led to the Pacific War was its invasion of China in 1937. After gaining control of Manchuria, the Japanese army set out to extend Japan's control into north China. Finally, in July 1937, Japan launched a major military campaign in China. This led to strained relations with the United States and other Western nations that had vested interests in Asia. In 1939 the United States abrogated its commercial treaty with Japan and imposed a limited trade embargo on Japan. In September, Japan moved into North Vietnam. In March 1941, negotiations for a new commercial treaty between Japan and the United States commenced, but certain issues, in particular, the U.S. proposal for Japanese withdrawal from China and the question of the applicability of the Tripartite Pact against the United States, could not be resolved. During the course of the negotiations, Japan moved into South Vietnam. This was clearly an indication of Japan's plan to move into Southeast Asia to gain access to the raw materials of the region, particularly oil. The United States froze Japanese assets in the United States and imposed an oil embargo on Japan.

This diplomatic impasse led to the resignation of Konoe as prime minister in October 1941. He was succeeded by General Tojo Hideki, who represented the hard-line officers in the army. When the negotiations reached a deadlock, Japanese government leaders, led by General Tojo, obtained the emperor's approval to go to war with the United States. The war commenced with the attack on Pearl Harbor on December 7, 1941.

After a series of successful campaigns at the outset of the war, the tide turned against the Japanese forces as U.S. military supremacy, especially on the sea and in the air, led to decisive U.S. victories. Then came total defeat and a devastated nation—and with that, the chance to start over from ground zero in 1945. The people of Japan had to cope with the discredited legacy of the cult of the emperor and the failures of major political and social beliefs, which had been embodied in authoritarianism, militarism and ultra-nationalism, imperialism, and the Confucian-based social ideology. A cultural and ideological vacuum thus pervaded Japanese society when the American forces arrived to remake and reshape Japan. Developments in Japan from that time through the mid-1990s are surveyed herein.

1

The End of the Pacific War

Japan had been in a virtual state of war since 1931, when it launched military operations in Manchuria. The Japanese then staged a massive invasion of China and successively conquered all of Southeast Asia, extending their military perimeter into the western Pacific. In 1942, Japan was forced to adopt a defensive strategy, after which it steadily lost its Pacific island bases. By August 1945, the Japanese were ready to end the war. After quibbling about the wording in the Potsdam Declaration, the Japanese government decided to accept the terms of surrender. Thus, Japanese military actions in East Asia, in which millions of people had been killed, were ended.

Exact figures on the number of deaths caused by Japanese military action are difficult to compute, but a United Nations (UN) estimate concluded that 9 million Chinese were killed in the war in China from 1937 to 1945. Counting the disruption and famine caused by the Japanese invasion, estimates of loss of life run anywhere from 11 to 15 million. Estimates of lives lost due to Japanese military actions in Southeast Asian countries run into the hundreds of thousands. Counting those who were killed by the Japanese forces and those who died of forced labor, starvation, and disease, it is estimated that 3 million people lost their lives in Java alone. Overall, it is estimated that 18 to 19 million people died in the military zone established by Japanese forces.

Korea, which was colonized by Japan in 1910, had millions of its people conscripted for military service and used as forced labor during the war. Over 230,000 Koreans were drafted into the Japanese army after 1938, and over 1 million were recruited to work in mines, factories, and on constructrion projects. After 1939, more than 140,000 people were conscripted to serve as workers in the military zone. About 150,000 of the Koreans drafted into the army died and of those conscripted to serve as laborers, 60,000 perished. Moreover, as will be discussed further on, thousands of women were conscripted to serve as "comfort women" for the Japanese troops in the numerous military zones.

Estimates of the numbers of Japanese lives lost are not precise either, but the Japanese government calculated the war dead in 1937–1945 to be 1,740,955. The number of military war dead in the Sino-Japanese War in 1937–1941 is calculated as 185,647. Army losses in the Pacific War are estimated to number 1,140,429, and navy losses, 414,879. Japanese civilian casualties in the Pacific war zone may have been as high as 650,000. Ten thousand civilians in Saipan and 150,000 Okinawans died in the battle zones. Those who succumbed to U.S. air attacks are estimated to number over 115,000 in Tokyo, over 70,000 in Nagasaki, and over 260,000 (including those who died later from the effects of atomic radiation) in Hiroshima. The total number of Japanese military and civilian deaths in the war is estimated at 2.1 million.[1]

Physically, Japan was in a shambles. The country had been devastated by the air raids, and most of its major cities lay in ruins. In all, 81 cities had been damaged by air raids. Tokyo had lost 57 percent of its dwellings, and Osaka, about 60 percent. Nationally about 20 percent of the houses had been destroyed by the air attacks, and roughly 8 million people had become homeless. Three years after the end of the war, 1 in 4 families still did not have regular dwellings. Those who had lost their homes lived in shacks, packing crates, corrugated iron lean-tos or slept in railroad station passageways. Makeshift huts remained in the major cities even a full decade after the war's end. The transportation system, telephones, power plants, and utilities were all on the verge of breaking down, having been subjected to maximum use without repair during the war. The U.S. air and naval attacks had destroyed 30 percent of Japan's industrial capacity, 80 percent of its shipping, and 30 percent of its thermal power. At the end of the war, industrial production stood at scarcely 10 percent of the normal prewar level. In January 1946, production was still severely depressed and had climbed to only 18.3 percent. In 1946, for the entire year, it remained at 30.7 percent of the 1934–1936 level.

Territorially, Japan had reverted to its status when Commodore Perry arrived in 1853. Japan had been compelled to relinquish Formosa, the Pescadores, Korea, and southern Sakhalin Island. The Kurile Islands were now occupied by the Soviet Union, and Okinawa was placed under American administration. Millions of soldiers and civilians from the former colonies and the occupied areas of the Asian mainland and Southeast Asia began to return to the already crowded Japanese islands.

The immediate problem—and a matter of life and death for the urban populace—was the food shortage. Bad weather had caused rice production to drop 27 percent below that of 1944, to a level about 32 percent below the prewar average. Having lost its colonial possessions, Japan could no longer obtain additional food from Korea, Formosa, or Manchuria.

The fishing industry, which Japan had relied on as a major source of food, had also deteriorated and was functioning about 40 percent below normal. Official food rations for each person per day came to 1,050 calories. The chief preoccupation of urban dwellers was scurrying about in search of additional food: "Housewives with babies on their backs lined up quietly for hours to obtain rice, sweet potatoes . . . Many people spent an inordinate amount of time in trains, jammed into unbelievably crowded cars, sitting on coach roofs, or clinging to engine 'cow-catchers,' on their way to scrounge for food in the countryside."[2] Hungry people scoured the black markets or went out into the villages to obtain sweet potatoes from the farmers, a venture that frequently ended in failure. A person who obeyed the law and abstained from getting food on the black market was apt to starve to death. One such man of principle, a judge in a Tokyo court, died of malnutrition in November 1947. He left behind a diary in which he had written:

> The food control law is a bad law. But as long as it is the law of the land we must observe it strictly. Regardless of how much agony it causes me I will not buy food in the black market. I have always respected Socrates' spirit when he readily accepted the punishment imposed on him though he knew it was a bad law. Today it is especially essential for people living in the land where the rule of law prevails to possess this spirit. I have decided to fight the black market and accept death by starvation. I live each day in the presence of death.[3]

Mass starvation of the Japanese people was avoided, however, because the American occupation authorities began transporting food to the country after spring 1946, following General Douglas MacArthur's request for emergency shipments of food and medicine. About eight hundred thousand tons of food was shipped to the country during the following year.[4]

The shortage of basic necessities and the issuance of a large amount of currency caused serious inflation. In 1945, the amount of currency in circulation was 14 times greater than in 1937, and by 1949, it was 6.5 times greater than it had been in 1945. The occupation authorities sought to impose price controls and curtail the flow of currency, but the cost of living continued to rise by approximately 10 percent each month for about two years. The wholesale price index in 1945 was 3.5 times that of 1934–1936, and in December 1949, it was 212.8 times; the consumer price index during the same period rose to 240 times the prewar level. Eventually the yen, which was worth about 25 cents before the war, was fixed at 360 yen to the dollar.

The Arrival of Occupation Forces

In the throes of a virtually collapsed economy and under a politically impotent government, the thoroughly bewildered and apprehensive Japanese people awaited the arrival of the occupying forces. In preparation for the unprecedented event, Prince Higashikuni Naruhiko (1887–1990) was appointed prime minister immediately after the termination of the war.

On August 28, 1945, the first contingent of occupation troops arrived at the Atsugi air force base outside of Tokyo. Eventually two hundred thousand U.S. troops were stationed throughout Japan.

On August 30, General MacArthur, who had been appointed the supreme commander of the Allied powers (SCAP) as well as the commander of the American military forces in the Far East, arrived at Atsugi. Corncob pipe in hand and dressed casually in work clothes, the new ruler of Japan stepped off his plane. Thus began the Occupation of Japan that was to last until April 28, 1952. General MacArthur established his headquarters across from the imperial palace in the Daiichi Insurance Building and commenced his tour of duty as supreme commander.

The general was supposedly acting on behalf of the Allies, whose policies were theoretically formulated by the eleven-member Far Eastern Commission. In fact, however, the United States government held the ultimate authority. If, for example, the commission failed to agree on a matter of policy, the United States was empowered to issue "urgent unilateral interim directives." There was also an advisory council in Tokyo, the Allied Council for Japan, consisting of representatives of the United States, the British Commonwealth, the Soviet Union, and China, but it had little real authority over General MacArthur. Essentially, the council became primarily a forum in which the Soviet Union berated American occupation policies. The strong personality of General MacArthur made the Occupation seem like a one-man show. His forceful leadership, self-assurance, dignified bearing, sense of mission, and astute political acumen won him the respect of the Japanese and made his "reign" a highly successful one.

The directive outlining General MacArthur's authority as supreme commander of the Allied powers in Japan was prepared jointly by the U.S. State, War, and Navy Departments and approved by President Harry S. Truman. The message transmitted to the general by the chiefs of staff stated

> 1. The authority of the Emperor and the Japanese Government to rule the State is subordinate to you as Supreme Commander for the Allied Powers. You will exercise your authority as you deem proper to carry out your mission. Our relations with Japan do not rest on a contractual basis, but on an unconditional surrender. Since your authority is supreme, you will not entertain any question on the part of the Japanese as to its scope.
>
> 2. Control of Japan shall be exercised through the Japanese Government to the extent that such an arrangement produces satisfactory results. This does not prejudice your right to act directly if required. You may enforce the orders issued by you by the employment of such measures as you deem necessary, including the use of force.[5]

Regarding his policies and objectives, General MacArthur states in his memoirs:

> From the moment of my appointment as supreme commander, I had formulated the policies I intended to follow, implementing them through the Emperor and the machinery of the imperial government. The reforms I contemplated were those which could bring Japan abreast of modern progressive thought and action. First destroy the military power. Punish war criminals. Build the structure of representative government. Modernize the constitution. Hold free elections. Enfranchise the women.

Release political prisoners. Liberate the farmers. Establish a free and responsible press. Liberalize education. Decentralize the political power. Separate church and state.

Writing about Japan's cultural tradition, he explained, "I carefully abstained from any interference by edict with the cultural traditions or the personal Japanese way of life. In frequent public statements I advised the Japanese people to seek a healthy blend between the best of theirs and the best of ours."[6]

The policies to be implemented in Japan had been decided upon by the Washington policymakers. General MacArthur had been given an advance copy of the Initial Surrender Policy for Japan en route to his new command. The measures described therein had been hammered out in Washington over the course of several years, with considerable input from New Deal thinkers.

After President Truman approved the policies formulated by the Joint Chiefs of Staff, a military order, JCS 1380/15 (Post-Surrender Directive to SCAP) was presented to General MacArthur. It spelled out in detail his duties in Japan,[7] the chief objectives of which were to demilitarize and democratize the country. General MacArthur then set out to fulfill his orders.

Contrary to the expectations of some Americans who had been awed by the fanaticism of Japanese soldiers in the imperial army, the Japanese people cooperated willingly with the occupation authorities. In fact, the initial occupation period was characterized by a remarkable degree of harmony. Of course, the emperor's acceptance of defeat and his submission to the Allied authorities made it easier for the people to do likewise. Moreover, the Japanese were already conditioned to bow to authority and accept an established order. In times of extreme stress they might resort to desperate and fanatical actions, but under normal circumstances, the Japanese behave as a highly practical people and are very rational and sensible, as well as friendly, cooperative, and courteous. The defeat and devastation of war had swept away the self-confidence and the psychological props that had for so long sustained the Japanese people. Now that these were suddenly removed, they lacked the will to resist the conquerors. However, defiance grew as time passed and the Japanese regained their self-assurance. It was then that demonstrations against the U.S. military bases started.

Sakaguchi Ango (1906–1955), a member of a group of young postwar writers referred to as the *burai-ha* (the decadents)—young writers who rebelled against the prevailing mores and trends—commented on the Japanese people's reaction to the occupation authorities as follows:

Of all peoples the Japanese basically muster up the least hatred and maintain it for the shortest time. Yesterday's enemy is today's friend; this easygoing optimism is a reality and not a counterfeited emotion. To cooperate with yesterday's enemy—no, to become bosom friends—is an everyday occurrence, and the more bitter the enemy, the more intimate we become. We want to serve a second master just as soon as the first one is out of the way, and we even want to serve yesterday's enemy.[8]

Cooperation with the occupying authorities was facilitated by the fact that the conquerors themselves displayed very little rancor or hostility toward the Japanese people. The general friendliness and spontaneous warmth manifested by the occupying troops made the relationship between the two peoples relatively harmonious. The U. S. military did not display the kind of pomp and ceremony or the overbearing haughtiness that had so frequently characterized the tyrannical rule of the Japanese military over conquered peoples. The ends pursued by the occupation authorities were not vengeance or exploitation; instead, reforms that would enable Japan to achieve a free and democratic society were to be introduced. Even if some of the measures and methods used to realize these ends lacked good sense from the Japanese point of view, no other conquered people in history was treated more humanely or benefited more at the hands of its conquerors. And people enjoyed the climate of freedom the occupation authorities brought to Japan.

A writer who returned to Tokyo from the countryside observed,

> It appears that the reason young people consider Tokyo to be a delightful place is because they were liberated from the oppressive forces by America. The police could no longer strut around arrogantly, neither could the teachers and principals. The young could behave as freely as they desired so long as they did not break the law. The pleasures of youth and freedom—Tokyo now seemed ready to freely grant these to them.[9]

In theory, the occupation authorities were not to function as a military government. SCAP was to exercise supervisory authority, while the task of governing the country was to be left to the Japanese government. In fact, however, there was no question but that the real power in Japan resided with SCAP, whence all important directives ordering Japanese government implementation emanated.

As noted, General MacArthur observed in his memoirs that SCAP's objective was to "first destroy the military power." Thus, SCAP set about demobilizing the Japanese forces, beginning with the 3.7 million Japanese troops at home. The job of repatriating Japanese forces from abroad was also undertaken by U.S. military authorities. This meant transporting approximately 3.3 million troops and 3.2 million civilians back to Japan. This task was largely completed by the beginning of 1948.

Most of those who had not been repatriated by then were prisoners of war in the Soviet Union. By May 1949, a total of 900,000 people had been repatriated from Soviet-controlled territories. This still left, according to Japanese estimates, 420,000 unaccounted for. The Soviet Union claimed to have only 105,000 more prisoners and returned 95,000 by the end of 1949. It is estimated that 55,000 people died while in Soviet detention camps. Disclosures after the collapse of the Soviet Union indicated that as many as 500,000 Japanese captured after the war had died while in forced labor in the Soviet Union.

In contrast to the Soviet performance, repatriation from China went much more smoothly, despite the fact that the largest contingent of Japanese overseas troops had been located in China, and the largest number of people had been killed there by Japanese troops. The return of Japanese prisoners was facilitated by the goodwill and magnanimity of Chiang Kai-shek, who told his fellow countrymen to cease regarding the Japanese as enemies and treat them as friends.

Japanese military installations and equipment were destroyed during the occupation, and the remaining navy vessels, with the exception of those ships needed by the occupation forces to carry out their assignments, were divided among the four principal Allied nations.

The War Crimes Trials

One of the key objectives of the Allied powers was the prosecution and punishment of those who had committed war crimes. Two generals had already been tried and executed by ad hoc military courts established by General MacArthur in the Philippines immediately after the end of the war. These were Generals Yamashita Tomoyuki and Homma Masaharu, who were held responsible for the atrocities committed by the Japanese troops in the Philippines—even though Yamashita was not in the Philippines when the atrocities were committed.

The International Military Tribunal for the Far East was created by the Allied powers for the purpose of trying political leaders responsible for "crimes against peace." Twenty-eight major, or Class A, war criminals were characterized as a "criminal, militaristic clique" that dominated in the Japanese political world from January 1, 1928, to September 2, 1945. They were charged with variously planning, preparing, initiating, or waging aggressive war. Most of these men were also charged with violations of the laws and customs of war as well as with crimes against humanity, which, as defined by the Allied powers, meant "inhumane acts committed against any civilian population, before or during the war."[10]

The trials were presided over by eleven justices, one each from Australia, Canada, China, France, Great Britian, India, the Netherlands, New Zealand, the Philippines, the Soviet Union, and the United States. The proceedings, led by chief prosecutor Joseph B. Keenan, opened on May 3, 1946, and were not concluded until April 1948. Defense attorneys protested the trials on the grounds that they were based on ex post facto laws, but their objections were rejected. The sentences were finally handed down in November 1948. Seven persons were sentenced to death by hanging, starting with General Tojo Hideki, who had been prime minister and war minister in 1941–1944. War with the United States was begun under his premiership. Sixteen were senteneced to life imprisonment; one was given twenty years; another, seven years; two died during the trial; and one person, Okawa Shumei, went insane.

On September 22, 1948, the seven men who had been sentenced to death were hanged. Among them were General Tojo and five other generals: Itagaki Seishiro, who instigated the Manchurian Incident and also served in China and as war minister in 1938–1939; Doihara Kenji, who served in Manchuria and

China; Matsui Iwane, commanding general of the forces that assaulted Nanjing; Muto Akira, who was chief of the Military Bureau 1939–1942, and also served in the campaigns in the Dutch East Indies and the Philippines; Kimura Heitaro, vice minister of war, 1941–1944, and commanding general of the Japanese forces in Burma. The only civilian hanged was Hirota Koki, foreign minister, 1933–1936, and prime minister, 1936–1937.

The close verdict of 6 to 5 to execute Hirota was the most controversial of the decisions. As foreign minister during the Nanjing Massacre of 1937, he was judged to have been "derelict in his duties" for not insisting that the cabinet take action to end the atrocities. He was also found guilty of "conspiring to commit aggression."[11]

All those who were executed, except Hirota, composed a short poem before they were hanged. Tojo's poem reads: "From tomorrow, without offending anyone, I shall rest in peace, beside the Amida Buddha."[12]

Among those who were sentenced to life imprisonment were Kido Koichi, lord keeper of the Privy Seal from 1940 to 1945, and the closest adviser to the emperor during this period; Hiranuma Kiichiro, prime minister in 1939 and ultranationalist leader; General Araki Sadao, war minister, 1931–1934, and leader of the militant army circle, the Imperial Way faction; General Koiso Kuniaki, prime minister 1944–1945; General Umezu Yoshijiro, who commanded military forces in China and Manchuria and served as army chief of staff in 1944; and Colonel Hashimoto Kingoro, a militant army officer who was charged with the bombing of the British gunboat *Ladybird* during Japanese military action in China. Former Foreign Ministers Togo Shigenori, a career diplomat and ambassaor to Italy in 1939, and Shigemitsu Mamoru, career diplomat and foreign minister, 1943–1945, were sentenced to prison for twenty years and seven years, respectively.

Eight of the eleven justices fully supported the tribunal's decision, but three dissented. Justice Henri Bernard of France dissented on the grounds that the emperor had not been tried and "no direct proof was furnished concerning the formation among individuals known . . . of a plot the object of which was to assure to Japan the domination . . . of some part of the world."[13] What was proven, he held, was only the desire to do so. Justice B.V.A. Roling of the Netherlands dissented over the issue of civilian responsibility for military acts; he held that indicted civilians like Hirota and Kido were innocent. Although Roling agreed that aggressive war was a crime, he dissented on the reasoning behind the finding that aggressive war was a crime. Justice Radhabinod Pal of India believed that the accused were innocent on all counts: The existence of a conspiracy had not been proven, aggressive war was not a crime in international law, and none of the conventional war crimes charges had been proven.[14]

Also charged as Class A war criminals were Matsuoka Yosuke, delegate to the League of Nations when Japan withdrew from the league in 1933 and foreign minister, 1940–1941, Admiral Nagano Osami, navy minister, 1936–1937 and chief of the navy general staff during 1941–1944, and Okawa Shumei, an ultranationalist leader. However, during the trial Matsuoka and Nagano died, and Okawa succumbed to mental difficulties. Prince Konoe, who had been prime minister at the outbreak of the 1937 Sino-Japanese War and again in 1940–1941 just prior to the war with the United States, committed suicide when he discovered that he was to be arrested. Tojo also attempted to commit suicide before his arrest and shot himself in the heart, though not fatally.

In 1957, the sentences of all classes of war criminals who had been tried in Tokyo and had been sentenced to imprisonment were commuted. Many had died during incarceration, but some managed to return to play active political roles after their release.

The question of trying the emperor as a war criminal was raised, but the idea was quashed by American officials; they concluded that if this were done it would make the work of the occupation forces in Japan virtually impossible. In his *Reminiscences*, General MacArthur wrote:

> There had been outcry from some of the Allies, notably the Russians and the British, to include [the emperor] in this category [of war criminals]. Indeed the initial list proposed by them was headed by the Emperor's name. . . . When Washington seemed to be veering toward the British point of view, I had advised that I would need at least one million reinforcement should such action be taken. I believed that if the Emperor were indicted, and perhaps hanged, as a war criminal, military government would have to be instituted throughout all Japan, and guerrilla warfare would probably break out.[15]

Yoshida Shigeru, who served as prime minister during 1946–1947 and 1948–1954, reflected, in his memoirs: "The fact remains that the respect and understanding shown by the General towards the Emperor from all and any relationship with war crimes did more than anything else to lessen the fears of the majority of the Japanese people in regard to the Occupation and to reconcile them to it. . . . It was the attitude adopted by General MacArthur towards the Throne, more than any other single factor, that made the Occupation an historical success."[16]

There was strong sentiment in the United States favoring the trial and punishment of the emperor, especially from the China specialists both in and out of government. Before the decision to exclude the emperor from the list of war criminals had been made, members of the prosecuting team prepared briefs for his trial. Colonel Henry Sackett, a member of the military tribunal's prosecution team, interrogated Kido Koichi at length about the emperor's political role. Sackett's interviews make clear that the emperor had been informed of all the decisions on military action made by the army and navy general staff. When Colonel Sackett asked Kido if the emperor knew about the plan to attack Pearl Harbor, Kido replied, "I believe he did know about the attack on Pearl Harbor." The decision had already been made not to try the emperor when Colonel Sackett interrogated Kido.[17]

   The emperor met with General MacArthur soon after the general's arrival in Japan. General MacArthur recalled in his memoirs that the emperor had said to him, "I come to you, General MacArthur, to offer myself to the judgment of the powers you represent as the one to bear sole responsibility for every political and military decision made and action taken by my people in the conduct of war."[18] This is affirmed by George Atcheson, political adviser in the diplomatic section of SCAP, who reported in a memorandum to the State Department that General MacArthur had told him that when he met the emperor, the latter stated he assumed full responsibility for the war on behalf of the Japanese people.

   However, "the Emperor said that he had not intended that the attack on Pearl Harbor take place before receipt by the U.S. Government of the Japanese declaration of war on the United States but Tojo had tricked him."[19] The emperor's stance contrasts with Tojo's position: At the war crime trials, Tojo "took pains to protect the imperial position and to present his arguments in such a way as not to compromise the person of the Emperor."[20] During Tojo's interrogation, Prosecutor Keenan asked, "Was that the will of Emperor Hirohito, that war should be instituted?" and Tojo responded, "It may not have been according to his will, but it is a fact that because of my advice and because of the advice given by the High Command the Emperor consented, though reluctantly, to the war."[21]

   Those who would like to absolve the emperor of responsibility contend that his decisonmaking power was circumscribed by the Meiji Constitution and that he was thus bound to approve decisions made by government officials. When questioned about why he was able to make the decision to end the war but did not oppose the decision to go to war in 1941, the emperor justified his position by saying that the decision to go to war had been made by the government and military leaders, therefore he had no option but to endorse their decision. In 1945, however, government and military leaders were unable to agree on whether to end the war, and Emperor Hirohito was asked by Prime Minister Suzuki Kantaro to decide whether to accept the terms of the Potsdam Declaration. Thus the emperor claimed he was acting in accord with the Japanese Constitution. Emperor Hirohito clearly saw his position as that of a constitutional monarch whose authority was circumscribed. This is proven by his support in the prewar years of the "emperor organ theory," espoused by a scholar of constitutional law, Minobe Tatsukichi (1873–1948), who held that the emperor was not above the state but was one of the organs of the government. By endorsing Minobe's thesis, the emperor asserted the following belief: "To hold that sovereignty resides not in the state but in the monarchy is to court charges of despotism."[22]

   Emperor Hirohito was educated and trained to be a ceremonial head of government. When he showed an interest in history in his youth, the court advisers diverted his attention from that subject and encouraged him to pursue his interest in marine biology. The most influential of these advisers at the imperial court after Hirohito became emperor was Prince Saionji Kimmochi (1849–1940), the last of the genro. He and the other court advisers sought to prevent the emperor from getting personally involved in controversial political issues. Experience had taught them this would only cause trouble. For example, at the outbreak of the Manchurian Incident, the emperor presented a statement to the prime minister and war minister expressing his wish to have the incident brought under control, and the perturbed militarists then blamed the court advisers. The advisers therefore concluded that it would be best to prevent the emperor from issuing any more statements, unless absolutely necessary. After the outbreak of the conflict with China in 1937, Prince Saionji advised the emperor not to participate in the discussions at Imperial Military Headquarters but merely to listen.

The emperor was aware, of course, that he could exercise decisive influence if he chose to express his views, as the following examples illustrate. In 1928, when Japanese military officers assassinated the Manchurian warlord, Zang Zou-lin, the emperor displayed his displeasure with Prime Minister Tanaka Giichi for making contradictory reports about the incident. Out of respect for the imperial throne, Tanaka felt obligated to resign. In 1936, radical military officers attempted to stage a coup détat, but the movement was quashed when the emperor took a strong stand. In this case, the chief court advisers as well as government leaders had been killed or incapacitated to create a power vacuum. Emperor Hirohito was therefore compelled to assert his leadership. In sum, the emperor was aware that government leaders like Tojo would carry out his wishes with alacrity if he made them known. A court attendant noted in his diary that the emperor said in 1946 that no one listened to what he had to say as faithfully as Tojo or carried out his wishes as swiftly.[23] Thus, the emperor could have dissuaded Tojo from deciding to go to war with the United States if he had so desired. The fact remains that regardless of whether Emperor Hirohito played an active role in the decisions that led to aggression and war in Asia and the Pacific region, he was the head of state and the military had direct access to him through the mechanism of the "independence of the supreme command." War was declared in his name, hundreds of thousands of Japanese soldiers and sailors died in the belief that they were fulfilling his wishes, and millions of Chinese and other people were killed in his name.

During the war crimes investigations, hundreds of people were indicted as Class B and Class C war criminals. About twenty high-ranking military officers were labeled Class B criminals, that is, they were accused of violating the laws and customs of war and were charged with command responsibility for the troops that had committed atrocities. They were all acquitted. Lesser officers and soldiers were indicted as Class C criminals, meaning that they were accused of crimes against humanity, such as mistreating prisoners of war and committing minor atrocities. They were tried by military commissions under the United States Eighth Army and by the Allied military authorities in the places where the crimes had been committed. Estimates vary, but somewhere between 5,500 to 6,000 people were charged and tried for war crimes. Over 930 people were executed, and the vast majority of the rest were sentenced to prison for varying lengths of time. Among the executed were 23 Koreans and 26 Taiwanese who had been conscripted to serve in the Japanese army. The war crimes trials held in Japan were completed by fall 1949. Unlike the Germans, the Japanese did not conduct war crimes trials on their own initiative.[24]

There were considerably arbitrary and irregular proceedings in the trials conducted in countries that Japan had invaded during the war, with innocent people unable to receive due process because of the bitterness about Japanese actions and atrocities. In the United States and Great Britain, soldiers in the armed forces have the right to disobey their superiors' orders if the actions the orders specify are contrary to standard regulations. In France, if soldiers commit illegal acts by obeying an officer's order, they are not punished; the superior officer who gave the order is held responsible. However, in the imperial Japanese armed forces, the troops were required to obey their superiors' orders without question. In the postwar trials, Japanese underlings were held responsible for their actions, even though they might have been following their superiors' orders.[25]

According to the practice of the Allied powers, commanding officers were held responsible for atrocities committed by the troops under their command. But in the Nanjing Massacre, the supreme commander of the army, Prince Asaka Yasuhiko, was not charged as a war criminal by the Tokyo tribunal. He was exempted, it is believed, because he was a royal prince. It is contended that those who had engaged in bacteriological experiments on the Chinese in Manchuria were not tried in return for their turning over the data to U.S. authorities.[26]

In addition to trying and punishing war criminals, the occupation authorities, in accordance with the directives of the U.S. government, sought to remove from positions of responsibility and leadership all those who had been exponents or agents of militarism or of militant nationalism. This entailed the purging of all high-ranking army and navy officers, as well as most of the high government officials and leaders of business and industry and right-wing nationalists. Those purged also included politicians who had been affiliated with the Imperial Rule Assistance Association, organized in 1940 under Prince Konoe's leadership in order to galvanize the people behind the imperial state.

SCAP's directive to the Japanese government to proceed with the investigation of those who fell in the stipulated categories was issued in January 1946. By May 1948, some 220,000 people, including 180,000 former military officers, were purged. SCAP also banned from the political scene a number of political leaders who were seeking to play a key role in the postwar era by restructuring the prewar political parties. For example, 262 out of 274 Diet members of the newly formed Progressive Party were purged, as were 30 of the 45 Liberal Party members and 11 out of 17 Socialist Party members. Those purged were forced to remain inactive until they were rehabilitated in 1950–1951.

The other objective of SCAP—the freeing of political prisoners—was implemented at the outset of the Occupation. SCAP immediately issued directives to the Japanese government to release all political prisoners, rescind the Peace Preservation Laws that Japan had enacted to imprison political dissidents and harborers of "dangerous thought," and abolish the special political police which had hounded harborers of "dangerous thought." The police-state system that had existed in prewar and wartime Japan was to be abolished. Prime Minister Higashikuni found these directives unacceptable because he believed in preserving the Peace Preservation Laws to curb left-wing activists, so he resigned. As a result of the SCAP directives, political prisoners who had been imprisoned, such as the Communist leader, Tokuda Kyuichi, were released from prison. In addition, scholars who had lost their teaching positions because of their political beliefs were restored to their positions.[27]

SCAP Reforms

The reforms to be introduced in Japan by the occupation authorities were to be implemented through the Japanese government. SCAP therefore issued directives to the Japanese government to implement a range of political, social, economic, and cultural reforms. On October 11, 1945, when Prime Minister Shidehara Kijuro called on General MacArthur, the general handed Shidehara a document that outlined five basic social reforms: (1) emancipating women through their enfranchisement; (2) encouraging unionization of labor; (3) opening the schools to more liberal education; (4) abolishing the police-state system, protecting the people from despotic, arbitrary, and unjust methods; and introducing the concept of habeas corpus; and (5) democratizing the economic system and ending monopolistic control over industry.[28]

Shidehara Kijuro (1872–1951) succeeded Prince Higashikuni as prime minister. Shidehara had been foreign minister in the 1920s and pursued a policy of international cooperation. The process of instituting reforms began with political reforms, that is with the democratization of the political institutions and practices. First of all, it was considered essential to disabuse the people of belief in the sanctity and divine status of the emperor. General MacArthur was opposed to "the doctrine that the Emperor of Japan is superior to the heads of other states because of ancestry, descent or special origin."[29] On New Year's Day 1946, SCAP encouraged Emperor Hirohito to publicly announce the fact that he was not divine. On this occasion the emperor stated, "The ties between us and our people have always stood upon mutual trust and affection. They do not depend upon mere legends and myths. They are not predicated on the false conception that the Emperor is divine and that the Japanese people are superior to other races and fated to rule the world."[30]

General MacArthur also set out to curb state support of Shintoism and sever the religious ties between the government and Shinto shrines. To this end, he issued an order, the Abolition of Governmental Sponsorship, Support, Perpetuation, Control, and Dissemination of State Shinto. Government funds were not to be provided to Shinto shrines, and "all propagation and dissemination of militaristic and ultranationalistic ideology in Shinto" was prohibited. In addition, another pillar of imperial authority, the peerage, or the nobility, was eliminated. As a result, 913 families, ranging in rank from barons to princes, lost their special status and privileges.[31]

Administratively, the Ministry of Home Affairs (Naimusho), which controlled the nation's police force and operated the special political police, was abolished; its functions were allocated to other ministries. However, the bureaucrats who had controlled domestic affairs under the former Ministry of Home Affairs continued to serve in the newly established ministries, carrying on in their traditional bureaucratic mode.

In December 1947, a new police law was enacted. The police, formerly under the control of the Ministry of Home Affairs, were now placed under the authority of local governments. In 1954, the system was revised, and the independent municipal police force was replaced by a prefectural police force. Local communities found it difficult to finance their own police force, which caused the local police authorities to weaken, whereupon the central government's authority over the police force was enhanced.

To ensure the civil rights of citizens, judicial and legal reforms were introduced. The new Japanese Constitution, discussed further on, provided for civil and individual rights, but prior to its introduction, SCAP convinced the Japanese government to institute certain judicial reforms. The concept of judicial review was introduced, and the Supreme Court was made "the court of last resort with power to determine the constitutionality of any law, order, regulation or official act."

Another important change introduced by SCAP was separating the courts from the Ministry of Justice, which freed the courts from the political influence of the government. Revisions in the Criminal Code entailed the abolishment of lèse-majesté (offense against the dignity of the emperor), heavier punishment for officials who abused their authority, and elimination of the provision that provided for the criminal liability of married women, but not married men, who committed adultery. Perhaps the most important legal provision enacted to protect the people's civil rights was the 1948 law on habeas corpus that bolstered the bill of rights introduced in the new constitution.

Still another aspect of instituting the new administrative reforms involved relaxing the central government's tight control over local and prefectural governments that had been imposed through the Ministry of Home Affairs. Formerly, prefectural governors were appointed by the central government, but under the reform, they were to be elected by prefectural voters. Further, the governors were to be responsible to the prefectural assembly members, also elected by the people. Governors also lost their power to override the prefectural assemblies. Fewer changes were introduced in municipal and village governments, which had already enjoyed relative autonomy under the old system. However, mayors were now elected directly by the voters rather than by the town or village assemblies, as had formerly been the rule. In addition, the principles and procedures of referendum, initiative, and recall were introduced at the municipal and prefectural levels.

In the electoral system, the most significant change was the introduction of women's suffrage. Universal male suffrage had been adopted in 1925, but the franchise was not granted to women. In December 1945, the election law was revised to provide for women's suffrage, as well as for lower voting age. The Civil Code provided for the equal rights of women and men in legal capacity, marriage, divorce, and authority over family matters.

Freedom of the press and freedom of speech were to be ensured in accordance with the August 29, 1945, U.S. Initial Post-Surrender Policy for Japan. That document states: "The Japanese people shall be encouraged to develop a desire for individual liberties and respect for fundamental human rights, particularly the freedoms of religion, assembly, speech and the press."[32]

Having been granted freedom of speech and press, the Japanese press began to express opinions that SCAP considered irresponsible. For example, the national press network, Domei, declared that "the end of the war had come about because of the Emperor's benevolence, rather than through Allied military superiority, and occupying Americans were merely guests of the Japanese Empire." It also professed the belief that "Japan might have won the war but for the atomic bomb, a weapon too terrible to face and one which only barbarians would use."[33]

Faced with these and other "irresponsible" statements by the press, SCAP decided that closer adherence to the civil liberties directive issued on September 10, 1945, had to be observed. General MacArthur called for responsible reporting of the news: "The Japanese Imperial Government will issue the necessary orders to prevent dissemination of news, through newspapers, radio broadcasting or other means of publication, which fails to adhere to the truth or which disturbs public tranquility." MacArthur also banned discussion in the media of such matters as "Allied troop movements which have not been officially released, false or destructive criticism of the Allied Powers, and rumors."[34] On September 15, *Asahi Shimbun,* Japan's largest daily newspaper, criticized the U.S. use of the atomic bomb, and on September 20, published an item by Hatoyama Ichiro (who later became prime minister) criticizing the atomic bombing of Hiroshima and Nagasaki. As a result, on September 21, SCAP issued a more specific guideline, a ten-clause press code stating that the "news must adhere strictly to the truth."[35]

Thus SCAP was placed in the awkward position of championing freedom of the press and speech but at the same time censoring material that could undermine public tranquility. For example, SCAP introduced a system of prepublication censorship, deemed particularly necessary as Communists who had been released from prison and given their freedom were beginning to become more active. SCAP's rationale was that as the occupying power of a defeated nation, the need to ensure the security and safety of its forces was unquestionable. But such actions did provide critics of the American forces with an excuse to criticize SCAP's "authoritarian" rule.

The scope of censorship was gradually extended to cover books and movies. For example, samurai movies were banned, as was Erskine Caldwell's *Tobacco Road* because it showed the dark side of American life. *Das Kapital* was suspended briefly. The Japanese government joined in, banning Norman Mailer's *The Naked and the Dead* (this ban was overruled by SCAP) and D. H. Lawrence's *Lady Chatterley's Lover.* In addition, foreign magazines, books, and motion pictures were not allowed into Japan if they were judged "detrimental to the purpose of the Occupation." When a Japanese crew made a documentary film on the effects of the atomic bombing of Hiroshima and Nagasaki, SCAP sought unsuccessfully to curb its production. After the film was produced, SCAP confiscated it and sent it to Washington. The film was not returned to Japan until 1967. There was a virtual blackout on any information about the atomic bomb until September 1949, when the Soviet Union exploded its atomic bomb.

Initially, SCAP censorship was administered fairly sensibly. Eventually, however, when the job was taken over by young officers who were ignorant about newspaper publishing, censorship turned capricious and onerous. Walter Lippmann's columns were frequently censored, and even Ripley's "Believe It or Not" cartoons were censored. Public discussion about the constitution and the law on economic deconcentration was restricted. SCAP was also sensitive about reports sent to the United States concerning its occupation policies. A reporter for the *Chicago Sun-Times,* Mark Gayn (author of *Japan Diary*), who wrote critical articles about the occupation, got in trouble with SCAP for posing "a constant menace to security regulations." He lost his position with the *Sun-Times* and his credentials to work as a reporter in Japan.[36]

Economic Reforms

Initially, in accordance with U.S. government policy, SCAP had arranged for Japan to pay reparations in the form of industrial equipment to nations that had been victimized by Japanese imperialism. This policy was advocated vigorously by members of the special reparations committee, headed by oil entrepreneur Edwin Pauley. Among the most determined advocates of punishing the Japanese business conglomerates was Owen Lattimore, an authority on Asian affairs.[37] The reparations plan called for the transference of selected industrial plants to the poorer nations that had been devastated by Japanese aggression and occupation. It was anticipated that reparations would propel all of "Eastern Asia [toward] political stability and peaceful progress," and that Japan would be kept from recovering "in a form which will allow her to gain control, or to secure an advantage over, her neighbors." General MacArthur, however, was opposed to dismantling the Japanese economic system because he was convinced of the need to stabilize the Japanese economy. Therefore, the plan to ship industrial tools and machinery out of Japan was abandoned by May 1949. Japan's total reparations settlements with the Asian countries came to little more than $1 billion.[38]

The U.S. government's program to democratize Japan included instituting "democracy" and freedom in the economic sector, which meant breaking up the stranglehold on the economy held by the giant business conglomerates, the *zaibatsu*. Included among those purged for militaristic and imperialistic activities were business executives, especially those affiliated with the big industrial and commercial complexes that constituted the *zaibatsu* and those who had played a part in Japanese expansion overseas.

In order to ensure the rise of democratic elements by effecting a wider distribution of both income and of the ownership of the means of production and trade, the U.S. Initial Post-Surrender Policy for Japan of August 1945, directed SCAP to pursue policies that "permit a wide distribution of income and of the ownership of the means of production and trade." To this end, SCAP was "to favor a program for the dissolution of the large industrial and banking combinations which have exercised control of a great part of Japan's trade and industry."[39] On November 1, 1945, a Basic Directive of the Joint Chiefs of Staff was sent to General MacArthur, directing him to persuade the Japanese government to submit "plans for dissolving large Japanese industrial and banking combines or other large concentrations of private business control."[40] Both of these directives were prepared by the State, War, and Navy Coordinating Committee (SWNCC). This approach, in essence, left it up to the Japanese agency to decide which industrial and banking combines were large concentrations that should be dissolved.

The experts in the State Department and the Antitrust Division of the Justice Department decided that the directives were inadequate and needed closer scrutiny, so in January 1946, they sent a mission headed by Corwin Edwards of Northwestern University to Tokyo to study ways to deal with the *zaibatsu* issue. There were diverse opinions on *zaibatsu*-busting. Assistant Secretary of State Will Clayton favored trust-busting and fostering free competition. Edwards also believed firmly in the system of free competition as the essence of democracy. On the basis of the report that Edwards submitted, the State Department formulated a plan for *zaibatsu*-busting and instituting free competition, in order "to destroy any and all excessive concentrations of economic power."[41]

SCAP then proceeded to implement its policy of dissolving the *zaibatsu*. Among the *zaibatsu* firms were the huge corporations like Mitsui, Mitsubishi, Sumitomo, and Yasuda. First, the Holding Company Liquidation Commission—a Japanese "public agency" created by SCAP in its November 1945 directive—designated 10 conglomerates for dissolution. The top 4 combined had a total of 761 subsidiaries. In all, 45 holding companies were dissolved. They were required to dispose of their stock in sales to the general public; the Holding

Company Liquidation Commission conducted sales of these shares. This, in turn, laid the foundation for the emergence of the massive Tokyo stock exchange system.[42]

The second step taken to dissolve the monopolies was the passage of the anti-monopoly law, which prohibited such practices as the formation of trusts and cartels, the interlocking system of corporate controls, and collusive agreements to restrain trade. These measures were implemented without much controversy, but the third phase, the plan to break up big business enterprises, aroused opposition from some sectors of the American government and business circles. The move to curb excessive concentration was based on the premise that "big is bad." The measures to curb excessive concentration were formulated in a policy paper known as FEC-230 (Policy on Excessive Concentrations of Economic Power in Japan, submitted to the Far Eastern Commission). In April 1947, Edward Christy Welsh was sent to Japan to take charge of SCAP's Antitrust and Cartels Division to implement this policy.

Welsh first proceeded to dissolve the two big *zaibatsu* trading complexes, Mitsui and Mitsubishi, which before the war had handled about 70 percent of Japan's foreign trade. He then set out to implement the deconcentration program, convincing SCAP to direct the Japanese government to pass the Deconcentration Law in December 1947. In early 1948, 325 companies—257 industrial firms and 68 companies in the distributive and service fields—that accounted for 80 percent of all of Japan's industrial, financial, and commercial enterprises were designated for deconcentration. It was reported that the commission was contemplating the dissolution of as many as 1,200 companies. The program aroused considerable opposition among American business and political leaders, who complained that the plan was socialistic and as such would retard the economic recovery of Japan. Consequently, a review board was created in May 1948 to reexamine the program for massive deconcentration. As a result of the investigation, most of the 325 companies originally slated for dissolution were removed from the list, although a few, such as Nippon Iron and Steel, Mitsubishi Heavy Industries, and Oji Paper, were dissolved.[43]

Nonetheless, the old *zaibatsu* control over the Japanese economy was loosened significantly. As a result of the general *zaibatsu*-busting, deconcentration, and antimonopoly measures, 83 *zaibatsu* holding companies were either dissolved or reorganized, and about 5,000 other companies were forced to reorganize to comply with the provisions of the deconcentration and antimonopoly laws. The Mitsui and Mitsubishi conglomerates, for example, were fragmented into 240 separate companies. Fifty-six family members of 10 *zaibatsu* conglomerates were compelled to relinquish their stock holdings and were banned from holding company positions. One-half of the relinquished stock was sold to company employees; the remaining stock was sold to the general public.[44]

The effort to eliminate big business conglomerates, however, turned out to be the least enduring of the occupation reforms. Most of the old *zaibatsu* firms reunited, albeit in a looser form, after SCAP departed. Such mergers increased with the rapid economic growth of the late 1950s and 1960s. However, the cartel-busting program did foster free competition and opened the way for individuals and independent companies like Honda, Subaru, Sony, and Matsushita to emerge as major players in both the Japanese and the world economy.

Land Reforms

The land reform program was another economic measure designed to bring about a more equitable distribution of wealth, and it turned out to be much more effective than *zaibatsu*-busting. In fact, it was perhaps the most successful reform measure introduced by SCAP. A memorandum issued by SCAP on December 9, 1945, asked the Japanese government "to take measures to insure that those who till the soil of Japan shall have a more equal opportunity to enjoy the fruits of their labor."[45] The Japanese government had begun to draft a land reform plan even before Washington and SCAP moved to initiate action. There were pro-tenant bureaucrats in the Ministry of Agriculture who, during the war years, had sought to implement policies favorable to tenants. When the opportunity for land reforms arose with the advent of SCAP, these officials were more than willing to cooperate and advance the reforms. At the end of the war, 70 percent of the farmers were either tenants or rented some land to augment their own holdings. About 46 percent of the cultivated land was tenanted, but there were no gigantic landowners. Only about 2,000 landlords owned as much as 100 acres; most individuals owned no more than 10 acres.

SCAP's land reform plan was formulated under the direction of Wolf Ladejinsky and was promoted by General MacArthur, who insisted on swift action. The proposal was presented to the Japanese government, and the Diet passed the Farm Land Reform Law in October 1946, which prohibited absentee landlordism. A landlord who lived in the community where he owned land could hold a maximum of 2.5 acres. An active farmer could own a maximum of 7.5 acres for his own use, plus an additional 2.5 acres that he did not cultivate. (Landowners in Hokkaido were allowed to own more acreage.) The government purchased the land from the landowners and sold it to former tenants, who were then required to repay the government over a thirty-year period at an interest rate of 3.2 percent. The transfer of land was managed by 13,000 locally elected land commissions.

However, skyrocketing inflation and the consequent decline in the value of money between the time when the amount of compensation was determined and when the transaction was actually completed resulted in landowners receiving practically no compensation. In some instances, the price per acre that was paid to the landowners was the same as the cost of a carton of cigarettes on the black market. This, of course, made it possible for any tenant, no matter how impoverished, to purchase his share of land. By August 1950, when the transfer of land was completed, about 2.8 million acres of rice land and 1.95 million acres of upland had been purchased from 2.34 million landowners and resold to 4.75 million tenants and farmers who possessed less land than the legal maximum. Only 12 percent of all arable land remained under tenancy, and low rents were fixed by law on this land. The percentage of full tenants dropped from 27.7 percent of the farmers in 1941 to about 5 percent in 1950. In addition, 600,000 acres of pasture land were acquired by the government for redistribution.

Labor Reforms

Another feature of the U.S. policy to strengthen democratic forces and create a more equitable distribution of wealth was the attempt to foster an independent trade union movement in Japan. The Japanese labor movement had emerged in the late nineteenth century, but labor faced the continuous opposition of the government and business interests. By the 1930s, the movement had essentially been emasculated, with workers being denied the right to strike because of the "national emergency" created by Japanese military actions on the continent. Agitation by labor leaders regarded as procommunist organizers was made illegal and punishable by imprisonment. With the end of the war and SCAP's pledge to foster democracy and freedom, labor union leaders, including Communist Party leaders who had been released from prison, set out to revitalize the union movement. A noncommunist labor leader, Matsuoka Komakichi, revived the Japan Federation of Labor (Sodomei) and the Communist leaders just released from prison set out to organize a Communist-led union movement. By mid-1946, a major Communist labor union, the Sanbetsu (Congress of Industrial Unions), was established with a membership of 1.6 million.

In accordance with SCAP's directives, a number of labor laws were enacted by the Japanese Diet. The Japanese government wanted to reserve the right of the government to intervene in labor disputes and restrict the right of government employees and workers in the public service sector to strike, but SCAP opposed imposing any restrictions. This was not surprising because at SCAP, the Labor Division of the General Headquarters was staffed by officials who had ties with labor or had worked for the U.S. Labor Department.

In December 1945, a trade union law was passed that guaranteed workers, including public service employees and teachers, the right to organize, engage in collective bargaining, and strike. In 1946, legislation was enacted to set up grievance procedures for the settling of labor disputes, at the same time denying public-safety and administrative employees the right to strike. In 1947, the Labor Standards Law was enacted, setting minimum standards for working hours, vacation, safety, and sanitation safeguards, sick leaves, accident compensation, and restrictions on the hours and conditions under which women and children could work. The law "significantly exceeded the U.S. Fair Labor Standards Act in coverage."[46]

It was through SCAP's paternalistic policies that Japanese workers acquired the protection and rights that had been denied them under the old regime. The number of unions and union members mushroomed by virtue of these sanctions, and by 1949, more than 6.5 million out of a total of 15 million industrial workers were enrolled in the more than 35,000 unions.

Educational Reforms

As noted previously, the memo handed to Prime Minister Shidehara by General MacArthur called for liberalization of education. The object was to remove militaristic and ultranationalistic influence from the schools and to inculcate democratic values in the students. The bureaucrats in the ministry of education, as might be expected, resisted introducing radical changes. The Minister of Education believed that it was necessary to stress the 1890 Imperial Rescript on Education to combat "the root of our recent moral decay." Until the end of the war, it had been traditional for public school children to recite the Imperial Rescript on Education, written in archaic literary style, every day before the start of class. However, General MacArthur and the officials at the general headquarters were determined to build the educational system on new premises. In October 1945, in his directives on educational reforms, General MacArthur ordered the Japanese government to revise the content of all educational instruction "in harmony with representative government, international peace, the dignity of the individual, and such fundamental rights as the freedom of assembly, speech and religion."[47]

In March 1946, an educational mission headed by George D. Stoddard, New York State commissioner of education, submitted a report to SCAP recommending that militaristic, ultranationalistic teachers be purged from the schools, that textbooks be revised, and that numerous changes be made in the curriculum. The report also recommended the extension of compulsory education to nine years; decentralization of control; and establishment of more institutions of higher learning. Stoddard's group advised the fundamental revision of the basic educational program, which stressed rote learning, and its replacement with a program that would encourage students to think by responding to new situations and by taking the initiative in exploring new ideas.

In order to remove militaristic and nationalistic concepts from the curriculum, General MacArthur directed that "new curricula, textbooks, teaching manuals, and instructional materials designed to produce an educated, peaceful, and responsible citizenry . . . be prepared." The Japanese government set out to revise the textbooks on its own, but the minister of education insisted that Japanese textbooks must "defend and promote the mythic imperial polity (*koku-*

tai), and high moral education." The revisions based on these principles were found unacceptable by SCAP officials. They concluded that "all the textbooks in morals, Japanese history and geography . . . had proved to be most pernicious." General MacArthur suspended the teaching of morals and Japanese history and geography until new textbooks were written. The revised Japanese history textbooks were examined meticulously to remove any passage that made "the Emperor or Japan in general sound too positive." The teaching of morals was eliminated from the curriculum.

The school system was reorganized in accordance with the American 6–3–3–4 (elementary, junior high, senior high, and college) system instead of the former 6–5–3–3 (elementary, middle, higher, and college) system. Control of the public elementary and secondary schools was turned over to locally elected boards of education. Prefectural boards, which were elected by the people, were established to coordinate the educational program in each prefecture, to certify teachers and administrators, and to approve all the textbooks. The control that the Ministry of Education had formerly exercised was eliminated; that body was now to provide only technical aid and professional counsel to the boards. It was no longer to write public school textbooks, although it was allowed to retain the practice of certifying them. The Ministry of Education issued a curriculum guide that the prefectural and local school boards used for guidance.

To increase the number of institutions of higher education, 68 new national universities and 99 other new universities were established in 1949. Junior colleges came into existence in 1950 and 205 of them had been founded by 1952. However, the quality of many of these institutions was poor, as they had formerly been higher schools, normal schools, and technical institutions. Consequently, the prestige of the older institutions was enhanced even further. This led to fierce competition among young students aspiring to enter the prestigious institutions.

A new force in the educational field emerged as another product of the postwar changes. This was the Japan Teachers' Union (Nihon Kyoshukuin Kumiai), a militant labor union strongly influenced by left-wing politics. It has continually kept a watchful eye on any trend that might presage a reversion to the former ways of imperial Japan. The militancy of this union's leaders was heightened by the government's campaign in 1949 to remove all Communists from the school system. At the college level, another powerful political force emerged in the form of a student organization. The National Student Federation (Zengakuren), organized in September 1948, provided forceful leadership in staging political demonstrations to combat whatever it deemed as undemocratic.[48]

A New Constitution

The most significant effort to democratize the Japanese nation occurred in the political realm. In this area, the United States set the following course of action: eliminate the power of the emperor, make the executive power of the government responsible to the people or their representatives, establish a legislative body that would be directly responsible to all adult citizens, and develop democratically controlled political parties. To accomplish this transformation, the essential undertaking was the adoption of a new constitution.

The U.S. government had not formulated any plan to revise the Japanese Constitution, so the planning committee on Japanese occupation, the SWNCC, did not specifically mention constitutional revisions in its directive to SCAP. General MacArthur took the initiative to revise the constitution in order to accomplish the goal of democratizing the country. In early October 1945, Prince Konoe met with General MacArthur, and the latter evidently encouraged Konoe to explore the question of constitutional revision. Konoe therefore set out to work on drafting possible constitutional changes. The general also advised Prime Minister Shidehara to work on constitutional revisions. The prime minister then appointed a Tokyo Imperial University law professor, Matsumoto Joji, to study the matter. Thus, there were two separate Japanese groups working on the project. Konoe's draft contained hardly any changes from the Meiji Constitution. Nonetheless, his role in revising the Japanese Constitution soon became a nonissue, because shortly thereafter he was designated a war criminal, and he subsequently committed suicide.

The Matsumoto version, as the newspaper *Mainichi Shimbun* reported, took 39 of the 76 articles directly from the Meiji Constitution. It held Japan to be a monarchy with the emperor as the sovereign authority. Yoshida Shigeru, who was foreign minister at that time, recalls that Matsumoto maintained that "no change was to be made to the principle of sovereignty residing in the Emperor."[49] This, of course, conflicted with the SCAP principle that sovereignty resided in the people. It was inevitable that SCAP would find the Matsumoto draft unacceptable, with its unchanged role of the emperor and its close adherence to the Meiji Constitution.

After General MacArthur was presented with the Matsumoto draft, he decided to have SCAP officials draft the constitution, instructing the chief of the Government Section, Major General Courtney Whitney, to work on the project. Whitney was told to incorporate three principles: limited monarchy, renunciation of war, and abolition of feudalism.[50] Whitney appointed a three-man committee to work on the project. One short week later, they had completed the draft, which consisted of 92 articles.

The Japanese authorities were disturbed by the SCAP draft and attempted to modify it by using carefully chosen Japanese terms in the translation in order to render it closer in meaning to their version. The new Japanese Constitution was made public on March 7, 1946, and was presented as a creation of the Japanese government. However, the public suspected that it was a product of SCAP because the text read like a translation. One distinctive feature of the new constitution was its use of colloquial Japanese, the first official document to be so written.

The draft constitution was then turned over to the Diet for consideration and adoption. After lengthy deliberation about the wording of the translation, the House of Representatives of the Diet adopted the new constitution on August 21, 1946, by a vote of 429 to 8. Five of the nay votes were cast by Communists, who opposed preserving the imperial institution. On October 6, the House of Peers approved the new constitution.

Records of the closed debates in the subcommittee that examined the American draft were sealed until 1956. The inherent linguistic differences between English and Japanese made for ambiguities and resulted in some changes in meaning. Professor Kyoko Ionue, who has compared the English version and the Japanese (translated) version sees differences in illocutionary force. She concludes that in drafting a democratic constitution "the Americans used, to a considerable extent, the language of their own Constitution. This, however, resulted in an inconsistency in the illocutionary force of the Japanese Constitution as drafted in English."[51]

The new Japanese Constitution changed the identity and role of the emperor from that of an absolute monarch to "the symbol of the State and unity of the people." Sovereignty was now vested in the people. The cabinet was made directly responsible to the Diet, which was made "the highest organ of state power." The members of the two houses were to be elected directly by the people. The upper house (House of Councillors) was given less power than the lower house (House of Representatives), which could override a negative vote in the upper house by passing a bill a second time with a two-thirds majority.

In the committee discussions, Article 24, which deals with marriage and equality of the sexes, caused much debate because Diet members found it difficult "to understand the idea of individual dignity, or its relation to the idea of equality of sexes." Their major concern was preserving the tradition of familism. One Diet member asserted, "I cannot help having considerable doubts about whether the traditional family system can be maintained under this draft." The debate proceeded with the understanding that "dignity of the individual" referred to the ethical character of the individual, and the phrase did not imply the American view that "individual dignity refers to the right of the autonomous individual to think for themselves, make their own decisions, and live their own lives as they see fit. The Japanese interpretation is closer to a sense of duty or responsibility than to [a] right."[52]

The Japanese Constitution provides comprehensive coverage of the rights of the people. In addition to the rights and liberties provided for in the American Bill of Rights, the Japanese Constitution has provisions for social welfare. It states that "All people have the right to maintain the minimum standards of wholesome and cultured living. In all spheres of life, the State shall use its endeavors for the promotion and extension of social welfare and security, and of public health." It also guarantees the people's right to an education, the right of labor to organize and engage in collective bargaining, and the equality of husband and wife. In addition, it provides for full legal protection against arbitrary arrest and punishment. In other words, rule of law had finally become a reality in Japan.

Although the draft prepared by SCAP disturbed many of the Diet members who wished to retain the Meiji Constitution, it was finally passed and proclaimed the law of the land on November 3, 1946. It went into effect in May 1947.

A unique feature of the new Japanese Constitution is contained in Article 9, the "no-war" clause:

> Aspiring sincerely to an international peace based on justice and order, the Japanese people forever renounce war as a sovereign right of the nation and the threat or use of force as means of settling international disputes.
>
> In order to accomplish the aim of the preceding paragraph, land, sea and air forces, as well as other war potential, will never be maintained. The right of belligerency of the State will not be recognized.

Japanese officials, including Ashida Hitoshi, who later became prime minister, inserted the clause "in order to accomplish the aim" to leave open the possibility of arms for self-defense. Yoshida Shigeru was opposed to the idea of limiting the no-war clause only to aggressive war because, he contended, wars can be started in the name of defense.[53] Article 9 later proved to be an embarrassment for the United States, which, in the course of the growing tension with the Communist powers, began to favor rearming Japan. Consequently, a tortuous reinterpretation of the clause condemning war was made, in order to enable Japan to maintain "self-defense" forces.

Finally, as already noted, changes were introduced at the local level to strengthen the autonomy of local governments and foster democratic procedures. In particular, the authority that the Ministry of Home Affairs had formerly exercised over local governments was removed.

Social Reforms

In the realm of social reforms, the most significant legal changes were introduced into the family system, particularly affecting the status of women. The equal rights of husband and wife were guaranteed. A wife gained the rights to own property independently and to obtain a divorce on the same grounds that men could use. Primogeniture was abolished, and daughters were given the right to inherit the same share of the family property as sons. The authority formerly held by the head of the stem family was removed. Family registries were to be compiled on the basis of the nuclear, conjugal family. The legal age for marriage without the consent of parents was changed to eighteen for males and sixteen for females. However, these legal changes, of course, did not bring about an immediate end to the old ways.

Among the social reforms initiated by the Japanese was the antiprostitution law of 1956, which finally removed the many brothels that had occupied fixed quarters of the towns and cities for centuries. The birth control movement gained popular support, resulting in the legalization of abortion in June 1949. The campaign to limit birth has enabled Japan to reduce its birth rate drastically, as discussed later on.

The Japanese Government During Occupation, 1945–1952

The reason the United States carried out its policies through the Japanese government was to avoid establishment of a military government. The cabinet and the Diet were essentially handmaidens of SCAP until the peace treaty went into effect in April 1952. Many of the reforms ordered by SCAP were adopted or set in motion by the Shidehara government. With the lifting of political barriers, a host of new and revived political parties emerged. The former members of the prewar Seiyukai, led by Hatoyama Ichiro, formed the Japan Liberal Party (Jiyuto). Former members of the prewar political party, the Minseito, formed the Japan Progressive Party (Shimpoto); Shidehara became its president after the first head was purged by SCAP. The Socialists organized the Japan Socialist Party, with Katayama Tetsu chosen as leader. The Communists, led by Tokuda Kyuichi, who had just been released from prison after eighteen years of incarceration, formed the Communist Party.

Faced with political opposition over reforms such as the revision of the constitution, Prime Minister Shidehara dissolved the Diet and held a national election in April 1946. In intense competition, 2,770 candidates ran for the 466 Diet seats. There were 363 participating political parties, many of which were one-person parties. In the election, the Liberal Party won 140 seats; the Progressive Party, 94; the Socialist Party, 92; and the Communist Party, 5. The Communist leader Nozaka Sanzo (1892–1993), home from years of exile, played up the idea of the "lovable Communist Party," but the voters did not seem to buy that concept.

When the Progressive Party gained only 94 seats, Shidehara resigned as prime minister. Hatoyama expected to become the next prime minister, as his party had won the largest number of seats, but he was purged by SCAP for his prewar political activities, such as dismissing a liberal Kyoto University professor in 1933 while he was minister of education. Shidehara favored Yoshida Shigeru (1885–1954) as his successor.

Yoshida had a distinguished career as a foreign service officer, but he had been incarcerated by Tojo during the war for being involved in a plan to end the war. Although he was not a member of any political party, Shidehara persuaded him to take on the presidency of the Liberal Party and assume the premiership. Hatoyama later claimed that Yoshida had agreed to turn over the premiership as soon as Hatoyama had been rehabilitated. Yoshida reflects that "Mr. Hatoyama probably imagined that my tenure as president of the Liberal Party would last only until the opportunity came for him to reenter public life and resume that position; I myself certainly had no idea at that time that I should retain the presidency of the party and the Premiership for very long."[54]

The first Yoshida cabinet remained in office for one year. During this period, many of the reforms that had been initiated during the Shidehara regime were adopted. The land reforms were begun, implementation of the new educational system occurred, and the Diet approved the new constitution. During this period, labor unions led by the Communists and left-wing Socialists began to challenge the government, staging a general strike over the government's policy of denying government and public service workers the right to strike. This resulted in SCAP banning the general strike scheduled for February 1, 1947, as is discussed more fully further on.

The new constitution was to come into effect in May 1947, so SCAP ordered new elections in April of that year. In March, some splinter groups from other parties joined the Progressive Party and formed the Democratic Party. In the April elections the Socialist Party emerged as the big winner, earning 143 seats. The Liberal Party won 131 seats, and the Democratic Party, 124. The Communist Party managed to garner only 4 seats, despite the strikes and demonstrations that were being staged by the party and its allies in the labor movement. Another offshoot of the prewar political parties, the Cooperative Party, won 31 seats.

The Socialist Party, as the party with the largest number of seats, was given the task of forming a new cabinet, with Katayama Tetsu (1887–1978) chosen as prime minister. Some have contended that SCAP favored a Socialist government, in the belief that it would be more effective than a conservative government in keeping labor under control.

Katayama organized his cabinet by forming a coalition with the Democratic Party, which was headed by Ashida Hitoshi (1887–1959), and the Cooperative Party. Thus, the first and, until 1994, the only Socialist government came into existence in May 1947. Under the Katayama cabinet, the old Ministry of Home Affairs, as previously noted, was abolished, and civil and criminal law codes were revised. The Socialists favored nationalizing the key industries, but the legislation they drew up failed to pass the Diet. Katayama was challenged by the left-wing Socialists over his policy of moderation. The Katayama cabinet, like other postwar governments, was beset with problems, particularly unemployment, food shortages, inflation, and labor unrest. When Katayama sought to raise railroad and postal fees, the left-wing Socialists opposed him, and he was forced to resign.

The Socialist, Democratic, and Cooperative Parties formed a coalition to enable Ashida, Democratic Party head and foreign minister in the Katayama cabinet, to form a new cabinet. Ashida sought to bring labor under control and revive the economy, but he was forced to resign when a scandal involving government officials, including him, was exposed. These officials had received bribes from a chemical fertilizer company (Showa Denko) to help the company obtain loans from the Reconstruction Finance Bank. Thus, the Ashida government had a short reign of only seven months, from March to October 1948.

The Liberal Party and a faction of the Democratic Party had merged to form the Democratic Liberal Party in March 1948. It is said that the Government Section of SCAP did not favor the conservative Yoshida, but as the head of the Democratic Liberal Party, he managed to gain sufficient support to form his second cabinet in October. From October 1948 to December 1954, Yoshida was able to remain in office for a six-year period, which was longer than any previous prime minister. His government played a major role in Japan's political and economic recovery.

Immediately after forming his second cabinet, Yoshida dissolved the Diet and held a national election in January 1949. His party won a decisive victory then, increasing its number of Diet seats from 152 to 264, thereby becoming the first party to win an absolute majority in the 466-member postwar Diet. The Communist Party managed to win strong support in the inner-city districts of Tokyo and Osaka. Still the "reformist parties" did poorly in general in this election, presaging the ascendancy of the conservative parties during the postwar years. Yoshida's victory in this election also dates the rise of the former bureaucrats; sixty-two Diet members were former bureaucrats. This election marks the formation of the triangular power bloc composed of conservative party members, bureaucrats, and business interests that dominated Japan for the next four and one-half decades.

Yoshida formed his third cabinet in February 1950 and concentrated on preserving political stability and advancing the country's economic recovery. He was faced with opposition from the Left, from the Communists in particular, who accused him of pursuing a "reverse course policy," that is, of seeking to undo many of the reforms introduced by SCAP. Pursuing a policy of retrenchment recommended by Joseph Dodge, a Detroit banker sent by the United States to study the Japanese financial situation, in 1949 the Yoshida government adopted a plan to reduce the workforce in state-run enterprises by 260,000 workers.[55] The government began implementing its plan by dismissing the national railroad workers. This led to a number of violent incidents that intensified the confrontation between the government and the labor unions. It also gave the Communists a popular cause with which to challenge the Yoshida government. With the growing militancy of the Communists and the outbreak of the Korean War, SCAP decided to recommend the purging of Communists from government positions and government corporations. Thus, the Yoshida government instituted the Red Purge in mid-1950, driving the Communist leaders underground.

In June 1950, the Korean War broke out. Japan became an important staging zone for U.S. forces as well as an essential source for military procurements. This gave a tremendous boost to the Japanese economy, which had been plagued with shortages and inflation ever since the end of the war.

One of Yoshida's cardinal objectives was the signing of a peace treaty to end the presence of U.S. occupation forces, something the United States was also aiming for. The U.S. policy toward Japan had shifted from the original objective of keeping Japan from reemerging as a military power to rebuilding its economy instead. With the outbreak of the Korean War and the stage set for the Cold War, the United States began to see the transformation of Japan in a different light. Japan could become an important bastion in the anticommunist bloc that the United States wanted to forge. Thus, from the U.S. perspective, the conclusion of a peace treaty with Japan was essential to strengthen ties in preparation for confrontation with the Communist powers.

The Peace Treaty

The United States had achieved its major objectives, the demilitarization and democratization of Japan, and Japan, under the firm leadership of Yoshida, was achieving a significant degree of political, social, and economic stability. General MacArthur was convinced that a prolonged occupation would have adverse effects, and as early as spring 1947, he began advocating the conclusion of a peace treaty. He believed that the "consummation of a just peace for Japan is one way—possibly the most dramatic and dynamic way open at this time—of asserting our leadership and regaining our lost initiative in the course of Asian affairs."[56]

In spring 1950, Secretary of State John Foster Dulles was assigned the task of preparing the groundwork for the peace treaty. The plan worked out by Dulles entailed linking the peace treaty with the conclusion of a security pact, granting the United States the right to maintain military bases in Japan. Okinawa was to remain under U.S. trusteeship, with the United States retaining the right to maintain military bases there.

A key issue was whether all the powers concerned, including the Communist nations, should participate in the signing of the peace treaty. Realizing that the effort to convince the Communist powers to participate would require lengthy negotiations and delays in the conclusion of the treaty, Prime Minister Yoshida sent his minister of finance, Ikeda Hayato, to Washington to ask for an early conclusion of the peace treaty even if it meant nonparticipation by the Soviet Union. Yoshida had decided to agree to allow U.S. military bases to remain in Japan. He was most interested in concentrating on domestic developments, and relying on the United States for Japan's defense would further his domestic projects. Debate among U.S. officials about whether conclusion of the peace treaty was premature suddenly ended when the Korean War broke out in June 1950. Conclusion of the treaty was now seen as an urgent matter.

The Soviet Union did not stand alone in having reservations about concluding peace with Japan. However, Dulles negotiated with Australia, New Zealand, the Philippines, and England and received their agreement. The knotty issue of whether Taiwan or the Communist government in China should conclude a peace treaty with Japan was left for Japan to decide in the future.

A meeting was scheduled to sign the peace treaty in San Francisco in September 1951, and invitations were sent to fifty-five nations. Forty-eight nations signed the peace treaty with Japan. The Soviet Union attended the conference but did not sign the treaty because its request to amend provisions of the treaty was denied. Neither the Chinese Communist government nor the Taiwan government was invited. Later in 1951, after being urged into action by the United States, Japan signed a peace treaty with the Taiwan regime. In the peace treaty signed in San Francisco, the issue of the four Kurile islands occupied by the Soviet Union at the end of the war was not resolved nor was the question of reparations addressed. Each nation was to negotiate directly with Japan, and it was understood that reparations would take the form of industrial assistance rather than monetary compensation.

On the same day the peace treaty was signed, agreements on a mutual security treaty were concluded between Japan and the United States. The document provided for the continued U.S. military presence in Japan, to protect Japan from external aggressors and internal rebellions supported by external powers. The terms of the security agreement were spelled out in an administrative agreement signed in February of the following year.

The conservative parties favored ratification of the peace treaty, but the Socialists divided on the question. Right-wing Socialists favored ratification without Soviet participation but opposed linking the treaty to the security agreement. Left-wing Socialists opposed signing the peace treaty without Soviet participation and objected to the security treaty. The Communist Party opposed ratifying a treaty that did not include all the powers concerned and rejected a security treaty that provided for the continued U.S. military presence in Japan. Yoshida had sufficient support in the Diet to get the peace treaty ratified in October 1951; the treaty went into effect on April 28, 1952.

Thus SCAP ended its tenure as de facto ruling power in Japan. Its presence during the Occupation had brought about a truly revolutionary change in the country. The mandate given SCAP had been accomplished, resulting in the end of militarism and imperialism and the building of the superstructure for a democratic government and society. In sum, Japan now had a new constitution, land reforms, and a liberalized education system. The monopolistic economic control of the *zaibatsu* had been loosened. The reforms had elevated the status of women, the common people, and the working class. The police state had dissolved, and a protective bill of rights and the principle of habeas corpus had been instituted. Individualism and equality had become new social characteristics. These, among others, were the measures initiated and effected by a governing authority that accomplished a revolution without bloodshed.

Regardless of the natural tendency of some Japanese to minimize the positive role of SCAP and despite the expected opposition and negativism of the Left, no one can deny the truly remarkable achievements of the occupation authorities. Even the Japanese are compelled to admit the striking contrast between the occupation policy, conduct, and record of the United States in Japan and the Japanese occupation record in China and Southeast Asia during World War II.

General MacArthur, the man most responsible for the transformation of Japan, was gone from the country when the peace treaty was signed. He had been relieved of his post in April 1951 because of his disagreement with President Truman over the Korean campaign. He had been succeeded by General Matthew Ridgway.[57]

2

Political Developments
After Independence

Freed from the authority of SCAP in April 1952, the Yoshida government moved to revise some of the reforms that had been introduced, thus giving rise to a trend that the opposition labeled a "reverse course." The confrontation between the government and its critics, led by the opposition parties, labor unions, students, and intellectuals, became increasingly acrimonious.

The Yoshida Years

On May Day 1952, the first of a series of violent confrontations between demonstrators and the police erupted, touched off by labor union antagonism toward the Yoshida government and cultural and intellectual leaders' strident opposition to the projected law on the prevention of subversive activities. The opposition forces also strenuously objected to the government's agreement to permit American military bases to remain in Japan. Any move by the United States to increase its military facilities in Japan provoked massive demonstrations led by left-wing politicians, labor leaders, students, and intellectuals.

At the same time, a series of confrontations between Yoshida and the opposition parties rocked the Diet. The prime minister sought to enact legislation to modify some of the laws that had been passed during the occupation era. In addition to the bill banning subversive activities, Yoshida sought to introduce restrictive legislation in education. He claimed to be concerned about

the decline in public morals, the need for curbing excesses arising from a misunderstanding of the meaning of freedom, the neglect into which respect for the nation and its traditions had fallen due to mistaken ideas of progress, the biased political

41

outlook prevalent among university students . . . the need for raising the standards of teachers.[1]

Yoshida's primary object, however, was to curb the influence of communism in the public school system. To this end, he introduced two bills. The first one prohibited teachers of elementary and junior high schools from engaging in political activities, and the second prohibited the teachers' union from introducing educational material on politics into the curriculum. There was much opposition to the bills, but after some modifications, they were passed by the Diet in May 1954.

Yoshida's critics charged that the enactment of the subversive activities law in July 1952 was clearly an indication of an overall plan to reverse the course of reforms. Another controversial Yoshida-sponsored measure was the plan to centralize the police. Yoshida contended that fragmentation of the police into local units caused inefficiency and prevented the police force from being used effectively on a national scale. Opponents of this plan feared that Yoshida's move was really an effort to return to the prewar system in which the police suppressed political and ideological dissent. The bill was nevertheless introduced in the Diet. It was vigorously opposed by opposition party members, who ultimately resorted to physical obstruction to prevent its passage. However, in June 1954, the bill was passed while its opponents boycotted the session. The measure provided for the abolition of municipal police and their replacement with prefectural police forces whose activities would be coordinated at the top level by the National Public Safety Commission and the national police.

At the onset of the Cold War, SCAP wanted to establish a 75,000-man Japanese security force to replace the U.S. troops that had been dispatched to Korea. Thus in October 1950, the National Police Reserve was established. Yoshida was opposed to rearming because he was convinced that it would hinder his plan to rebuild the economy. He was counting on the Socialists to oppose this move for rearmament.

The proponents of the creation of the police reserve contended that it was not rearmament but was designed to maintain order within Japanese territory and therefore did not violate the no-war clause of the Japanese Constitution. Soon after the peace treaty went into effect, the police reserve manpower was increased to 110,000. The maritime reserve, which functioned as a coast guard, was also strengthened by the loan of eighteen frigates and fifty landing craft from the United States. In 1954, in order to be eligible for further military aid, Yoshida signed the Mutual Security Treaty with the United States. The agreement provided for the extension of military aid to countries prepared to defend themselves, and called for the United States to help Japan defend itself in case of aggression by a third power. In return, Japan was to purchase American surplus agricultural products, expand its land and sea defense forces, and acquire coast guard vessels and submarines from the United States. Yoshida then submitted two bills to the Diet to transform the police reserve into a defense force. These were the Defense Agency Establishment Bill and the Self-Defense Force Bill.

As Yoshida had hoped, the Socialist party vigorously opposed the bills, asserting that they were the first step in the rearmament of Japan. The Progressive Party, led by Shigemitsu Mamoru (1887–1957) who had signed the surrender document on the *Missouri* as foreign minister, supported the bills and managed to get them passed, thus establishing the Defense Agency. The new agency was charged with the task of defending the peace and independence of Japan. The Ground Self-Defense Force, the Maritime Self-Defense Force, and the Air Self-Defense Force were established under the aegis of the Defense Agency. The apparent violation of Article 9 of the Japanese Constitution, which expressly prohibits the maintenance of military forces, was dismissed by the creators of the defense forces, who argued that the Japanese Constitution did not rule out self-defense. Yoshida, insisting that there was a difference between rearmament and the creation of self-defense forces, remarked that "the idea of rearmament has always seemed to be one verging on idiocy."[2] The pressure to rearm was exerted with greater intensity by the United States as the Cold War became more critical to U.S. interests.

Yoshida's political difficulties began shortly after the peace treaty was signed, when he began to face growing opposition within his party. The forces of opposition had begun to coalesce in mid-1951, when former politicians who had been purged were rehabilitated. Among them were Hatoyama and his supporters, conservatives who regarded the Yoshida government as temporary—a regime to be replaced as soon as Hatoyama could return to political life. These politicians expected Yoshida to relinquish his post when Hatoyama was rehabilitated. Although Hatoyama suffered a mild stroke just before the purge was lifted, his faction still wanted Yoshida to turn over the premiership to him. Hatoyama, who disapproved of Yoshida's policy of cooperation with the United States, favored establishing diplomatic ties with the Soviet Union, revising the constitution, and rearming Japan. The other conservative party, the Democratic Party, merged with two minor parties and formed the Progressive Party (Kaishinto).

Faced with opposition from the Hatoyama faction, Yoshida sought to increase his support in the Diet and dissolved it in August 1952. The Liberal Party lost 45 seats, dropping from 285 to 240. Of these, 73 were Yoshida supporters, 68 were for Hatoyama, and 99 were neutral.[3] One hundred and thirty-nine of the winners had just been rehabilitated, so it appeared that the old-line politicians were making a comeback. Nevertheless, the Hatoyama faction could not rally enough support to replace Yoshida, who was then able to form his fourth cabinet.

Yoshida was forced to dissolve the Diet again, however. The Socialists, angered because Yoshida called one of their members a "damn fool," called for and achieved a no-confidence vote. In the election that followed in April 1953, the Hatoyama faction, which had formed its own Japan Liberal Party, ran a campaign calling for constitutional revision and rearmament. The same policies were advocated by the Progessive Party. The Yoshida faction opposed constitutional revision and called for a gradual expansion of the self-defense force. The election resulted in Yoshida's Japan Liberal Party winning 199 seats, less than a majority.[4]

Yoshida formed his fifth cabinet, this time with minority support in the Diet. In order to get Shigemitsu's support, Yoshida agreed, as noted, to upgrade the Reserve Police Force, turning it into the Self-Defense Force, and established the Defense Agency as well. He also persuaded Hatoyama to rejoin the Japan Liberal Party, and in return, he agreed to establish a constitutional study committee.

Although Yoshida was a strong leader, he was not very popular personally. He was tactless, cocksure, and autocratic, and his critics charged him with conducting a "one-man" government. The left-wing parties in particular constantly clashed with him, but lacking the voting strength to prevent him from passing "reverse course" measures, they could only demonstrate their opposition by physically disrupting Diet proceedings. Labor leaders were also hostile to Yoshida for such actions as passing the law prohibiting strikes by electric power and mine workers.

Opposition to Yoshida from the Hatoyama faction in his own party continued. Kishi Shinsuke (1896–1987), who had been incarcerated as a war criminal for his prewar and wartime activities, was released from prison in 1948. He joined the Liberal Party in March 1953 and became a supporter of Hatoyama. The two men formed the Japan Democratic Party in November 1954 with the intent to oppose Yoshida. Then, in cooperation with the Socialist parties they called for yet another no-confidence vote against Yoshida in the Diet. Yoshida sought to counter this by dissolving the Diet, but big business interests opposed the move because they favored unity, not conflict among the conservatives. Faced with opposition from members of his own party as well, Yoshida was forced to resign in December 1954. He then severed ties with the Liberal Party and played the role of an elder statesman until his death in 1967.

The Post-Yoshida Years

Yoshida, who had guided Japan for the six years that spanned the difficult occupation period, set the nation on the path to self-sufficiency and independence. He maintained close ties with the United States, kept military spending to a minimum by relying on the United States to protect Japan, concluded the peace treaty, and signed the security pact with the United States.

Yoshida was succeeded as prime minister by Hatoyama. Hatoyama appointed mainly prewar politicians to his cabinet, in contrast to Yoshida, whose key cabinet members were bureaucrats. Unlike Yoshida, Hatoyama favored revising the constitution, rearming Japan, and pursuing an independent course in foreign policy. He therefore departed from Yoshida's policy of close cooperation with the United States and set out to normalize relations with the Soviet Union and Communist China.

Hatoyama's Japan Democratic Party (the former Japan Liberal Party) lacked a majority in the Diet, which he dissolved shortly after taking office, hoping to strengthen his party's position. In the election held in February 1955, his party emerged with 185 seats, becoming the largest faction, though still lacking a majority.

Japanese business interests wanted the conservative parties to merge to check the power of the left-wing groups. Thus pressured by business organizations, the leaders of the two major conservative parties set aside their personal rivalry, agreeing to the merger. In November 1955, the Liberal Democratic Party (LDP) was born. This merger set the basis for the one-party control that dominated the Japanese political stage until 1993, referred to as the "1955 system."

Just prior to the conservative party merger, the two Socialist parties also united, for the next thirty-eight years functioning as the major opposition party to the dominant LDP. At this point in 1955, the conservatives held roughly two-thirds of the Diet seats, and the Socialists, one-third. This configuration remained more or less intact until 1993. At the same time, Communist leaders resurfaced after having gone underground during the Red Purge of 1950, as is discussed later on.

Hatoyama pursued his goal of revising the constitution—namely deleting Article 9 (the antiwar clause)—to make it possible for Japan to rearm. He also pushed for educational changes, aiming to make the school board members appointed rather than elected and to institute stricter government control over public school textbook content. In the face of heavy opposition, he managed to pass a law providing for the former but failed on the latter issue. In October 1956, the minister of education issued a decree on textbook certification.

To pursue his goal of normalizing relations with the Soviet Union, Hatoyama initiated talks with the Soviet government. When the two sides failed to agree on the disposition of the southern Kurile Islands, which were still under Soviet control, Hatoyama decided that in order to avert a breakdown in the discussions it would be wise not to press the issue. In October 1956, he traveled to Moscow and personally concluded an agreement normalizing relations between the two countries, which included arrangements on commerce and fishing. Trade between the two countries began to increase slowly.

In December 1956, Hatoyama was forced to resign because of poor health. His successor remained in office for only two months and also left office because of illness.[5] The LDP then turned to Kishi, who, upon release from prison, had made a comeback in the political world as an active member of the Liberal Party. He had left that party to join Hatoyama's Democratic party, but when the two conservative parties merged to form the Liberal Democratic Party in November 1955, he became its secretary-general.

Kishi as Prime Minister

Kishi remained in office from February 1957 to September 1960. He believed that the constitution needed revision in order to enlarge the emperor's authority somewhat and restrict the Diet's power. He also favored increasing the power of the police and removing Communists from the schools. When faced with strong opposition from the Socialists, he dissolved the Diet. In the May 1958 election, his party lost 10 seats and dropped to 287 seats in the lower house. The Socialists won 166 seats, and the Communists 1.

In the realm of foreign affairs, as noted later in Chapter 3, Kishi sought to adjust Japan's ties with South Korea and the Southeast Asian countries. His policy toward the Communist powers adhered closely to the U.S. anticommunist line. Although he wanted Japan's foreign policy to be in tune with U.S. policy, he felt it necessary to revise the security treaty in order to place Japan on a more equal footing with the United States. Negotiations were conducted with the United States, and in October 1959, the two nations agreed on the terms of revision. The treaty provided for the continued use of Japanese bases by U.S. forces, but the United States agreed to confer with Japan before dispatching the U.S. troops posted in Japan to military operations abroad. A time limit of ten years was set for the treaty, after which either side could cancel it on one year's notice. Kishi and his supporters hailed the new security agreement as an improvement over the former treaty because it was a pact concluded between equals.

But the Socialists, labor leaders, Communists, students, intellectuals, cultural leaders, and pacifists objected vociferously. They contended that the provision stipulating cooperation between the two countries to maintain peace in the Far East created a tacit agreement that drew Japan into a military alliance against the Communist nations, particularly Communist China. A massive campaign was launched to prevent ratification of the treaty. Those who opposed the pact not only feared the revival of militarism and the possibility of being drawn into a war, but many also distrusted American foreign policy which, they held, represented the forces of imperialism. This attitude toward the United States was matched by a tendency to view the Communist nations as the friends of peace.

Starting in late 1959, street demonstrations organized to oppose the security treaty grew larger and more frenzied. The treaty opponents persuaded the labor unions to strike in protest against the pact, and millions of workers went on strike in June. Student demonstrators clashed with police in front of the Diet building; one student was killed in the turmoil.

Kishi, however, remained resolute in his decision to have the treaty ratified, and he whipped into line those conservative party members who were wavering. The left-wing Socialists were bent on blocking ratification, by using physical obstruction if necessary. On May 19 and 20, 1960, the Diet was turned into a virtual combat zone as both supporters and opponents of the treaty ignored parliamentary protocol and resorted to violence. Diet members literally wrestled with one another while thousands of demonstrators snake-danced outside, voicing their angry opposition to the pact. The opponents sought to block the treaty by preventing the Speaker from occupying his chair. Finally, Kishi's faction summoned the police, who removed the obstructionists and escorted the Speaker to his chair. Then, while the Socialists boycotted the session, the Liberal Democrats approved the treaty.

It is understood in Japanese political procedure that a simple majority in the Diet does not entitle the majority party to ignore the wishes and interests of opposition party members. According to one scholar, "In this sytstem if you win sixty percent of the vote you are allowed to carry out sixty percent of your program, not one hundred percent."[6] Hence, when Prime Minister Kishi rammed the revised Mutual Security Treaty through over the frenzied opposition of the other parties, he was charged with behaving undemocratically. A tumultuous uproar ensued, and a movement to unseat him gained force.

Political agitators as well as radical leaders of the National Student Federation organized mass demonstrations against Kishi. There was also widespread public support for the movement "to defend democracy." The demonstrations began taking an increasingly anti-American cast, and on June 10, President Dwight D. Eisenhower's press secretary, James Hagerty, who was in Japan to prepare for the president's visit, became the target of a student demonstration. Hagerty was forced to escape the mob by helicopter. A few days later, after violence erupted again between demonstrators and the police, Eisenhower's visit was canceled. The protest movement finally subsided when the treaty went into effect on June 19, 1960. The demonstrators may have failed to prevent the ratification of the Mutual Security Treaty, but they did succeed in bringing about the downfall of Kishi, who resigned as soon as Japanese and U.S. ratifications were exchanged on June 23.

Kishi was the last of the prewar and wartime political leaders to assume power in postwar Japan. In 1993, political analysts evaluating the significant political accomplishments of the postwar years included Kishi's conclusion of the Mutual Security Treaty as one of the most important achievements.

Following Kishi's resignation, a political struggle for the premiership among rival factions in the Liberal Democratic Party ensued. The intraparty power struggle among factions, which began when the Hatoyama faction challenged Yoshida's leadership, continued to characterize the LDP.

To become a serious contender for party leadership, a faction leader had to have scores of supporters in his group, and to gain such support, he needed access to financial sources in order to underwrite his supporters in their own election campaigns. The source of funding, of course, was big business, which therefore had significant leverage over party affairs. Business interests wanted to prevent the conservative party from breaking up into separate parties. Thus, there were limits to the amount of factional power struggle they would tolerate. Dissolution of the conservatives alliance, as had previously occurred in

November 1955 with the formation of the Liberal Democratic Party, was viewed as intolerable. As long as party factions did not split from the party, LDP control of conservative party power would be allowed to continue. The LDP's 1955 power construct held until 1993, when splinter groups left the party.

Under the restraints imposed by big business, then, the power struggle to succeed Kishi raged. The contest was finally won by Ikeda Hayato (1899–1965), who assumed the premiership in July 1960 and remained in office until November 1964. As an official in the Ministry of Finance, he had risen throught the ranks of the bureaucracy. He represented the party leaders with similar bureacratic backgrounds and was supported by Kishi and Sato Eisaku, another future prime minister. And he had the support of business interests. Ikeda avoided Kishi's confrontational tactic vis-à-vis the Socialist Party and adopted a conciliatory approach. One concrete result of this approach was his success in settling the miners' strike against the Mitsui-owned Miike Mine, which had been going on since January 1960. He arranged negotiations and settled the dispute soon after he took office.

Ikeda did not push for constitutional revision or rearmament, as had Hatoyama and Kishi. He replaced Kishi's focus on foreign policy with emphasis on economic expansion, pledging to double the national income in ten years. As discussed later in the section on economic developments, the economy had been expanding throughout the 1950s, but Ikeda planned to accelerate the growth by liberalizing government controls and instituting greater government investments.

The general economic prosperity wrought by the conservative parties in the 1950s and 1960s had made their grip on the reins of power secure. The Socialists continued to wallow in their doctrinaire quagmire, failing to make any inroads into the electoral base of the conservatives. Even after acrimonious confrontations during the first six months of 1960, the Socialists were unable to broaden their power base when Ikeda dissolved the Diet in the fall. The Socialists had expected that the bitterness that split the country over the Mutual Security Treaty would redound in their favor, but it did not turn out that way. The LDP won a resounding victory in the fall 1960 election, gaining 296 seats, compared to the Socialist Party's 145.

Just prior to the election a young right-wing fanatic stabbed Asanuma Inejiro, a leader of the Socialist Party. A few months before this, Kishi had also been attacked and injured. In February 1961, another fanatical right-wing youth charged into the home of the publisher of an influential journal, injuring the man's wife and killing a housekeeper. The extremists attacked the publisher for publishing a story that the assassin considered akin to lèse-majesté, that is, the story was an offense against the emperor. Although these incidents caused some people to fear the revival of the type of right-wing fanaticism that had prevailed in the prewar years, that view was held by only a small minority. Such fears virtually disappeared with the high-speed economic growth under Ikeda.

Ikeda's income-doubling plan even convinced bitter opponents of the Mutual Security Treaty—like the Socialists and labor union leaders—to play down political issues and focus on economic growth. Ikeda's initiative in launching Japan on the path of high-speed economic growth resulted in Japan's emergence as a world-class economic power. In this sense Ikeda's assumption of the premiership in 1960 can be regarded as a milestone in postwar Japanese history.

However, despite Ikeda's success in economic planning, factional strife in the party did not cease. The term of office for the LDP party chairman was two years, after which he could be reelected or be succeeded by someone else. Ikeda was chosen to continue as head and prime minister in 1962, but Sato Eisaku (1901–1975) expected Ikeda to turn over the leadership to him in 1964. When Ikeda gave no indication of doing so, Sato began to challenge him. He criticized Ikeda's high-speed economic growth policy, saying that social issues deserved greater attention. Sato challenged Ikeda for the party leadership in the late 1963 party election, but Ikeda won by a mere 3 votes. Ikeda then formed his third cabinet in January 1964. Both Ikeda and Sato spent money lavishly to win over party members, setting the pattern for subsequent party leadership contests.

Ikeda's third term as prime minister did not last long; he was afflicted with cancer of the throat and had to resign in October 1964. With Yoshida's backing, Sato succeeded Ikeda as prime minister and remained in office for nearly eight years, the longest continuous tenure of any Japanese prime minister. He was able to do so because there were no strong rivals in his party; the old-line party leaders had passed from the scene. Sato, who had risen through the bureaucracy like Ikeda, was elected to the Diet in 1949 and was a follower of Yoshida. In addition, as Kishi's brother he had a strong power base.

The Sato Government

Sato followed Ikeda's policy of expanding Japan's economy, but he also devoted more attention to foreign affairs. He visited the United States to negotiate the return of Okinawa and the Bonin Islands to Japan, and he set out to adjust relations with South Korea.

In the lower-house Diet election of February 1967, a new party, the Komeito (Clean Government Party), sponsored by the Soka Gakkai (Value Creation Society), an organization linked to the Buddhist Nichiren sect, ran candidates for the Diet for the first time and captured 25 seats. The LDP lost some seats, as did the Socialist Party, which continued to lose voter support in succeeding elections. This was undoubtedly because the party continued to adhere to its doctrinaire Marxist stance at a time when the Japanese economy was expanding rapidly and the standard of living was rising. The Communists won only 5 seats.

In the prefectural and municipal elections, the Socialists and Communists were fairly successful. In the April 1967 election for the governor of Tokyo, a liberal intellectual won with the support of the Socialists and the Communists. Urban population growth and increased urban problems enabled "reformists" to win mayoral elections in Osaka, Kobe, Kita Kyushu, and Yokohama.

After successfully negotiating the return of Okinawa, Sato dissolved the Diet in early 1970, hoping to increase the number of LDP seats. In the subsequent election, the LDP managed to gain a solid majority with the addition of a number of independents.[7]

With a solid majority in the Diet, Sato was able to renew the Mutual Security Treaty with virtually no opposition. He, like other conservative leaders, had followed the U.S. leadership position in dealing with Communist China. Thus, he lost face when the United States suddenly changed its position and U.S. President Richard M. Nixon visited China to establish friendlier relations with the Communist government. After nearly eight years in office, Sato was beginning to decline in popularity. Other party leaders aspiring for the premiership were getting restless. Sato therefore used the occasion of the official return of Okinawa to Japan to resign. He was awarded the Nobel Peace Prize for "insuring that Japan would not develop nuclear weapons and for signing a treaty restricting the spread of nuclear technology."[8]

The Tanaka Government

Sato was succeeded by Tanaka Kakuei (1918–1993), who had served as minister of finance in the Sato and Ikeda cabinets. Tanaka was regarded as an anomaly because he did not rise up through the elite ranks like previous prime ministers. Further, he was not a graduate of the University of Tokyo, nor had he ever been a bureaucrat. Although he had received only an elementary school education, he made a fortune in the construction business. He was ambitious and a man of action. He succeeded politically by making use of his financial resources, becoming a shrewd populist politician who had mastered the art of "money politics," pork barrel politics, and patronage. He not only got money from donors but set up bogus companies and dealt in real estate and stocks, using funds from these companies for his political activities. Thus he created a strong and supportive faction in the LDP. When he became prime minister in July 1972 in his midfifties, he was the youngest postwar premier ever elected.

As soon as Tanaka became prime minister, he flew to Hawaii and met with President Nixon, then flew to China to normalize relations with that country. In domestic affairs, he had formulated a plan for the "reconstruction of Japan" that entailed dispersing industrial plants throughout Japan rather than their being concentrated in existing major industrial centers along the Pacific coast. His plan also involved building railroads and freeways in regions not yet connected to the urban industrial centers. These plans, however, were never adopted.

Tanaka dissolved the lower house and held an election in December 1972. This time the LDP lost 17 seats, and the Socialists gained 18. The Communists won 38 seats and 10 percent of the popular vote for the first time. Their success was the result of urban discontent, which stemmed from overcrowding, pollution, inflation, and the high cost of housing.

As part of his plan to "reconstruct" the nation, Tanaka increased the budget by 25 percent over the previous year in order to build up the infrastructure. One of his projects was to build a railroad to his home base, which cost the government a fortune. This resulted in increased inflation, particularly in real estate. After this, Tanaka was confronted with the oil crisis of 1973, when the Organization of Petroleum Exporting Countries (OPEC) reduced oil production. Oil prices rose very rapidly from the 1973 price of $2 a barrel, ultimately reaching $35 a barrel by 1981.

Japan, which was heavily dependent on oil imports for its burgeoning industries, imported 99.7 percent of its oil. In order to remain on good terms with the oil-producing Middle Eastern nations, Tanaka was compelled to divert from the pro-Israel line followed by the U.S. He dispatched the head of the Japanese Agency for Science and Technology to the Middle East to win recognition from the Muslim states as a "friendly nation." Tanaka sought to deal with the oil crisis, which caused panic buying and inflation, by regulating and reducing Japanese oil consumption. His finance minister proceeded to cut government allocations that had been set aside for Tanaka's reconstruction plan. But inflation could not be reined in, and in 1974, wholesale prices rose 31 percent over the previous year.

To gain public backing during the economic crisis, Tanaka vigorously campaigned in the upper-house election of 1974, spending the huge sum of 50 to 100 billion yen ($175–$350 million). Two top cabinet members who objected to his activities resigned from their posts. A journalist exposed Tanaka's shady financial dealings. Tanaka's reputation as a political manipulator of financial deals and corruption was ruining his political standing—even big business turned away from him. As a result, he resigned in November 1974, soon after President Gerald Ford visited Japan. During his tenure, Tanaka had one accomplishment to his credit, namely, the enhancement of the welfare system. He instituted free medical care for the elderly; hence 1973 is regarded as "year one" of the welfare system.

Political behavior in the Tanaka government revealed the financial shenanigans that Japanese party politicians of the time engaged in to build up their power position, for example, using links to big business as sources of money and tying in with key bureaucrats to gain influence over important political and economic sectors. Opposition parties also engaged in the same kind of networking for fund-raising.

Although Tanaka gave up the premiership, he remained a power in the party as the leader of the biggest faction. In 1976, the Lockheed bribery scandal involving high government officials, including Tanaka, was exposed, and Tanaka was indicted. He was judged guilty and sentenced to four years in prison, but he continued to exercise power as a "shadow shogun." While he was appealing the decision in 1985 he suffered a stroke and finally lost power over his faction to one of his followers, Takeshita Noboru.

Post-Tanaka Musical Chairs

Miki Takeo (1907–1988), who succeeded Tanaka as prime minister in 1974, did not have a strong power base, but because his two major rivals within the party blocked each other, he was selected as a compromise choice. He belonged to the more liberal wing of the party and was viewed as a "clean" politician. He sought to reconcile the contending factions by distributing cabinet and government posts to members of key factions.

Miki continued his party's policy of cooperating with the United States in foreign affairs. In 1975, he visited the United States to confer with President Ford, and agreed to the importance of cooperation and ensuring the security of South Korea. Miki established the policy of limiting defense expenditures to 1 percent of the gross national product (GNP). This, however, did not mean a reduction or a low ceiling on defense spending because the GNP continued to rise year after year.

Miki also sought to curb monopolistic control of the market by big business and regulate cartel-like groups. To accomplish this, he introduced antimonopoly legislation in the Diet in April 1975. His measure passed the lower house but was defeated in the upper house. Miki also attempted to mollify government enterprise workers who were seeking to remove the 1948 ban on strikes by public enterprise employees, but he failed to persuade his party members to support this policy.

The Lockheed scandal involved Lockheed's bribery of government and businessmen to effect the sale of Lockheed Tristar planes to All Nippon Airways and the Defense Agency. Lockheed had spent over $12.6 million, most of it in payoffs, to complete the sales. Miki pushed to expose the facts and prosecute the wrong-doers, among whom was Tanaka, charged with accepting a bribe of 500 million yen (about $4.5 million). This investigation caused Tanaka supporters to call for Miki's resignation. Business leaders were eager as well to oust Miki because of his antimonopoly position. Moreover, the old-line political pros opposed Miki's policies because he favored political reforms such as setting restrictions on political fund donations, introducing reforms in the electoral process and in the method of choosing the party chief, and so on.

Hoping to win public support, Miki dissolved the lower house of the Diet. However, in the ensuing election of December 1976, the LDP lost 22 seats, winning only 249 seats—less than a majority of the 511 seats.[9] The Lockheed scandal was undoubtedly the cause of the decline in the LDP's popular vote, which fell to 41.8 percent. With the poor showing in the election, Miki resigned.

One of the chief faction leaders, Fukuda Takeo (1905–1995), defeated his rival, Ohira Masayoshi (1910–1980), by a slim margin and became prime minister in December 1976. Fukuda thereupon promised to turn over the premiership to Ohira after his two-year term expired. Fukuda had risen through the bureaucracy; he was a Kishi follower and was regarded as being hawkish since he advocated giving more authority to the joint military council. His move to legalize the adoption of an era name for each imperial reign—a practice that had merely been customary since the Meiji era—was also regarded as a rightist move. The system was legalized in 1979 by Ohira, who succeeded Fukuda.

In foreign affairs, Fukuda visited the United States to meet with President Jimmy Carter. He formulated a contingency plan for cooperation between the United States and Japan in case joint defensive measures became necessary. His critics attacked the plan, contending that it would draw Japan automatically into any conflict that involved the United States. But the opposition parties were ineffective in opposing the Fukuda government, mainly because labor was concentrating on cooperating with business interests to help Japan cope with economic difficulties resulting from the oil crisis. Further, student radicals were now more interested in advancing their careers by joining elite business companies.

Fukuda also concluded a diplomatic treaty with Communist China in 1978. The signing of the treaty was delayed after Tanaka's visit to China in 1972 because China had wanted to include a criticism of hegemonic powers (directed at the Soviet Union) in the agreement. But by 1978, China's leader, Mao Zedong, had passed away, and the extremist Gang of Four had been removed from power. Deng Xiaoping was interested in cooperating with Japan to develop China's economy. All of these factors facilitated agreement on the treaty.

Although Fukuda had agreed to turn over the premiership to Ohira after two years, he began to shift his position after the LDP did well in the upper-house election. He wanted to dissolve the lower house and hold an election to strengthen his party power base. Naturally enough, Ohira objected to this. He persuaded the party to decide on party leadership by holding a nationwide primary vote, in which party members and affiliates of the party were entitled to vote. This system was adopted in 1977 to replace the former practice, in which only party members serving in the Diet chose the party head and prime minister. The new system of choosing the party head would, it was assumed, make the process more democratic and would also eliminate the practice of buying the support of Diet members. The new system, however, did not weaken vote buying. Instead, political support money was spread around even more widely as the numbers of party voters inflated—aspirants for party leadership created bogus party members and affiliates. The party electorate ballooned to 1.5 million. Ohira's scheme succeeded. He defeated Fukuda, receiving 550,000 votes to the latter's 470,000. Fukuda then resigned, and Ohira assumed the premiership in December 1978.

Prime Minister Ohira sought to deal with the government deficit by enacting a consumption tax, but he had to abandon his plan because of the opposition parties. The opposition then presented a no-confidence vote. Ohira thereupon dissolved the Diet, hoping to receive a strong mandate from the voters. Nonetheless, in the election held in October 1979, he failed to increase the LDP seats and his party gained no new seats, holding 248, as before the election.[10] In the prefectural elections held earlier that year in April, the left-wing groups had lost some of the prefectural and mayoral offices that had been traditional leftist strongholds. For example, the candidate for the Tokyo governor's office backed by the Socialists and Communists lost to the LDP candidate. In Osaka as well, the incumbent backed by the Communist Party lost to the LDP candidate. These developments were indicative of the positive effects on voters of economic growth; the popularity of the anticapitalist forces was beginning to erode.

In May 1980, the opposition again called for a no-confidence vote on Ohira because more information on LDP members' involvement in the Lockheed scandal had surfaced during the trial. The no-confidence vote passed, largely because about 70 LDP anti-Ohira Diet members abstained from voting. Again, Ohira was forced to dissolve the Diet. The Fukuda-Miki faction considered forming a splinter party to face the electorate. However, big business prevented the split by making political donations to the election campaign—donations contingent on retaining unity in the party. In the midst of the campaign in June 1980, Ohira died of a heart attack. This event led to tighter unity among the LDP members, and public sympathy for the late Ohira appeared to have helped the LDP in the election. The party gained 36 seats, winning an absolute majority in the Diet with 284 LDP seats.[11]

As Ohira's successor, Tanaka backed Suzuki Zenko (1911–), a member of the Ohira faction. Suzuki became prime minister in July 1980. In May 1981 he visited the United States and met with President Ronald Reagan. The term "alliance" was used in the joint statement issued after their meeting. This touched off vociferous criticism by the opposition, and Suzuki's foreign minister was forced to resign. Suzuki also increased the defense budget while freezing the other government ministries' budgets. To appease the right wing in the LDP, he and his cabinet members worshipped at the Yasukuni Shrine, where the war dead are honored, on the anniversary of the end of the war.

The Suzuki government's tilt to the right was apparent in the Ministry of Education's more stringent scrutiny of school texts. For example, the Ministry changed the phrase "invasion of China" to "advance" into China. It also called for changes in textbook discussion of the atrocities committed by the Japanese troops in Nanjing in 1937 (Nanjing Massacre), in the 1915 Korean resistance against the Japanese colonizers, and so forth. Suzuki was also beset by public outrage when U.S. Ambassador Edwin Reischauer revealed that American naval vessels with nuclear weapons were sailing over Japanese waters and docking in Japanese ports. In general, the pressure from the Tanaka faction to lean to the right evidently made Suzuki so uncomfortable that he decided not to seek a second term.

Nakasone and His Successors

Nakasone Yasuhiro (1918–), another Tanaka follower, was chosen to succeed Suzuki, and he took office in November 1982. Nakasone was a strong, hawkish leader and, unlike Suzuki, did not adopt a low-key approach. He made effective use of the media and seemingly loved being in the spotlight. His cabinet was dominated by Tanaka supporters. Immediately after taking office, he indicated his willingness to revise the constitution. He expressed the desire to clear the deck of all postwar political issues, which some people thought meant that he would reexamine all postwar political changes, including the revisions to the constitution. Earlier, he had told Yoshida that "as long as the current Constitution exists, the state of unconditional surrender persists."[12]

In November 1983, Nakasone dissolved the lower house of the Diet. The LDP did not do as well as in the previous election because of continuing revelations about party members' involvement in the Lockheed scandal and their questionable financial dealings. The LDP received 45.8 percent of the popular votes, 2.2 percent fewer votes than in the previous election; the party won only 250 seats, down from their previous 284 seats.[13]

Although indicted and sentenced to prison over the Lockheed affair, Tanaka continued to have strong popular support in his home district and won as representative in the lower house of the Diet by more votes than when he was prime minister. He continued to exercise power from behind the scenes in his party and was regarded as a "shadow shogun," but he suffered a stroke in early 1985, relieving Nakasone of the burden of having to defer to him.

Nakasone's defense policy involved strengthening the defense force and increasing the defense budget above the 1 percent of the GNP limit that Miki had imposed. He encountered strong opposition in the Diet but still managed to increase the defense budget to just slightly above 1 percent. He allowed U.S. warships with nuclear weapons to dock in Japanese ports and agreed to conduct joint naval maneuvers with the United States in Hokkaido. To display his "patriotism," he took part in the national Founding Day ceremony at the Yasukuni Shrine.

Among Nakasone's domestic accomplishments was his policy of privatizing state-run enterprises. In April 1985, he privatized the tobacco industry, which had been a state monopoly. The state-run Telegraph and Telephone Public Corporation was also privatized and became the Nippon Telegraph and

Telephone Company, Japanese National Railways, also state-run, was split into seven private companies, that is, six passenger-train companies and one freight-train company.

Nakasone sought to be a major player in foreign affairs. In January 1983, he visited South Korea and pledged to maintain close ties with that country. Immediately afterward, he visited the United States and established a close rapport with President Reagan, commenting that he planned to serve as President Reagan's "catcher." He made a statement to the press that he intended to make Japan an unsinkable aircraft carrier in the event of any Soviet bomber attack. He also said he would close the Straits of Japan to Soviet submarines.[14]

In 1984, Nakasone easily won reelection to a second term as party head and prime minister. In 1986, he dissolved the Diet. In the lower-house election, the LDP won 300 seats, 50 more than in the previous election. The Socialists suffered a significant loss, going from 112 to 85 seats.[15] His electoral victory allowed Nakasone to extend his tenure one year beyond the usual two-year term.

After suffering heavy losses, the leaders of the Socialist Party resigned their party posts, and for the first time, a woman, Doi Takako, was chosen as the head of a major party. Doi's tenure was short-lived, however. Because her party suffered losses in local elections, she resigned as party head in June 1991.

Takeshita Noboru (1924–), formerly a close follower of Tanaka, was chosen by Nakasone as his successor. Takeshita had forged a support base in his own party by splitting off some Tanaka supporters to join his own circle. He was regarded as an expert in *nemawashi*, the networking of all elements concerned to form a consensus. One notable event that captivated the public's attention during Takeshita's premiership was the news of the emperor's ill health and of his ultimate death in January 1989.

During this time period, a small group of ultranationalists belonging to a party called Kominto (Imperial Subjects Party) often cruised through the streets of Tokyo with loudspeakers to trumpet their cause. Kominto disapproved of Takeshita for having "usurped" Tanaka's leadership in the Liberal Democratic Party and decided to discredit Takeshita, sending sound trucks out to criticize him. But their anti-Takeshita activities suddenly ceased. Later, it was revealed that Takeshita's ally and party fund-raiser, Kanemaru Shin, had contacted Sagawa Kyubin (Sagawa Express Delivery), an organization that had ties to the head of the second-largest *yakuza* (organized crime syndicates) gang. Sagawa Kyubin effectively quashed the Kominto's anti-Takeshita campaign.[16]

Takeshita pushed through a 3 percent consumption tax, simultaneously reducing the progressive income tax rate. Thus, the burden of taxation was shifted onto the poor and the rich benefited. He also sought to decentralize authority by turning over more government functions to local governments, but he failed to accomplish this because of opposition from entrenched bureaucrats in the central government.

Takeshita fell from power when the Recruit scandal, as it was dubbed, was exposed. In 1984, Recruit Cosmos, a real-estate subsidiary of the real estate firm, Recruit, had sold unlisted Recruit shares to politicians and bureaucrats, including Takeshita, Nakasone, and Miyazawa Kiichi (another future prime minister), to enable them to make huge profits when the stocks were traded over the counter. Again, in 1986, Recruit passed shares on to politicians and individuals with political clout, for example, newspaper executives.[17] Members of the opposition parties were also involved in the Recruit plot to buy influence. The exposure of the Recruit scandal led to Takeshita's resignation.

As Takeshita's successor, the LDP selected Uno Sosuke, Takeshita's foreign minister. But Uno remained in office for only two months, from June to August 1989, because a geisha went public about Uno's dalliance with her. That this affair became a public issue and Uno was subjected to criticism, especially by women, is indicative of the changing mores in Japan. Formerly, such relations were politely overlooked, and geishas remained mute about their relations with highly placed public figures. The revelation forced Uno to resign.

Kanemaru Shin (1914–), who had become the "king maker" after Tanaka suffered a stroke and was the "money man" for the LDP, chose to replace Uno with Kaifu Toshiki (1933–), who was seen as a noncontroversial choice. Kaifu's position as prime minister was precarious, however, and because he was not one of the faction leaders, his status depended largely on Kanemaru's backing. Despite the scandals involving shady financial dealings and corruption that plagued the LDP, when a Diet election was held in February 1990, the party won 275 seats, 18 more than a simple majority, although 20 fewer than its holdings before the election.[18]

In the international arena, Japan's role in the Persian Gulf War of early 1991 was a matter of controversy both at home and abroad. The United States wanted Japan to participate in this UN military venture, but the Japanese Constitution with its no-war clause forbade the settling of international disputes by force. The Kaifu government dispatched nonmilitary personnel to aid the UN effort, but even this caused criticism at home as being a violation of the spirit of the constitution.

Kaifu, who had a reputation for indecision, was not a key leader among the power brokers in the party. When his two-year term was up, Takeshita abandoned him and threw his support behind Miyazawa Kiichi (1919–), one of the party workhorses. Miyazawa assumed office in November 1991.

Miyazawa had served in a number of cabinets as director general of the Economic Planning Agency and as finance minister. He was fluent in English, so it was assumed that he would be able to communicate more effectively with U.S. officials than previous prime ministers. He, too, had been involved in the Recruit scandal, and when news of the scandal broke during the Takeshita reign, Miyazawa was compelled to resign his post as finance minister. Nevertheless, this did not undermine his political standing sufficiently to prevent his rise to the premiership, a post he had hoped to gain when Nakasone had left the position in 1987.

In August 1992, not long after Miyazawa had assumed office as prime minister, another major scandal involving the LDP was uncovered. The news broke that Kanemaru Shin, who had become the power behind the scenes as the master of money politics after Tanaka's demise, had received about $4 million from Sagawa Kyubin—funds that had been earmarked for party political activities. As noted previously, the investigation revealed Kanemaru's role via Sagawa Kyubin to use *yakuza* gang members to quash right-wing opposition to Takeshita. It was already known that some local politicians had ties to *yakuza* gangs, but this was the first time that links between the *yakuza* and national political leaders were exposed publicly. Kanemaru was fined a few thousand dollars. He tried to continue as party leader and Diet member, but public criticism forced him to leave the political arena. The investigation revealed that Kanemaru had received a fortune in illegal donations from companies that counted on government contracts, especially construction companies, many of which were linked to *yakuza* gangs.

Construction companies have been politically influential in Japan because they employ about 9 percent of the workforce, that is, over 6 million workers. They depend heavily on government contracts, and for that reason, they donate large amounts of money to key politicians. Even though a limit of $13,000 per year was set as the amount each politician was allowed to receive as donations, there is no limit to the number of support groups a politician can create, and each of these can receive the maximum amount.[19] This widespread illegal fundraising is attributable to the system of multiseat electoral districts, in which three to five Diet members are chosen from each district. Faction leaders of the various political parties seek to ensure the victory of as many of their followers as possible in each district. Thus, the election becomes a contest among factions within the party, in addition to being an interparty contest. Each faction has to go about raising money to grease the campaign process.

The Kanemaru scandal contributed seriously to the downfall of the LDP, which had controlled the government since 1955. The intraparty squabbles caused one party leader, Ozawa Ichiro, to break with the Liberal Democratic Party and form his own Japan Renewal Party (Shinseito). He become a supporter and one of the powers in the coalition that emerged under the leadership of Hosokawa Morihiro (1938–).

Miyazawa's troubles as prime minister multiplied. While confronted with political scandal and intraparty factional strife, he was faced with the task of dealing with the trade surplus with the United States, which was resulting in increasingly strident complaints by U.S. officials and business leaders. He hosted a visit by President George Bush in 1992, but their discussions resulted in no more than a general agreement about redressing the situation.

The election for upper-house members in July 1992 resulted in a surprisingly strong showing for the LDP—despite the scandals and the growing concerns about the economic slowdown. The opposition had conducted its campaign by attacking Miyazawa's proposal to allow Japanese military personnel to participate in UN peacekeeping operations. Nonetheless, this issue did not affect the LDP unfavorably.

Miyazawa's euphoria over election results did not last long however; the LDP began to encounter more defectors to newly organized splinter parties. Among these new parties was the Japan New Party (Nihon Shinto), formed in May 1992 by Hosokawa Morihiro, a former LDP upper-house member and governor of Kumamoto Prefecture. As the descendant of a prominent Tokugawa daimyo family and the maternal grandson of the prewar political leader Prince Konoe, Hosokawa had the right pedigree—and an aristocratic demeanor that the Japanese public loves.

In addition to Ozawa's Japan Renewal Party, another group of LDP defectors formed the Sakigake (New Harbinger) Party. Miyazawa was thus faced with a shrinking majority in the Diet. In June 1993, the opposition managed to pass a no-confidence vote against Miyazawa. Fifty members of the LDP bolted from the party. Miyazawa called for an election of the lower house of the Diet in July. The LDP suffered a serious defeat, winning only 223 seats, which was a loss compared to the 275 seats it had won in the 1990 election. The party was 33 seats short of a majority in the 511-seat lower house. For the first time in thirty-eight years, the LDP lacked a governing majority.[20] Thus came the end of conservative party rule and the collapse of the 1955 system.

The Emergence of Splinter-Party Governments

Miyazawa and the LDP leaders hoped to stay in office by forming a coalition with one of the minor parties, but the effort failed. Instead, the minor parties rallied behind Hosokawa and his Japan New Party to forge a coalition of parties with diverse interests and principles, which included the Socialists and Komeito. A new political era thus dawned in Japan in 1993.

As the new prime minister, Hosokawa set the objectives of ending LDP one-party rule, bringing more women into politics, and wiping out corruption. Ironically, Ozawa, one of his key backers, was a Kanemaru disciple and had taken money beyond the legal limit from a construction company.

Hosokawa's reform bill to limit political contributions and change the electoral districts to the single-seat system met with opposition from parties that felt they would be disadvantaged by the changes. LDP members objected to stringent limits on political donations; small parties objected to the single-seat system. The reform bill was expected to redress the imbalance in electoral representation between sparsely populated rural districts and heavily populated urban areas. The imbalance had occurred because the allocation of Diet seats had been made in 1947 when the rural population was still large. As the population shifted to the urban centers, the old system was adjusted only slightly. The result was serious imbalance in representation. For example, in 1992, a district in the Yokohama area had nearly 2 million residents per Diet seat. In comparison, in the outlying district of Tottori Prefecture in western Honshu, there were only slightly over 300,000 residents per seat. Each vote in this district had 6.5 times the weight of a vote in the Yokohama district.

The reform bill passed the lower house but failed to pass the upper house. However, in early 1994, a compromise bill was passed. It granted more flexibility in political donations and provided for both single-seat electoral districts and districts that had proportional representation along party lines.

The Hosokawa government was very short-lived. Hosokawa was forced to resign when financial scandals from his earlier years were exposed. He was then succeeded by Hata Tsutomu (1935–) of the Japan Renewal Party, who patched together a coalition of minor parties and formed a cabinet in spring 1994 without a majority in the Diet. But the Socialists left the coalition, suspecting that Ozawa and Hata were planning to forge a party to rival the LDP without including their party. The Socialists also disagreed with the government leaders' plans to increase the consumption tax while reducing the income tax and to join the United States in pressuring North Korea on its nuclear policy. Saddled with an ungovernable minority in the Diet, Hata resigned at the end of June, after only two months in office.

In order to regain its power, the LDP formed a coalition with its perennial rival, the Socialist Party. To obtain the cooperation of the Socialists, the LDP leaders supported the chairman of the Socialist Party, Murayama Tomiichi (1924–), for the prime minister's post. Thus, for the first time since spring 1948, when the Katayama cabinet fell, a Socialist became the head of government. The LDP and the Socialists had taken opposite sides on almost all the major issues, but political expediency triumphed over principles, as usual. The LDP, with Diet membership of 200, embraced the Socialist Party, with its 74 members. The objective of the LDP was essentially to prevent the Socialists from forming a coalition again with the rival groups that had split off from the LDP.

The Socialist Parties

SCAP's policy of fostering democracy in Japan had given all the former political groups that had been stifled under the prewar militaristic power structure the freedom to engage in unhindered political activities, propagate their political ideas, and pursue their objectives. The Socialists organized the Japan

Socialist Party in November 1945, and with the support of labor leaders, they emerged as a force ready to challenge the conservative political parties that were being organized by prewar political leaders. As noted, following a strong showing in the April 1947 election, the Socialists were given the chance to take over the government in May 1947, aided by the Democratic and Cooperative Parties. But the Katayama government fell when the party split over the budget.

Disagreement between the left and right wings of the party plagued the Socialists throughout the postwar years. In December 1948, a group split off from the party and formed the Labor-Farmer Party. The dissension did not help the Socialists, and the party lost in the January 1949 election, dropping from 111 seats to 48. The right-wing Socialists favored democratic socialism and adopted an anticommunist stand, objecting to the Communists' opposition to liberalism and democracy. The right wing recognized private property and favored following a peaceful, parliamentary route to establish a welfare state. Unlike left-wing Socialists, right-wing Socialists favored rearmament and revision of the constitution. In general, right-wing Socialists were more pragmatic in their policies than the more doctrinaire left-wing Socialists.

The left-wing Socialists adhered to Marxist concepts and opposed Japanese capitalists, whom they regarded as the handmaidens of American imperialism. The left wing had the support of the Sohyo (General Council of Japanese Trade Unions), a major labor union federation. It was also favored by intellectuals and "men of culture," who favored neutralism in the East-West conflict and sympathized with the Third World stance represented by India and other non-Western nations. In October 1951, the Socialist Party split into rightist and leftist Socialist parties.

The left and right wings disagreed over the crafting of the 1951 peace treaty. The left wing objected to a treaty that did not include the Soviet Union and China, whereas the right wing favored the treaty but agreed with left wing objections to the security pact with the United States. The leftist Socialists actively opposed the presence of U.S. military bases in Japan, and their flank of the party gained in popularity as public sentiment against Japanese entanglement with U.S. Cold War policies gained force.

The rise in the leftist Socialists' popularity was linked to the young generation that opposed Japanese involvement in the East-West Cold War struggle. As the left wing gained strength, the right wing came to accept the idea of a merger. In October 1955, the two Socialist parties decided to merge, since that would enable both factions to increase their Diet seats.[21] The party hoped that by merging it could eventually win enough seats to gain control of the government. Following the merger, the party program adhered to the moderate line of the right wing. The new party platform stated: "The fundamental task of our Party is to realize a socialist society by transforming the present capitalist society democratically and peacefully in accordance with the historical conditions of the present state of Japanese capitalist developments, that is, by carrying out the so-called peaceful revolution."[22] After the merger, the Socialists were able to occupy 156 seats in the Diet. Following the Socialist merger the two conservative parties, the Liberal Party and the Democratic Party, also merged, as previously noted. Thus the 1955 political configuration was established.

The pragmatic and doctrinaire differences between the left and right wings persisted, however. The pragmatists wanted the Socialists to appeal broadly to all classes, but the more doctrinaire Socialists held that the Socialist Party was a working-class party whose goal should remain transforming the capitalist system to socialist. The doctrinaire thinkers accused the moderates of abandoning socialism and striving for the establishment of a welfare system under capitalism. In the end, the moderates left the Socialist Party in 1960 and organized the Democratic Socialist Party.

In 1960, an old-time party leader, Asanuma Inejiro, was assassinated in the midst of the Mutual Security Treaty controversy. He was regarded by right-wing nationalists as a procommunist politician, as he had visited China in 1959 and had made a speech in Beijing to the effect that American imperialism was a common enemy of both the Japanese and Chinese people.

The popularity of the Socialists crested during the hubbub over the Mutual Security Treaty. When the economy began to grow very rapidly under Prime Minister Ikeda's income-doubling plan, voters' attention shifted to material goals rather than ideological objectives. Political gridlock ensued. The Socialist Party's popular vote hovered around the 20 percent mark, where it stayed after the 1960s.[23] The Socialists failed to benefit from the 1993 disarray of the LDP and won only 70 seats, with voters turning to the newly formed "reform" parties.

The failure of the Socialists to win power was undoubtedly related to Japan's economic expansion and the emergence of the nation as a major economic power in the 1960s. The ideological stance and idealism that the Socialists presented to the public by opposing capitalism during this period seemed to be at odds with Japanese social and economic life. The most important Socialist power base has been labor. Although Sohyo supported the party through the postwar years, labor also saw its clout diminish in the era of high-speed economic growth and prosperity.

As already noted, the Socialist Party joined the coalition of minor parties under Hosokawa in 1993, split with Hosokawa's successor Hata, and entered into a coalition with the LDP, which enabled Murayama to become prime minister.

The Communist Party

With Japan's defeat in the war and the arrival of SCAP to foster freedom and democracy in Japan, Communist leaders who had been imprisoned or forced to flee abroad ever since the late 1920s were now free to engage in political activities. Among the 439 political prisoners released was Tokuda Kyuichi (1894–1953), who declared his plan to organize the Japanese Communist Party. He and his cohorts demonstrated in the streets, calling for the abolishment of the emperor system, and gathered in front of SCAP headquarters to express their gratitude to the agency for securing their release from prison.

These rehabilitated Communists assumed that they would soon be able to establish a people's republic and called on the Socialists to form a united front. But they also attacked old-line Socialists leaders, labeling them as war criminals. Furthermore, they expected the Socialists to adopt their party agenda. In January 1946, Nozaka Sanzo (1892–1993) returned. He had fled Japan in the prewar years and had worked with the Chinese Communists from the 1930s until the end of the war. Just before returning to Japan, he went to the Soviet Union to confer with Communist leaders there about the line to pursue in Japan. He advocated establishing a program that would appeal broadly to the Japanese public and called for the organization of a Communist Party. Archival documents made available since the collapse of the Soviet Union have also revealed that Nozaka had agreed to serve in Japan as a spy for the Soviet State Security Committee (KGB).[24]

The Socialists agreed to form a united front with the Communists and establish organizations to foster a people's movement throughout Japan. They were especially successful in Kyoto, where Communist and Socialist activists engaged in labor activities and sought to deal with the food shortage crisis. Even after the party leaders discontinued the united-front effort, the leaders in Kyoto sustained the united front and in 1950 succeeded in electing a Communist governor and a Communist mayor of Kyoto.

Nationally, the Communist Party also intensified efforts to rally the people behind the Communist cause. The food shortages, inflation, unemployment, disruptions, and dislocations resulting from the war and Japan's defeat provided the Communists with many opportunities to stage demonstrations and rallies. In 1946, a May Day parade was staged for the first time since the early 1920s, and some 500,000 people demonstrated before the imperial palace. The Communists and Socialists took the leadership role in organizing labor unions and staging strikes. It was assumed by left-wing leaders that SCAP would not intervene in their efforts to stage a socialist revolution.

In August 1946 under the leadership of the Communists, the National Congress of Industrial Unions (Sanbetsu) was organized with 1.63 million workers. In October that same year, the unions in mining, the electrical industry, and the newspaper and broadcasting media staged strikes. This was seen as the preliminary step in staging a general strike. In January 1947, Sanbetsu made plans to stage a general strike on February 1. The plan was to bring down the Yoshida government and establish a Communist-Socialist united-front government. SCAP, which had taken the position of not intervening directly in labor disputes, decided to act to prevent the general strike. This strained the close relationship that had been developing between the New Deal thinkers at SCAP headquarters and the leftist Japanese parties. By the end of 1947, the Communists began to take an openly anti-SCAP stand. They spoke against allowing U.S. military bases to remain in Japan and called for national independence and an early peace treaty.

Labor agitation continued, and when the government set out to reduce the number of workers at state-run enterprises and dismiss a large number of them, a series of violent incidents broke out. Some union leaders who objected to Communist Party control of the Sanbetsu split off to form the Sanbetsu Minshuka Domei (Sanbetsu Democratization League) in 1948.

Because of the Cold War and the growing anticommunist ideology that came to govern U.S. thinking, as well as the continued agitation by the Communist-led unions, SCAP moved to curtail the activities of the Communists. The Communist leaders believed that the public was behind them. They were feeling optimistic because the party had won 35 seats in the January 1949 election, a substantial increase from the 4 seats held before the election. The Communists had done especially well in the lower-class sections of Tokyo and Osaka, so Tokuda planned to stage a massive antigovernment movement in September 1949 to bring down the Yoshida government. SCAP, however, scuttled the plans by launching a Red Purge campaign. A large number of government and private-sector employees were dismissed as Communists who posed a threat to the security and stability of the occupation program.

Instead of resisting SCAP's order for the Communists to register with the government, Tokuda allowed more than 100,000 party members to register, thus providing the government with the identity of the Communists to be purged from public life. SCAP also encouraged local government authorities to pass public-safety legislation to curb the activities of the Communists.

During 1949–1950, the Soviet Cominform called on the Japanese Communist Party to adopt more forceful action instead of following Nozaka's plan for a peaceful revolution. The leaders split between those who held the Cominform directive to be difficult to fulfill and the "internationalists," who held that they should follow Cominform directives. The former group was led by Tokuda; among the latter group was Miyamoto Kenji (1908–), who later became party head. The moderates were compelled to go along with the internationalists, and the party staged more forceful demonstrations and clashed with SCAP forces in May 1950. General MacArthur then purged the party's Central Committee members and the editors of the Communist journal *Red Flag* and banned the journal. In addition, about 12,000 Communists were fired from state-run enterprises and private companies. SCAP also ordered the dissolution of the Communist-led National Confederation of Trade Unions (Zenroren). Communist leaders like Nozaka and Tokuda went underground.

Communist Party members continued to follow the Cominform line and aspired to carry on a people's war to establish a Communist state modeled after the Chinese Communist system. They continued to organize workers and students to strengthen their support base. From January to July 1952, leaders urged students and workers to challenge the government and business authorities and provoked numerous incidents. The biggest incident occurred on May Day 1952, when the marchers clashed with the police before the imperial palace, which resulted in thousands of injuries.

These activities caused the government to pass a violence prevention act. Further, the public became disenchanted with the Communists' extremist activities. In the 1952 election, the Communists, who had won 36 seats in 1949, failed to capture a single seat. In the 1953 election, they managed to win only 1 seat. Their popular vote dropped from 2.98 million in 1949 to 0.65 million in 1953.

In 1953, Tokuda died in Beijing, where he had gone after being purged. Nozaka then reconciled the moderates and the extremists. Following Joseph Stalin's death and Nikita Khrushchev's anti-Stalinist campaign, the Japanese Communists shifted their goal of staging a revolution in Japan, intent upon combating American imperialism and Japanese capitalist support of American imperialism.

In 1955, the Red Purge was lifted, and Nozaka and others resurfaced. Nozaka was elected to the upper house and remained active in party affairs as chair of the Central Committee until 1982. In 1958, Miyamoto Kenji became the general secretary of the Central Committee and continued to push against American imperialism and Japanese monopoly capitalism. When the split between the Soviet Union and Communist China occurred, Miyamoto switched to a pro-China line, expelling those who disagreed with him. This line was adhered to until 1966, when Mao's great Cultural Revolution was launched. After that, Japanese Communist leaders began to relax their rigid pro-China, anti–Soviet Union line.

The voters' support for the Communist Party did not rise much above the 1953 level during the 1960s. The party's holdings in the lower house remained low. The Communists won 3 seats in the 1960 election, 5 in 1963, and 5 in 1967. In 1969, they won 14 seats. As noted earlier, they did better in 1972 than in most elections, capturing 38 seats. Their popularity continued to seesaw.[25] The collapse of the Soviet Union took the wind out of the Communist Party's sails; it was not even given a place in the new Hosokawa coalition in 1993.

Perhaps the discrediting of Nozaka Sanzo, whose life coincided with the history of the Japanese Communist Party, can be seen as symbolic. In 1992, Nozaka was expelled from the party—at age one hundred—when the Soviet archives recently opened to the public revealed that in the 1930s he had maligned a fellow Communist, Yamamoto Kenzo (1895–1942), who had fled Japan for the Soviet Union, informing Soviet authorities that he was a Japanese spy. This resulted in Yamamoto's arrest and execution by firing squad.[26]

Other Minor Parties

The Komeito (Clean Government Party) emerged on the political scene in 1964 as a branch of the Soka Gakkai, a secular arm of the Buddhist Nichiren sect. The Soka Gakkai had a strong following among poor urban residents. It had run candidates in the 1959 upper-house election and had won 6 seats and in the 1962 upper-house election had gained 9 seats. After organizing the Komeito, the Soka Gakkai, led by Ikeda Daisaku, decided to run candidates for lower-house seats. In its first such campaign, the party won 25 seats in 1967. Since then, it has managed to win in successive elections, capturing 50 seats or so per election. In the 1993 election, the Komeito won 51 seats, then joined the Hosokawa government as an important component of the seven-party coalition. In 1992, it claimed 14 seats of the 127 seats contested in the upper-house election, even though it was expected to suffer from the rift between the Nichiren priesthood and the Soka Gakkai. The Komeito has usually taken a moderate to conservative stand on key issues in the Diet. For example, it supported the LDP government's bill in 1992 to allow Japanese military personnel to participate in UN peacekeeping operations.

The Democratic Socialist Party, organized in 1959 by those who disagreed with the more doctrinaire leftist Socialists, generally adhered to a moderate line and frequently supported the LDP's domestic and foreign policies. The number of seats it managed to win in lower-house elections remained within the 20- to 30-seat range in the 1960s and 1970s, but began to slide downward in the 1980s, hitting a low of 14 in 1990 and 15 in 1993. The Democratic Socialist Party also joined the Hosokawa coalition.

Analysis of LDP Dominance

The LDP dominance of the political scene from 1955 to 1993 was facilitated in part by the economic growth and prosperity that prevailed in Japan from the 1960s onward. In addition, the protective umbrella that the United States provided Japan in the international arena made it possible for the governments in power to concentrate on economic expansion, which led to general public satisfaction. Furthermore, the linkage among conservatives, the bureaucracy, and business interests enabled the entrenched interests to fend off any challenges by opposition parties and labor unions, as well as to deflect criticism emanating from the intellectuals and men of culture.

The intraparty factionalism that characterizes the LDP, as well as the other parties, has kept the LDP from developing into a steamrolling power machine. The presence of factions within the party makes it necessary for party leaders to make compromises and effect mutual accommodations. The factions are not divided over ideological or policy matters, although differences in emphasis do exist. Instead, differences among factions center on personal and regional ties and historical antecedents. Many political ties are based on family relations. For example, the relationship between the behind-the-scenes party boss, Kanemaru Shin, and the money man, Takeshita, was cemented by the fact that the former's son was married to the latter's daughter.

Two critical factors that determine the choice of a given faction leader as prime minister are his ability to provide financial support and patronage and his effectiveness in dealing with people. Faction leaders covet the position of prime minister, but they are also eager to gain ministerial positions. Thus, factional struggles are not about principles and policies but rather concern the personal pursuit of power and status.

To establish a strong following and keep followers loyal, the faction leader must provide them with funds to enable them to win in electoral campaigns. A faction leader's success therefore depends on how much money he can raise. The strong leader Tanaka Kakuei, for example, was able to amass a huge financial reserve that enabled him to remain in power as the shadow shogun, even after he was forced to leave the government. The power that Kanemaru Shin exercised in the LDP resulted from a similar stash of funds.

The need to accumulate enormous amounts of money makes it necessary for the party to establish close ties with financial sources, for example, with big business interests and even with shady businessmen linked to the *yakuza,* in which case fund-raising becomes mixed with bribery. Thus, scandals of the sort already noted—the Lockheed bribery case, the Recruit scandal, the Sagawa Kyubin deal—were engaged in as a routine practice. The only difference between these and other such occurrences is that these scandals were exposed.

Ties with big business are of prime importance to Japanese political parties, and the LDP has benefited the most from such relationships. Not surprisingly, the LDP–big business link has been a significant factor in the LDP's successful control over political power for almost forty years. Business interests have supplied huge sums of money that have allowed the LDP to conduct election campaigns successfully. And to cover all bases, big business interests provide funds for the Socialists and other opposition parties as well.

There are several organizations made up of big business interests. The most important is the *Keidanren* (Federation of Economic Organizations), composed of powerful industrial organizations. Its membership includes more than 700 of the largest industrial, commercial, and financial corporations. Although the established interests play down the role of the *Keidanren* and big business in general in politics, the close linkage between big business and the LDP is undeniable. The *Keidanren* has a voice in selecting prime ministers and favors party leaders who have entered the party from the higher echelons of the bureaucracy.

The merger of the Democratic and Liberal Parties in 1955 was, in fact, brought about partly in response to pressure from business leaders, displeased about the split among conservatives. In addition, business interests have sought to minimize intraparty factional strife in the LDP. A conservative-led Japanese government never makes major economic decisions without consulting the top business leaders and the Federation of Economic Organizations, which collectively represent the major trade organizations and large corporations. Political contributions, marital connections, school ties, personal friendships, and business links all contribute to forging close ties between big business and the conservative Liberal Democratic Party.

The LDP has also had among its leaders many former government officials, who are, in general, preferred by big business interests. The factions led by Kishi, Ikeda, and Sato have had a notably high percentage of these men. However, by the 1980s, the ranks of these former high-ranking bureaucrats had thinned out due to old age and death.

Another reason for the LDP success in maintaining control of the Diet is the support it receives from rural areas. In 1988, about 80 percent of the Diet members came from agricultural constituencies with close ties to the LDP. Although the population per district in rural communities is much smaller than in urban districts, the number of seats per district is the same. Thus, the political influence of rural districts is greater than their population size would warrant. Accordingly, in order to win and retain the support of rural districts, the LDP has accommodated farmers with price supports on rice and restrictions on imports of farm products. The LDP has also had the support of white-collar workers, junior executives, and small shopkeepers, whose interests are protected by government restrictions on supermarket chains.

Some authorities attribute the LDP's success in sustaining its political dominance in the postwar years "to its ability to respond to popular and partisan pressures and demands" and "to the absence on the national level of a viable alternative government in the wings."[27] The lengthy entrenchment of the LDP and its mode of operation have caused other observers to conclude that

> the Japanese government is one of the most corrupt in the world. Not so much in the sense of graft and bribery—although there is enough of that too—corrupt in the sense that it is one-sided, biased, unfair, detrimental to the common good. Government works in the interest of big business and the large agricultural organizations, the latter largely to get the votes. The ruling alliance of the bureaucrats, government and big business is what has shaped present-day Japan.[28]

The Bureaucracy

Understanding the role of the bureaucracy is the key to deciphering Japanese economic and international trade policies as well as domestic policies. Political party leaders come and go, but bureaucrats are entrenched in key positions with lifetime tenure.

Even though Japanese bureaucrats do not have their own political party, in many respects they wield more power than the minor political parties, or even the major parties, when it comes to the formulation and implementation of foreign and domestic policies. Bureaucrats have the expertise and knowledge to make policy, draft legislation, and implement policy after it has been approved by the Diet. Since cabinet members come and go, they have little control over bureaucrats, who remain entrenched in their positions. The primary job of a cabinet minister is to be the spokesman for the ministry he is heading for the time being. His major concerns are patronage and politically sensitive programs.

From 1955 until 1993, Japan was ruled, it may be said, by the Liberal Democratic Party, big business, and high-level bureaucrats. In the mid-1980s, one out of every four LDP members was a former high-ranking bureaucrat. In December 1993, 76 of the 511 lower-house members were former bureaucrats. Likewise, a vast majority of the postwar prime ministers were former bureaucrats. Between 1955 and 1979, 40 percent of the cabinet members came from the same group. Party leaders and high-level bureaucrats generally work closely together.

It is contended by some analysts that top bureaucrats, rather than party leaders or cabinet members, actually run the government. In 1993, there were 861,000 bureaucrats entrenched in twelve ministries involved in regulating virtually all aspects of the Japanese public life. It is typical that "permission to move a bus stop can take two or three years; to start a resort project plans must be submitted to at least six ministries; dozens of licenses are needed to open a supermarket."[29]

Authorities state that the sources of bureaucratic power are threefold; including regulatory authority, budgetary discretion, and public esteem. In the realm of regulatory authority, the bureaucracy has the power to grant official approval and licenses. The Ministry of Transport possesses complete jurisdiction over the nation's air, rail, and bus services, "right down to the number of vehicles which may operate in a given area."[30] It has licensing and approval powers over 1,966 items. Prime Minister Hosokawa complained that when he was governor of Kumamoto he had to get permission from the Ministry of Transport to move a bus stop by 10 meters (10.94 yards). The number of taxis that can operate in a given area, the fares charged, and so on are regulated by the bureaucracy. To build a public park anywhere in Japan, the Ministry of Construction requires that there be benches, a swing set, and a slide.[31] It is recognized that the bureaucracy sets Japan's agenda. For example, in the 1970s, the bureaucrats decided a consumption tax was needed, so they persuaded the politicians in the Diet to pass such a tax—despite broad public opposition. The politicians risked public censure because they needed the bureaucracy to advance their own political agenda. Karel van Wolferen, a Dutch correspondent who has spent most of his career in Japan, writes, "Japanese government bureaux have extraordinary powers of awarding licenses and other permissions for commercial pursuits, and withholding advantages like subsidies, tax privileges or low-interest loans at their own discretion. Ministries can resort to 'administrative guidance' to force organizations in their realm of endeavour to adopt 'voluntary' measures."[32]

The most powerful bureaucrats are those in the Ministry of International Trade and Industry (MITI) and in the Finance Ministry, who together chart the general course of the nation's economy. U.S. frustration in negotiating with the Japanese government to try to convince Japan to ease its trade restrictions stems partly from the fact that it is not the political leaders but the bureaucrats who make the decisions. When Hosokawa became prime minister, he pledged to deregulate the economy—but he was forced to face reality. He could not get the bureaucrats to bend. The Finance Ministry bureaucrats were more interested in balancing the budget and increasing tax revenues than stimulating the economy.

The Finance Ministry plays a central role in drafting and implementing the national budget and collecting taxes. Japanese political parties, unlike those in the United States, have very little influence over the formulation of financial policies. The power that the Finance Ministry exercises has been likened to having the U.S. Treasury, the Office of Management and Budget, the Internal Revenue Service, and the Securities and Exchange Commission consolidated into one government department.

The Hosokawa-Hata splinter-party group failed to retain the support of the Socialists, who objected when the Hosokawa-Hata group went along with the Finance Ministry bureaucrats' proposal to enact a consumption tax to offset the temporary reduction in the income tax. The Socialists opposed imposing a sales tax and favored a permanent cut in the income tax.

MITI exercises tight control over foreign trade, and with its power to regulate foreign trade, it has authority over 1,915 items. Those companies wishing to import goods into Japan are required to navigate a maze of stringent regulations. Automobiles being imported into the country are individually inspected. Only in 1994 did the Ministry of Transport decide to allow blanket certification of Jeep Cherokee vehicles sold in Japan. Yet, it cannot be said that these bureaucratic regulations were designed solely to block the entry of foreign products. Japanese car-owners have to comply with the required strict inspection of the vehicle three years after purchase. Thereafter, they must have the car checked every six months in minor inspections, which costs about $136, plus any repairs the garage deems necessary. Then, every twelve months a major inspection must be done, which costs $200, plus repairs. In addition, every two years a comprehensive inspection is required, which costs $600, plus whatever repairs the garage mandates—and these often cost thousands of dollars.[33]

The Finance Ministry is supposed to oversee the securities industry. But a cozy relationship developed between the two groups over the years, and Finance Ministry bureaucrats allowed established securities firms to engage in whatever machinations they desired, a practice designed to keep new competing brokers from entering the market. In the 1990s, not a single new securities brokerage license had been issued since 1968. The only new entrants that have been allowed have been foreign securities firms, which do not pose a threat to the Japanese firms. In the late 1980s, a major scandal erupted involving one of the top securities firms, Nomura Securities. The firm had manipulated the stock market to increase the value of the stocks held by the *yakuza*. In addition, twenty-one securities firms had given improper compensation to special clients, such as Toyota Motors, Hitachi, and Matsushita, to cover their losses. The Finance Ministry claimed to have investigated and found no wrongdoing. Public pressure led to the establishment of a commission to investigate the securities industry, but a move to establish an independent securities commission like the U.S. Securities and Exchange Commission was blocked by the Finance Ministry.[34]

Local authorities and businesses, subjected to stringent, close inspections and controls covering 10,717 items by the government centered in Tokyo, have been fighting for more decentralization and deregulation, but thus far the entrenched bureaucracy has remained a formidable foe. The bureaucrats still retain the elitist mentality that the Meiji bureaucrats inherited from the samurai of the Tokugawa era. Most of the high-ranking bureaucrats are graduates of the elitist University of Tokyo and have prestige, status, and authority. Because many top political leaders are also graduates of the same university, school ties among group members also contribute to the cementing of close relations. The final link in the triangle—politicians, business leaders, and bureaucrats—is made when high-level bureaucrats find jobs in big business firms after retirement, where they engage in networking for their new employers. Japan remains "a country by bureaucrats, of bureaucrats and for bureaucrats."[35]

Because bureaucrats make their decisions in secret and enforce the adoption of measures they have formulated by this process, the outside groups and the common people have no recourse to challenge their actions. It is undeniable that "secrecy is an ingrained aspect of nearly every important institution in Japan." Since the 1980s, a grass-roots movement has emerged that is working to force government agencies to provide information to the public, which is of course affected by their decisions. Advocates of this strategy are confronted with a formidable body of entrenched bureaucrats who might as well say, "We control the information. The public has no right to the information."[36]

Party government officials have little control over the bureaucracy. When a cabinet member of the reform-minded Hosokawa government clashed with a top bureaucrat and forced the latter to resign over his interference in politics, the event became headline news. The angry bureaucrat went on TV, saying he had done nothing wrong; he had been simply following a long-practiced custom.

A politician who sits on a Diet committee that deals with issues over which a bureaucratic agency has jurisdiction can influence that agency's policies and decisionmaking. However, in order to do this successfully, the Diet member must gain knowledge and expertise in the issues and establish close personal relations with the bureaucrats concerned. These Diet members are referred to as *zoku-giin*, meaning members of the tribe.[37] Upon retirement, high-level bureaucrats frequently join a business corporation, which enables the corporation to have an inside track to the bureaucracy. Also, as noted earlier, many high-level political leaders have risen from the bureaucracy into the political arena: "In the higher reaches of the System, bureaucrats, former bureaucrats in top business positions, former bureaucrats turned politician and the former bureaucrats or bureaucratised businessmen who head the business federations are as one."[38]

3

Foreign Relations

During the Occupation, Japan, of course, could not follow an independent path in formulating its foreign policy; Japan's foreign relations were determined by SCAP. After the signing of the peace treaty in 1951 and the withdrawal of occupation authorities in 1952, Japan became free to pursue its own course. In reality, however, the Japanese government adhered to its policy of following the U.S. leadership, particularly vis-à-vis the Communist powers during the Cold War years. U.S. policy toward Japan shifted from focusing on demilitarization to rebuilding the nation to use it as a link in the anticommunist chain along the eastern Pacific rim. As early as 1948, U.S. Secretary of War Kenneth C. Royal called for such a change in policy. The United States began to build up its military bases in Okinawa to create an East Asian bastion after China fell to the Communists.

The United States

While the conservative-led Japanese government cooperated with the U.S. anticommunist policy, the Japanese opposition increasingly raised its voice against the U.S. military presence in Japan and Okinawa. In 1952, when the United States wanted to use an area near Kanazawa (along the Japan Sea) for target practice, the villagers got the support of the Communists, Socialists, and leftist labor groups (Sohyo) and aroused nationwide opposition to the plan. The village opposition was allayed temporarily with monetary compensation for use of the land, but in 1957, the United States abandoned the practice grounds. This controversy provided the left-wing opponents of U.S. bases in Japan with the impetus to stage numerous other demonstrations against military bases. At the same time, the Left used antinuclear testing as an issue to arouse popular opposition both to the U.S. military presence and to the Japanese government's cooperation with American anticommunist policies.

In 1954, the occupants of a Japanese fishing boat were exposed to radioactive ashes from the hydrogen bomb tests the United States had conducted at the Bikini Islands. The fishermen, who had suffered radiation burns, were hospitalized. Although the government had concealed this incident from the public, it was exposed by the Yomiuri newspaper. A nationwide movement was organized to protest nuclear bomb testing, and 30 million signatures were collected. In addition, a move to gain worldwide support for this movement was initiated. In 1955, participants from thirteen foreign nations and from Japan held the first world anti–nuclear bomb testing conference in Hiroshima.

The next issue that was used by the peace advocates, many of whom were ideologically motivated anti-U.S. partisans, to rally the public was the Mutual Security Treaty, signed by the United States and Japan along with the peace treaty in 1951. The security treaty made Japan part of the Pacific military network, but it also served as a check on Japan, preventing the country from reverting to militarism and posing a threat to the other Asian nations.

In June 1957, soon after Kishi became prime minister, he traveled to the United States to visit President Eisenhower. The two leaders issued a joint statement on establishing a committee to reexamine the security pact. Foreign Minister Fujiyama Aiichiro worked on the revision of the security treaty in February 1959 and made public his draft plan. The main points were these: to settle the Okinawa and the Bonin Islands issues, to spell out U.S. responsibility for the defense of Japan, to decide on the location of U.S. military bases by administrative agreements, and to fix the tenure of the treaty at ten years. The Liberal Democratic Party worked on the revision of the treaty on the basis of Fujiyama's plan. By May 1959, the United States and Japan had agreed on the terms of the treaty revision.

When Fujiyama made the agreement public, opponents of the treaty, led by the Sohyo labor union leaders and Socialist Party members, organized a national conference in March 1959 to oppose revision of the treaty, convincing over 130 organizations to join the move. The Communist leadership decided to join the conference, but the two unions affiliated with the Communist Party, the Zenroren and the Shinsanbetsu (New Congress of Industrial Unions), refused to participate.

There was also disagreement within the Socialist Party about the treaty. Nishio Suehiro, leader of the right-wing Socialists, asserted that he was not absolutely opposed to the treaty. However, he contended that if the Socialist Party was going to oppose the pact, it should have an alternative plan. He also opposed allowing the Communist Party to participate in the conference. As already noted, in January 1960, he split with the party and organized the Democratic Socialist Party with forty-five Socialist Diet members.

The Communist Party members also disagreed on this question. The extremist Trotskyite group, consisting mainly of radical students, was expelled from the party, after which that contingent organized the Japanese Communist Bund. The Trotskyites took charge of the zengakuren, the national student federation, and disagreeing with the plan devised by the National Council to block the pact by legal means, they moved to prevent the treaty from being approved—by physically disrupting the Diet proceedings. The National Council organized to prevent the revision of the Mutual Security Treaty and sponsored meetings throughout the country, attracting 3 million participants.

Among the vocal opponents of the pact were intellectuals, scholars, and men of culture, many of whom vented their anti-American sentiment by playing up the image of the United States as a nuclear terrorist and an imperialist power. Ironically, most of these opponents had remained silent about Japanese imperialism and atrocities during the war, and they continued to remain silent about the atrocities committed by Japan during its aggression in China and other areas of Asia.

In January 1960, Prime Minister Kishi traveled to Washington and concluded the agreement on the new Mutual Security Treaty. The treaty provided for cooperation between the two nations to counter threats to peace and security in the Far East. It also provided for political and economic cooperation between Japan and the United States. Compared to the 1951 security pact, this pact placed Japan on a more equal footing. The 1951 security pact had prohibited Japan from leasing military bases to other powers, but this provision was removed from the 1960 treaty. Japan's defense obligations were limited only to the main islands of Japan. In order for the United States to bring nuclear arms into Japan, it had to obtain Japan's prior approval. The pact provided for the continued stationing of U.S. troops in Japan, but again, prior consultation was required before major changes in the deployment of U.S. armed forces to Japan were made. In return for the U.S. commitment to defend Japan, the United States expected Japan to maintain an adequate defense force. The tenure of the treaty was ten years, after which time either party could abrogate it with one year's notice.

The treaty clearly linked Japan to the United States in the Cold War. Opponents of the pact contended that Japan would be automatically drawn into any war that involved the United States in the Far East. To improve the treaty, they wanted the perimeter of the Far East defined, and they questioned the effectiveness of the provisions for prior consultation.

When the content of the treaty was made public, the Chinese Communist government and the Soviet Union denounced it. The Soviet Union made it known that as long as foreign troops remained in Japan it would not return the four Kurile Islands to Japan. Cold War tension had intensified at this time because a U.S. U-2 spy plane flying over Russia was shot down in May 1960, and Khrushchev asserted that the Soviet Union would bomb spy plane bases. The

Soviet response concerned the opponents of the pact because U-2 spy planes were based at the Atsugi air force base in Japan.

Aside from the general concern about potential Japanese military involvement in the Cold War, other considerations surrounded the treaty negotiations. There was opposition to the possibility of militarization, and many Japanese wanted to be freed of American domination after the Occupation. Further, pro-communist sentiments, concern over domestic politics, and student discontent over the existing state of affairs all seemed to lend a part in creating the mass hysteria over treaty ratification. Despite massive opposition, Kishi got the treaty ratified on June 19. He then resigned as prime minister.

Following the Mutual Security Treaty controversy, U.S.-Japanese relations went back on track when Ikeda succeeded Kishi. Ikeda, as noted, concentrated on economic developments rather than foreign affairs. Ikeda's successor, Sato, was even more active in this area.

In November 1969, Sato traveled to the United States to confer with President Nixon. Two important issues were on the agenda: the question of the reversion of Okinawa to Japan, and the textile issue. In the 1968 presidential campaign, President Nixon had promised the southern states, where the textile plants were concentrated, that he would limit textile imports. In his discussions with Sato, Nixon therefore requested that Sato seek to implement voluntary reductions in Japan's textile exports to the United States. A misunderstanding developed, however, because Nixon thought that Sato had agreed to take steps to reduce textile exports to the United States, but Sato had meant only that he would give the request serious consideration.

The other matter concerned the reversion of authority to the Japanese over Okinawa and the Bonin Islands. Technically, the United States was exercising administrative authority over these islands for the UN, which had placed them under U.S. trusteeship. With the intensification of the Cold War, the U.S. National Security Council and the U.S. military hoped to maintain long-term control over Okinawa and began to strengthen and upgrade the bases there.

In the early 1950s, there had been some sentiment in Okinawa for complete independence rather than reversion to Japanese government authority. As Japan's economic condition improved, however, opinion shifted toward favoring reuniting with Japan, and the numbers of people signing petitions for reversion to Japan began to increase. Also, political and public opinion leaders in Japan began to call for resumption of Japanese control over Okinawa and the Bonin Islands. Nonetheless, the 1951 peace treaty left U.S. administrative control over Okinawa intact. Secretary of State Dulles held that the United States should retain control of Okinawa as long as the East Asian situation remained tense. However, the United States did return the Amami Islands just north of Okinawa to Japanese authority. In 1952, an Okinawa government was established under U.S. control, whereupon the Okinawan movement to rejoin Japan grew more active. The opponents of continued U.S. presence protested in particular the extensive use of Okinawan land—13 percent of the territory—for U.S. military bases.

The Japanese public, as well as the political leaders, did not raise the Okinawa issue until after the peace treaty had been signed. Then, as the movement for reversion intensified in Okinawa, the Japanese became more interested in the issue and began to call for the return of Okinawa to Japan. In 1956, the Diet passed a resolution calling for the return of Okinawa and the Bonin Islands.

In 1962, U.S. President John F. Kennedy formally acknowledged that Okinawa was part of Japan but held that it could not be returned to Japan immediately because of its strategic importance in the defense of the free world. He pledged to cooperate with Japan in aiding Okinawa economically and financially and in fostering the Okinawan right of self-rule. But the U.S. military favored retaining control over Okinawa and had congressional support of its position. The U.S. high commissioner maintained that the United States had trusteeship over Okinawa and took no steps to institute Okinawan self-rule. In Japan, this resulted in an outburst of demand for the end to U.S. occupation and removal of U.S. military bases.

Upon becoming prime minister, Sato made the return of Okinawa one of his goals. When he traveled to Washington in 1965 to meet with President Lyndon B. Johnson, he raised the issue of Okinawa. Johnson agreed to give Japan a greater voice in Okinawan affairs but made no specific commitment about returning Okinawa and to Japan. When Sato visited the United States again in 1967, an agreement was reached to finalize in two or three years the date for the return of Okinawa to Japan.

In 1969, when Prime Minister Sato visited President Nixon, the two leaders agreed on 1972 as the date for Okinawa's reversion to Japan. At the same time, an agreement was reached on the renewal of the Mutual Security Pact and its applicability to Okinawa. Sato wanted to ban nuclear weapons from Okinawa, but the joint statement on this point was vague. Japan could interpret the agreement as providing for Japan's prior right of refusal if the United States wanted to bring nuclear weapons into Okinawa. However, the United States could interpret the agreement as meaning that it was possible to introduce the weapons only with prior notification. The agreement was ratified by the Diet in 1972, and Sato fulfilled his objective of Japanese repossession of Okinawa.

Another matter that strained U.S. relations with Japan, at least with the radical student groups and left-wing parties, was the Vietnam War. The United States had used its bases in Japan for military operations in Vietnam. Okinawa, in particular, served as an important U.S. military base. Military procurements were made in Japan for the Vietnam War, and Japan also served as a rest and recreation center for U.S. troops serving in Vietnam. Those who opposed the Mutual Security Treaty and the presence of U.S. bases, as well as those who criticized the government for cooperating with the United States in this venture, organized the *Beheiren* (Citizens' Organization for Vietnam Peace) and staged anti–Vietnam War rallies and demonstrations. Among the organizers were members of the Communist and Socialist Parties, labor leaders of the Sohyo, and radical students.

The major focus of U.S.-Japan relations from the 1970s on shifted to trade between the two nations. The United States has remained Japan's biggest trading partner since the end of the World War II. In 1970, 30.7 percent of Japan's exports (in terms of dollar value) and 29.4 percent of its imports were to and from the United States. The figure remained in the 20 percent to 30 percent range until the 1990s. In 1992, Japan's exports to the United States came to 28.2 percent of total exports and imports from the United States amounted to 22.4 percent of the total. The disparity in export and import percentiles was reflected in the monetary balance in favor of Japan, which grew increasingly larger. In 1960, the balance of trade was in the United States' favor, amounting to $452 million, but by 1970, it was in Japan's favor by $380 million. Following the oil crisis of 1973–1974 the balance shifted back to the United States' favor (by $459 million). Since then, the trade surplus, in Japan's favor, has increased by leaps and bounds. By 1980, the surplus had risen to $6.959 billion. It rose to $39.485 billion in 1985, to $43.563 billion in 1992, and to $59.3 billion in 1993.

This shift has led the United States to demand that Japan redress the balance by removing stringent import restrictions and that it open up its market. The United States (and other nations) has pressured Japan to strengthen the yen in the international currency exchange market.

The precarious footing of the Japanese economy was exposed in August 1971, when President Nixon imposed a 10 percent surcharge on imports to the United States and exerted pressure on the Japanese government to revalue the yen upward. This touched off an acute economic crisis in Japan, which at the time was sending about 30 percent of its exports to the United States. The Japanese trade surplus with the United States continued to balloon. As a result, the imbalance of trade became a growing source of friction between Japan and the United States.[1] International pressure mounted on Japan to put the yen on a floating exchange rate like European currencies instead of having the yen fixed at 360 yen to a dollar. It was assumed that strengthening the yen would redress the trade balance that favored Japan. In December 1971, the finance ministers of ten industrial nations met in the United States and fixed the yen at 306 yen to a dollar. Even so, the value of the yen continued to rise, and by 1978, it had reached 210 per dollar. It reached 128 yen to a dollar in 1988. In 1994, the exchange rate went higher than 100 yen per dollar, but the strong yen still failed to correct the trade imbalance.

Automobile exports to the United States increased at a phenomenal pace, partly because the oil crisis of 1973 prompted Americans to purchase smaller cars. Japan was ready to supply these economical models to replace the gas-guzzlers that Detroit continued to produce, as U.S. manufacturers were convinced that Americans preferred larger cars. As Japanese cars began to flood the U.S. market, some congressmen began to talk about passing a law to limit Japanese car imports. As is discussed in Chapter 4, in order to prevent this the Japanese government imposed a voluntary quota of 1.85 million units on automobile shipments to the United States in 1986. The quota was voluntary and flexible. In 1990, the number of passengers cars sent to the United States had dropped to 1.719 million, down from the 2.383 million figure of 1986. Nonetheless, the Japanese automobile manufacturers' share of the U.S. car market continued to increase, especially because Japanese auto manufacturers began to establish factories in the United States to circumvent the possibility of U.S. import restrictions. Thus, by 1990, Japan had gained 25 percent of the U.S. automobile market. Slightly more than one-half of the 2.6 million Japanese cars sold in the United States in 1990 were manufactured in the United States. Forty-four percent of the Nissans sold in the United States were U.S. manufactured. Although such U.S.-manufactured cars are assembled in the United States, most of the parts are imported from Japanese automakers' subsidiary plants in Japan.

The number of Japanese exports began to slow down with the economic recession that started in Japan at the end of the 1980s. As the yen strengthened relative to the dollar, automobile exports, especially, began to decline. In April 1994, auto exports dropped 16.2 percent compared to the same month in 1993.[2] All the same, because of the sale of cars manufactured in the United States, the Japanese car producers' share of the U.S. market did not shrink. In 1993, Japanese car manufacturers held about 30 percent of the U.S. auto market, and this percentage had even increased somewhat by mid-1994.[3]

Before the 1970s, other Japanese export goods were a source of friction between the two countries. Initially, textiles were at issue. In 1969, the U.S. government asked Japan to impose voluntary export limits on its textiles. As noted, in 1969 Nixon and Sato discussed Japan's restricting its textile exports to the United States and a misunderstanding resulted. When Sato did not take immediate action, Nixon felt that Sato had broken his promise. After the second Nixon-Sato meeting in 1971, Japan did agree to restrict its textile exports to the United States, and an agreement was signed in January of that year. Next, steel and chemical products became important export items for Japan. These were followed by new export products—consumer electronics, automobiles, metalworking machines and other precision machines, and computer chips—all of which became major export items and contributed to increasing the trade surplus with the United States. Voluntary export restrictions were imposed on passenger cars, steel products, machine tools, color TV sets, and other items in the 1980s, but the Japanese trade surplus with the United States continued to increase. Japan imported mainly nonindustrial goods from the United States, whereas it sent industrial and high-technology products to the United States.

To redress the imbalance, the United States has requested that Japan not only reduce its protective tariffs but also revise the web of red tape that seems designed to keep out foreign goods. The policy on car imports, for example, rather than granting blanket approval on a given make and year of automobile, require car-by-car inspection. Only in 1994 did the Jeep Cherokee receive blanket certification. U.S. businesspeople complain that standards are manipulated against foreign products, that foreign investments are discouraged, and that the distribution network is virtually a closed system. Business dealings are often conducted through an old-boy network of personal friendships and traditional ties that constitute a "multilayered lattice." Murray Sayle, an Australian who has lived in Japan for a number of years, explains how the system functions in lower-level business transactions:

> In the village outside Tokyo in which I live there are four gas stations, offering gasoline at four different prices. The one I patronize charges three yen a liter more than the one that happens to be closest to my house. Why don't I switch? Because the Proprietor is a friend of mine (and how could he not be since we have done business for years?), but even if he wasn't, he would still be entitled by social convention to a cash payment in compensation for the loss of my business from my new supplier, which would have to be long and carefully negotiated between the two men. . . . While theoretically I am free to switch, village opinion is on the side of my staying where I am.[4]

Just as this "closed system" prevails within the country, Japan essentially maintains closure toward the external world, that is, the Japanese government, with the support of business interests and politicians, has maintained a protectionist policy.

As the trade imbalance between the two countries continued to grow, the U.S. pressure on Japan to relax its trade restrictions was intensified. In 1989, discussions on a new policy to open up the Japanese market, referred to as the Structural Impediment Initiative, were begun. Among the objectives are quick licensing of discount malls, overnight clearance of imports through customs, dismantling of the Big Store Law, which favors small-scale retailers over supermarkets and chain stores, and so on.

Critics of the Japanese distribution system contend that Japanese manufacturers and wholesale dealers have a stranglehold on the market, stifle competition, and keep foreign competitors out. Under the existing system of marketing, consumer prices for the Japanese buyer remain high. For example, in the mid-1980s, retail prices were 4.21 times higher than wholesale prices, whereas in the United States the difference was only twice as high.

In the 1980s, there were 2.4 million retail outlets and 400,000 different distributors in Japan. In the 1980s, small retail stores accounted for 56 percent of retail sales in Japan compared to 3 percent in the United States. For Japan, eliminating the Big Store Law means the eventual demise of the millions of mom-and-pop stores and their replacement with huge chains and supermarkets as in the United States, where, ever since the 1950s, the corner grocery stores have disappeared.

There was much heated discussion in the United States about Japanese restrictions on the import of farm products like beef, citrus fruits, and rice. In 1991, the ban on importation of beef and citrus fruits was finally lifted, though high tariffs remained; the tariff on beef, for example, remained at 70 percent. The ban on rice continued because of the stubborn opposition of the farm bloc. The Japanese electoral system is tilted heavily in favor of the rural districts, so politicians are hesitant about going against farmers' interests. The result is that consumers are compelled to pay an exorbitant price for rice. In 1992, an Osaka sushi vendor's plan to make sushi in California and ship it to Japan was blocked until the Finance Ministry relented. It was not until 1993, when a poor harvest resulted in a rice shortage, that the government, under Prime Minister Hosokawa, allowed some American rice to enter the Japanese market. Even so, the imported rice was purchased and distributed by the Food Agency of the Agriculture Ministry; it sold the imported rice at the same price as domestic rice, which costs six times more than rice grown by other nations. In accordance with the agreement concluded at the 1989 Uruguay world trade conference, Japan is committed to allowing 4 percent of its domestic rice to be imported by 1995. Over a six-year period, that ratio is to be raised to 8 percent. Of course, it is not unusual to have special-interest groups protect their turf. On a smaller scale, the story of U.S. peanut growers' success in restricting peanut imports is much like that of the Japanese rice farmers.

Despite the dispute over Japanese restrictions on imports of certain farm products, Japan has been, and still remains, by far the largest importer of American farm products. In 1989, Japan imported $10.3 billion worth of farm products from the United States. In 1990, Japan imported 20.5 percent of U.S. agricultural exports. In that year Japan imported, in terms of tonnage, 27 percent of all U.S. corn exports, 22.6 percent of all soybean, 56.5 percent of all beef and 63 percent of all pork. In 1989, on average, each Japanese consumer bought $361 worth of products made in the United States whereas the average U.S. consumer bought $378 worth of Japanese goods.

The removal of all restrictions on imports from the United States is not expected to redress the trade imbalance significantly, but it would at least remove the perception that the Japanese do not "play fairly." There is no question that the United States provided a wide-open market for Japan and thus enabled the Japanese economy to expand phenomenally after the 1960s. All one has to do to verify this is observe the blanketing of the U.S. market with Toyotas, Hondas,

Nissans, Mazdas, Cannon, Minolta, Nikon, Seiko, Sony, Panasonic, and Nintendo.

The U.S.-Japanese economic relationship is not as one-sided as is often perceived. For example, setting aside imports and exports, sales in 1990 by U.S. companies operating in Japan came to $80 billion a year in goods and services, compared to $14 billion in sales by Japanese companies in the United States. But Japanese investments in such highly visible American landmarks as Rockefeller Center, CBS Records, Columbia Pictures, MCA, Inc. (which aroused the public because MCA also owned facilities in Yosemite National Park) have heightened concern that the United States is being bought up by Japan, Inc., even though in reality Japanese investments were not as large as British and Canadian investments. Japan, however, directly invested $18 billion in the United States in 1991, a much larger amount than U.S. direct investment in Japan, which totaled $1.3 billion. The total investment Japan made in the United States between 1951 to 1990 came to $130.5 billion.[5] However, the buyouts and investments that were made during the boom years of the 1980s had abated by the 1990s when the Japanese economy began to cool down. Thus, the fear that some Americans had of a Japanese takeover of the U.S. economy appears to have been unfounded.

Because of the unfavorable trade balance and Japan's reluctance to open up its markets fully, U.S. lawmakers have been pushing for legislation to curb imports from Japan. In 1991, there were thirty bills in Congress to compel Japan to address the issue. To prevent unfavorable legislation from being passed, Japanese business firms have been lobbying intensively. Japanese companies have spent about $400 million annually in this lobbying effort. Still, some American firms have successfully broken into the closed system in Japan by hiring retired bureaucrats from MITI and the Finance Ministry, who have given them access to the corridor of power and have lobbied on their behalf.

The difficulties encountered in penetrating the Japanese market are not always Japan's fault. U.S. auto manufacturers have complained for years about the barriers imposed on their entry into the Japanese market. However, they have consistently sought to market left-hand drive automobiles—but the Japanese drive on the left side of the road, so right-hand drive is essential. Finally, in 1993, an American automaker, Chrysler, introduced a right-hand-drive vehicle, the Jeep Cherokee. In mid-1994, Ford Motor Company began marketing right-hand drive cars in Japan. In 1994, General Motors officials indicated that they were considering the production of right-hand drive cars for the Japanese market. But the cost of producing right-hand drive vehicles for a limited market was what kept U.S. automakers from moving more quickly in this direction. No amount of high-pressure tactics—such as all three auto company CEOs accompanying President Bush to Tokyo in 1992 to open the Japanese auto market—could prove effective without the manufacture of cars that are suited to the conditions in Japan.

In 1994, President Bill Clinton took a hard line in discussing the trade issue with Prime Minister Hosokawa. He demanded specific commitments and the implementation of quantitative targets rather than glossing over the lack of agreement with diplomatic generalities. The threat of a trade war, which both sides wish to avoid, appeared to have resulted in concessions by Japan on facilitating the marketing of Motorola cellular phones in Japan.

Although trade is the major issue of concern in U.S.-Japanese relations, military cooperation has also been a matter of ongoing concern, and the matter was aggravated further during the 1991 Persian Gulf crisis. The United States wanted Japan to play a more active role in the war against Iraq, but there was strong opposition in Japan to providing direct military assistance due to the antiwar clause in the Japanese Constitution. Even the Japanese government's decision to send minesweepers to the Persian Gulf was met with opposition. Further, many Asian nations that had been victims of Japanese aggression in the 1930s and 1940s indicated their concern about Japanese military participation in the Gulf War. Japan did contribute $13 billion to the Gulf campaign, but this was hardly appreciated by the U.S. officials.

Before the Gulf War, U.S. leaders had been calling on Japan to increase its defense budget to lighten the U.S. burden of providing a military umbrella for Japan. In 1976, the Japanese government imposed a ceiling of 1 percent of the GNP on defense expenditures. In 1992, Japan spent 6.3 percent of its government expenditures on defense, which worked out to slightly less than 1 percent of the GNP and amounted to $275 per capita. In the same year, the United States devoted 5 percent of its GNP, or $1,122 per capita, to defense.[6]

The difficulty in resolving the existing issues, especially in the areas of trade and economic reciprocity, has resulted in what the media describe as "Japan-bashing," that is, increasingly shrill criticism of Japan. A report written for the CIA by participants in a conference at Rochester Institute of Technology in 1991 described Japan as being nondemocratic and racist, as well as an "immoral, manipulative and controlling culture."[7]

In U.S-Japanese negotiations over trade and defense matters, differences in negotiating style have often produced misunderstandings. The Japanese shy away from blunt, explicit statements, whereas the Americans prefer to be candid and outspoken. A Japanese who says "yes" is likely to mean "I understand your point," not "I agree with you." But "yes" to an American implies assent. To a Japanese, "I'll try to do my best" really means "It will be difficult to do what you ask." Misunderstandings thus occur that lead U.S. officials or businesspeople to view the Japanese as being two-faced, or opportunistic, and lacking in principle. Ishihara Shintaro's insistence in his book *The Japan That Can Say 'No'* that Japan must learn to say no infuriated Americans, but he may be offering a positive suggestion. If the Japanese learned to do this, misunderstandings or charges that Japanese people are two-faced could be avoided.

For a U.S. official or businessperson, substance is important, whereas for the Japanese form or style tends to be of greater significance. The former U.S. ambassador to Japan, James D. Hodgson, concluded that "if you try to accommodate the Japanese in matters of style, they will usually try to accommodate you in matters of substance."[8]

The Soviet Union

Japan's relations with the Soviet Union had been estranged since the end of World War II. In April 1941, prior to the outbreak of the Pacific War, Japan signed a neutrality pact with the Soviet Union. As Japan's difficulties in the war mounted, Japanese officials attempted to convince the Soviet Union to act as a mediator between Japan and the Allied powers. However, Stalin had already made a commitment at Yalta in early 1945 to enter the war against Japan once Germany was defeated, so Japan's effort to get Russia to intervene on its behalf failed. On August 8, two days after the atomic bombing of Hiroshima, the Soviet Union declared war on Japan and moved its troops into Manchuria. At the end of the war the Soviet Union wanted to have Japan divided into occupation zones, as in Germany, but the United States did not acquiesce in this plan. The Allied Council for Japan, an advisory body to the occupation authorities, was established, with the United States, the British Commonwealth, the Soviet Union, and China as members. General MacArthur, however, ignored its presence, despite protests by the Soviet Union.

With the onset of the Cold War, the Soviet Union was virtually frozen out of occupation policies in Japan. After the Communist victory in China in 1949 and the outbreak of the Korean War, the United States concluded a peace treaty with Japan in 1951 and pursued its policy of building Japan into an important component in the chain of defense against the Communist powers in the Pacific.

The Soviet Union refused to sign the peace treaty, and relations with Japan remained strained. As agreed upon at Yalta at the end of World War II, the peace treaty provided for the transference of southern Sakhalin Island and the Kuriles to the Soviet Union. Japan held that four of the islands, Etorofu, Kunashiri, Shikotan, and Habomai, were not part of the Kurile Islands and were historically Japan's Northern Territories. This issue continued to be an impediment to efforts to normalize relations between the two countries even into the 1990s.

Prime Minister Yoshida followed a policy of adhering to the U.S. Cold War line, but when Hatoyama became prime minister in late 1954, he set out to normalize relations with the Soviet Union. Negotiations were conducted between Japanese and Soviet officials in London in June 1955. The talks stalled when Japan asked for the return of all four islands in the Northern Territories and the Soviet Union indicated its willingness to return only the two smallest, southernmost islands, Shikotan and Habomai. Negotiations were then discontinued.

The Socialists took a hard line and demanded that the Japanese government negotiate the return of South Sakhalin, as well as all of the Kurile Islands. Undoubtedly, they took this position to embarrass Hatoyama. The Liberal Democratic Party indicated that it would be content with the return of the four islands. Talks were resumed in January 1956 but were again discontinued, and the Soviet Union declared a ban against Japanese salmon fishing along its coast. Japan's minister of agriculture went to Moscow to negotiate the fishing issue, and an agreement was concluded that fixed a maximum limit on salmon fishing. Foreign Minister Shigemitsu was sent to the Soviet Union to resume negotiations on the islands in July 1956, but the issue could not be resolved. Then, U.S. Secretary of State Dulles told Shigemitsu that if Japan turned Etorofu and Kunashiri over to the Soviet Union, the United States would retain Okinawa as its territory. The U.S. State Department advised Japan that it should insist on getting all four islands back. In August 1956, Prime Minister Hatoyama traveled to Moscow and concluded an agreement that provided for the return of Habomai and Shikotan after a peace treaty between the two nations had been concluded. The fate of the other two islands was to be left to further negotiations. Relations between the countries were resumed, and the Soviet Union consented to the admission of Japan to the United Nations.

When Japan and the United States concluded the Mutual Security Treaty in 1960, Soviet leader Khrushchev informed Japan that the Soviet Union would only return the remaining two islands if Japan regained control over Okinawa and all foreign troops were removed from Japanese soil. Three decades later the two countries failed once again to agree on the island question when President Mikhail Gorbachev visited Japan in 1991, hoping to get financial assistance and attract Japanese investment in the Soviet Union. The talks ended without either issue being resolved. As a result, the Kurile Islands issue continues to remain unresolved in the 1990s and has prevented the conclusion of a formal peace treaty between the two nations.

So far as trade between the two countries is concerned, it has been limited. In 1990, before the Soviet Union collapsed, 0.9 percent of Japanese exports went to the Soviet Union, and 1.4 percent of Japanese imports came from that country. In 1992, after the breakup of the Soviet Union, 0.3 percent of Japanese exports went to Russia, and 1 percent of its imports came from Russia.

China

In its relations with the People's Republic of China, Japan followed the U.S. position even after regaining its sovereignty with the peace treaty in 1951.

Neither of the Chinese governments were signatories of the peace treaty, but in April 1952, Prime Minister Yoshida signed a peace treaty with the Chinese nationalist government in Taiwan.

The China market has traditionally been important for Japan. In the prewar years (1934–1936) 23.8 percent of Japan's export trade and 14.1 percent of its import trade was with China. Prime Minister Hatoyama favored establishing relations with Communist China. Thus, during 1954–1956 cultural and economic exchange between the two countries began to develop, and trade between them began to slowly increase.

Prime Minister Kishi, however, was opposed to establishing closer ties with China, so when Taiwan objected to the plan to allow China to open a commercial office in Japan, Kishi agreed to deny diplomatic status to Communist China. Angered by this, China discontinued the growing cultural and economic ties. After Kishi left his position, Ishibashi Tanzan (prime minister in 1956 and LDP party leader) visited China and conferred with Chinese leaders about resuming trade without establishing political ties. Zhou Enlai was amenable to the idea of establishing a nongovernmental, people-to-people relationship.

During this time period, China's relationship with the Soviet Union was becoming strained. In 1960, the Soviet Union withdrew its technical advisers from China and stopped providing economic assistance. Therefore, China became interested in developing economic ties with Japan. And Japanese business interests were also interested in the China market. In late 1962, a commercial agreement was concluded between the two countries. As a result, trade between Japan and China began to increase. In 1970, 3 percent of Japanese exports and 1.3 percent of the Japanese import trade was with China. Political ties, however, were not resumed, because Japan was following the U.S. policy of not establishing political relations with the People's Republic of China. China was critical of the Japanese government's political stance, and during the great Cultural Revolution of the mid-1960s, anti-Japanese sentiment was fanned by the Chinese authorities. They were even critical of the Japanese Communist Party for not joining China in criticizing the Soviet Union and expelled the Japanese Communist Party delegate from Beijing. In negotiating the renewal of the trade agreement in 1967, the Japanese delegates had to sign a statement critical of the Sato government's policy of adhering to the American anti-China line. In 1970 and 1971, Japan voted with the United States in the UN in opposing the expulsion of Taiwan and approving the seating of delegates from the People's Republic.

As a result, the Japanese leaders were caught completely off guard in summer 1971 when President Nixon suddenly announced his plan to visit China and establish U.S.-Chinese relations. The Japanese government was not consulted about this move, nor was it notified about it in advance. China had objected vehemently to the conclusion of the Mutual Security Treaty between the United

States and Japan. But President Nixon told Zhou Enlai that the treaty was designed to prevent the rise of Japanese militarism. Zhou accepted this explanation.

Following the change in U.S. policy toward China, Sato tried to establish ties with China but was rebuffed by Zhou. When Sato resigned and was succeeded by Tanaka Kakuei, Zhou indicated that he welcomed the change. Tanaka stated then that the normalization of Japanese-Chinese relations was one of his chief objectives. Zhou, interested in establishing better relations with Japan, announced the abandonment of the reparation demands for the damages Japan had caused during the war with China. Given the signal for better relations, Tanaka decided to travel to China.

Some members of Tanaka's party, led by Fukuda, opposed abandoning the Chiang Kai-shek government in Taiwan, pointing out that at the end of the war Chiang had facilitated the return of Japanese troops and civilians and had withdrawn reparations demands earlier. But Tanaka overcame their objections and notified Nixon of his plan when he met with him in Hawaii. In fall 1972, Tanaka travelled to Beijing and negotiated an agreement to normalize relations between the two countries. However, a peace treaty resolving all issues stemming from Japan's war against China was not signed at that time. The conclusion of a formal diplomatic treaty was left for subsequent negotiations.

China relinquished its reparation claims and Tanaka expressed regret for the suffering Japan had inflicted on the Chinese people. No explicit statement about Japan's relation with Taiwan was mentioned in the agreement, though China seemed to have tacitly accepted Japan's continued relationship with Taiwan. When the agreement to normalize relations between Japan and China was concluded in 1972, the Taiwanese government announced its decision to break off relations with Japan. But economic relations were sustained by the establishment of a nongovernmental organization for cultural and economic relations, and by an agreement to continue nongovernmental ties, signed in January 1973.

The conclusion of a formal peace treaty with China was delayed because China wanted a statement condemning "hegemony," which was directed at the Soviet Union, included in the treaty. Japan opposed doing this because it feared straining Soviet-Japanese relations. Following the departure of Mao Zedong and the hard-line Gang of Four from the Chinese political scene, a more moderate leadership under Deng Xiaoping emerged in China. Needing to gain economic and technical support from Japan, China was willing to modify the statement on hegemony. Hence, a formal treaty of peace and friendship was signed between the two countries in 1978. The clause on hegemony was modified to state that it did not apply to the signatories' relations with any third party. Political relations between the two countries remained harmonious after that. In 1987, Deng Xiaoping visited Japan, and in 1992, Emperor Akihito visited China. China, however, was not fully satisfied with Japan's recognition of the Japanese aggression and atrocities committed in the 1930s and 1940s. For example, when the Ministry of Education required a textbook publisher to change the phrase "aggression into China and Korea" to "advance" into those countries, the governments of China and South Korea protested vehemently.

The commercial relationship between the two countries continued to expand after Tanaka's visit to China. In 1970, 2.9 percent of Japan's exports went to China, and 1.3 percent of its imports came from that country. In 1984, the figures were 4.3 percent and 4.4 percent, and in 1992, 3.5 percent and 7.3 percent. By 1993, China had become one of Japan's largest trading partners with total import-export trade amounting to $37.8 billion (with the United States, it was $160.5 billion). Japan was important to China as a trading partner. In 1990, Japan imported 16 percent of China's total exports, and Japanese products constituted 15.1 percent of China's imports. Between 1951 and 1990, Japan invested a total of $2.8 billion in China—about 6 percent of its total investments in all Asian nations.[9]

Japanese business operations in China continued to increase. For example, as soon as the peace treaty was signed, a Japanese firm received approval to build a steel mill in Shanghai, and a joint venture to drill for oil off the China coast was started. By the mid-1980s more than 300 Japanese companies, like Sony and Mitsubishi, had offices in Beijing.

Although Japan's formal diplomatic relations with Taiwan were severed with the resumption of relations with the People's Republic of China, cultural and commercial relations continued. In 1992, Japan's exports to Taiwan amounted to 6.2 percent of its total exports, and its imports from Taiwan came to 4.1 percent.

The Republic of Korea

Relations with the Republic of Korea have been delicate because of the bitter memories harbored by the Koreans over the Japanese occupation of their country between 1910 and 1945. The continued discrimination against Korean residents in Japan, moreover, does little to improve relations between the two nations. Further, the recent revelations about the conscription and enslavement of thousands of young Korean women during the war to force them to serve as "comfort women" (a euphemism for prostitutes) for the Japanese armed forces, as well as the procrastination of the Japanese authorities in acknowledging such practices and paying indemnities, have continued to sustain the Korean distrust of Japan.

At the end of the war, there were over 1 million Japanese military personnel and civilians in Korea. Of these, the 170,000 troops and 500,000 civilians in South Korea were repatriated to Japan by early 1946. Of the 74,000 military personnel in the north, 56,000 were sent by Soviet authorities to work as slave laborers in

Siberia. The rest of the military personnel and 300,000 civilians were sent back to Japan in 1947. About 1,000 technicians were detained in North Korea.

About 2 million Koreans had been forced to go to Japan to work in factories, on construction projects, and in mines and labor camps in the prewar and war years. About 1.44 million returned to their homeland, but 600,000 stayed on in Japan, where they remained the object of social, economic, and political discrimination.

Politically, the leadership of Koreans who stayed in Japan split between the pro-North Korean (Japan Korean Federation) and pro-South Korean (Japan Korean Residents People's Organization) factions. The former worked closely with the Japanese Communist Party and actively engaged in anti-emperor, anti-establishment activities. Because of the procommunist activities of the Korean Federation, SCAP began cracking down on the group. It ordered its dissolution in 1949 and purged the leaders. At the same time, SCAP insisted that schools established to educate Korean children must adhere to the guidelines established by the Japanese Ministry of Education and denied autonomy to the Korean schools in formulating their educational curriculum. The schools run by the Korean Federation were closed down in 1949.

Japan's political and economic dealings with South Korea were conducted through SCAP until the end of the Occupation. In 1949, South Korean President Syngman Rhee visited Japan and met with Yoshida. The two leaders announced their common interest as members of the West in the East-West conflict, but Rhee called for the return of Tsushima Island, located in the straits of Japan, to Korea and also asked for reparations for the years of Japanese colonization. When Japanese fishing boats crossed over the coastal boundary between the two countries, established by SCAP, the South Koreans captured the vessels. In 1949, the South Korean government proclaimed the coastal area extending as far as 199 nautical miles as its coastal territory, in contrast to the commonly recognized three nautical miles, and continued to detain Japanese fishing vessels.

In the Korean War, Japan sided firmly with the United States and benefited greatly from U.S. Korean War procurements. South Korea did not participate in the signing of the peace treaty because of opposition from Japan and England. Bilateral negotiations were conducted between South Korea and Japan in 1952. However, the negotiations hit a snag when the Koreans demanded that Japan apologize for its annexation of Korea and pay reparations. Japanese officials contended that the colonization of Korea was based on a treaty between the two countries and was therefore not a violation of Korean rights. The Koreans denied the validity of the annexation treaty. The Japanese demanded the return of Japanese citizens' private property, which had been confiscated by the Korean government at the end of the war, claiming that the confiscation was in violation of the Hague Treaty of 1907. The Korean authorities rejected this claim.

Disagreements arose over other issues as well. South Korean officials requested that all the Koreans residing in Japan be certified as South Korean citizens. The Japanese rejected this demand. The South Korean government also requested that all the vessels that had been registered in Korea during Japanese colonial rule and that were in Korean waters at the end of the war be turned over to them. Japan agreed to turn over twenty-four vessels for the sake of economic cooperation. The first negotiations then ended in failure over the issue of reparations. The second and third rounds of negotiations also ended without agreement. The Koreans were angered in particular over the Japanese delegate's remark that Japanese occupation had been beneficial to Koreans. Hence, discussions broke down and were suspended until 1958.

In 1958, discussions were resumed under Prime Minister Kishi, but at the same time, Japan was negotiating with North Korea to allow the repatriation of those Koreans who wanted to return to North Korea. As a result, the South Korean government not only ended the discussions but also terminated commercial relations with Japan and ceased sending back Japanese fishermen who had been detained. The negotiations were resumed in 1960, but in the course of those discussions, the Syngman Rhee government was overthrown so negotiations were postponed.

Discussions were resumed between Syngman Rhee's successors and the Japanese government, but the question of reparations and the Rhee coastal boundary still presented obstacles to an agreement. However, Japanese business interests moved toward establishing commercial ties with South Korea.

After General Park Chung Hee took power in 1961, negotiations were resumed, and in 1963, agreement was reached on a reparations payment of $300 million, plus an additional $300 million in loans to be extended by Japan. In return, the Korean authorities agreed to limit the coastal boundary to twelve nautical miles. In Japan, the opposition parties objected to an agreement being concluded with a military government, and the Korean opposition, led by students, protested the small size of the reparations payment and the abandonment of the Rhee nautical boundary. As a result, the negotiations were once again discontinued.

In 1965, negotiations were resumed under the Sato government. To avoid admitting that the 1910 treaty that resulted in the annexation of Korea was invalid, the Japanese insisted on inserting a "no longer valid" clause, to the effect that the annexation became invalid when Korea gained independence in 1948. Thus, Japan could avoid paying reparations for the years when Korea was under Japanese rule, and instead, Japan could agree to provide grants and loans amounting to $700 million. In return, the Korean government agreed to provide financial compensation to individual Koreans who lodged claims against Japan, which worked out to be slightly over $16 million.[10]

The South Korean government requested that Japan recognize the South Korean government as the only legitimate government of Korea, thus denying the validity of the North Korean government. Japan acknowledged the UN resolution that the South Korean government was the only legitimate government of Korea but avoided acknowledging the South Korean government's sovereignty over all of Korea, recognizing its sovereign authority only south of the 38th parallel. The Rhee nautical line was reduced to twelve miles, and Japan agreed to return to Korea cultural artifacts in the possession of public institutions, like the Tokyo National Museum, but not those in private collections. As for Korean residents in Japan, those who had been in Japan since the prewar years and their offspring and grandchildren were granted permanent resident rights. But permanent resident rights were not granted to subsequent generations until 1991. Other discriminatory practices remained, such as denial of the franchise and of the right to work in government agencies and enterprises, and so forth.

Koreans, led by students, held that the agreement did not meet legitimate Korean demands, and they opposed the treaty. The Japanese opponents of the treaty held that the terms of the treaty would align Japan on the side of South Korea, pitting it against the North, and opposed its ratification. But Park stifled the opposition in Korea and had the treaty ratified. In Japan, the opposition parties boycotted the Diet. However, Sato and the LDP got the treaty ratified with the support of the Democratic Socialist Party. Thus, by the end of 1965, formal diplomatic relations were established between the two countries.

Economic relations between Japan and South Korea grew steadily after this period. In 1992, Japan's exports to South Korea amounted to $17.77 billion, or 5.2 percent of its total exports, and imports came to $12,339 billion, or 5.0 percent of its total imports. The trade surplus with South Korea from 1965 to 1991 amounted to $66.2 billion, causing South Korea to complain—like other nations—about Japanese market barriers.

Efforts to improve political relations between the two countries continued. When the president of South Korea, Roh Tae Woo, visited Japan in 1990, the emperor of Japan made a public apology for Japan's past actions against that country. During his visit to Korea, Prime Minister Kaifu also apologized for Japan's past actions. Japan had not still established official relations with the Democratic People's Republic of Korea (North Korea) by 1994. Informal discussions have taken place, but little progress has resulted because of North Korea's demand for war reparations and for recompense for damage caused after the end of the war by the political division of Korea into north and south.

Southeast Asia

Because of Japan's wartime activities in Southeast Asian countries, bitterness toward Japan persisted in this region. Japan had forced the people of the occupied countries to labor on its military projects, causing heavy losses in life. The growing economic penetration of Southeast Asia by Japanese business interests is regarded by some people in the region as an economic version of the wartime

Japanese political hegemony that was established in the name of the East Asia Coprosperity Sphere.

After the peace treaty was signed in 1951, Japanese authorities sought to establish ties with the newly independent Southeast Asian nations. In 1957, Prime Minister Kishi traveled to Southeast Asia, seeking to lay the foundation for economic cooperation. He also concluded agreements to pay reparations to Indonesia and South Vietnam.

Relations with Indonesia developed amicably despite the history of Japanese conscription of thousands of Indonesians to serve as forced laborers on the Asian mainland during the Pacific War. In 1959, President Sukarno of Indonesia, who had cooperated with Japan during the war in the expectation that Japan would aid in the liberation of Indonesia from Dutch control, visited Japan.

The Philippines, of course, was a key military target of the Japanese in World War II because it was a U.S. colony, and bitter fighting took place there, with many Filipinos fighting side by side with Americans. But some Filipino leaders, such as José Laurel, cooperated with the Japanese, believing in the Japanese promise of independence.

Thailand, which was an independent state, sought to remain neutral and did not oppose Japan during the war. Thus, it did not suffer from Japanese oppression as did other areas where the Japanese launched military campaigns to drive out the Western powers.

In the 1960s, the Japanese public's attention in Southeast Asia was focused on the Vietnam War, and as noted earlier, a mass protest movement was organized against Japanese government leaders for supporting U.S. war efforts in Vietnam. Following the end of the Vietnam War, Japanese efforts to develop close economic links throughout Southeast Asia gained momentum. In 1977, Prime Minister Fukuda visited the region, and in a speech in Manila, pledged friendship and cooperation. In 1987, Prime Minister Takeshita attended a summit conference of the Association of Southeast Asian Nations (ASEAN), including Thailand, Singapore, Malaysia, Brunei, the Philippines, and Indonesia. In 1991, Prime Minister Kaifu traveled to Southeast Asia and in a speech in Singapore expressed "sincere contrition" for Japan's past actions during the war. He also assured those Southeast Asians fearing the resurgence of Japanese militarism that the vast majority of the Japanese detest the thought of war.

Japan has sought to expand its commercial relations with the Southeast Asian nations and has also made capital investments in these countries. In 1992, Japanese exports to the Southeast Asian countries of Indonesia, Malaysia, the Philippines, Singapore, and Thailand came to 11.9 percent of its total exports, or $42.47 billion, and $30.194 billion, or 13 percent, of its imports. In 1990, oil from Southeast Asia accounted for 17 percent of Japan's oil imports. Indonesia alone accounted for 12.6 percent of Japan's total oil imports, and Japan imported 42.5 percent of Indonesia's total exports in 1990.[11]

Japanese investment in these countries has been increasing. Between 1951 and 1990, Japan invested $11.54 billion in Indonesia, $6.555 billion in Singapore, and $4.422 billion in Thailand. In 1990, about 15 percent of Thai workers in manufacturing plants were employed by Japanese firms. Japanese exports of automobiles and electronic products have been steadily increasing. In 1990, Japan sold 3.4 million automobiles to the Asian nations, and the TV market in Asia for Japan is ten times larger than the market for sales in the United States.[12]

Japanese businessmen who work in these countries have often been criticized for their condescending attitude toward the local populace, as well as for being cliquish, aloof, arrogant, and indifferent to local problems. There have been complaints about "sex tours" (i.e., trips to visit Southeast Asian brothels), the recruiting of women to serve as "entertainers," and other unsavory activities. It has been charged that Japanese wartime imperialism has been replaced by economic imperialism and that Japan's indifference to the plight of its fellow Asians was reflected in its virtual lockout of the Vietnamese refugees, the boat people. Asians who were victims of Japanese imperialism in the 1930s and 1940s contend that Japan has never acknowledged its past misdeeds, and they remain extremely sensitive to any possibility that Japan might reemerge as a military power.

A German Catholic priest who has lived in Japan since 1929 observed, "One thing that bothers me is that I do not think they [the Japanese] show much concern for the welfare of others in their international economic relations. They do not seem to show much responsibility for other people, unless it will bring them a profit."[13] That Japanese business people occasionally treat underdeveloped peoples less fairly than they do Americans and Europeans was demonstrated, perhaps, by the complaints of a Mexican textile manufacturer who had ordered advanced textile machines from a major Japanese trading company but instead was sent used, defective machines that brought about the ruination of his business. His repeated complaints got him nowhere, and he finally took the company to court in 1985.[14] A Philippine writer who spent some time doing research in Japan concluded that, "the Japanese will take advantage of those who are weak. It is therefore imperative for us to build strong societies so that we will not be sucked away. We must also continually remind the Japanese of what they did during the war and should not be deluded about their weeping over Hiroshima." He observed that Emperor Hirohito traveled to America and Europe, apologizing for what the Japanese army did in World War II—but he did not make a similar trip to Southeast Asia.[15]

Japanese leaders have been trying to take heed of these criticisms, and they have also been increasing Japan's contributions to international aid programs. In 1991, Japan contributed $10.95 billion in economic assistance to developing countries, surpassing the $9.6 billion contributed by the United States. In 1989, Japan became the second-largest stockholder in the World Bank.

When a labor shortage developed in Japan during the 1980s, workers from other Asian nations were allowed to enter Japan to meet the labor need. At the same time, the number of illegal immigrants began to increase. The treatment accorded the immigrants was less than fair, and they came to suffer the same kind of indignities that Asian residents in Japan have been subjected to.[16]

Australia

Japan's relations with Australia have been cordial, and trade has benefited both countries. In 1976, the two countries signed a treaty of friendship and co-operation. Economic ties between them have increased steadily. In 1970, Japanese exports to Australia came to $589 million, and imports reached $1.5 billion. In 1992, exports amounted to over $7 billion and imports, $12.447 billion. During that same year, 2.1 percent of Japan's exports and 5.3 percent of its imports were from trade with Australia. A large portion of goods imported from Australia consisted of foodstuffs, minerals, and coal. Automobiles and machinery were the major Japanese exports to Australia. Between 1951 and 1990, Japan invested $16 billion in Australia, about 5 percent of its worldwide investments. Interest in the Japanese language and in Japanese studies has increased enormously in Australia because of these close economic ties.

The Middle East

The other area of major concern for Japan has been the Middle Eastern Arab states because of Japan's heavy dependence on oil from that region. In 1990, 71.5 percent of Japan's oil imports came from the Middle Eastern nations, with the United Arab Emirates being the heaviest supplier, with 21.4 percent. Thus, Japan's interest in the area's political developments remains high, and it seeks to avoid getting involved in the political conflicts in that region. In the 1973 oil crisis that resulted from the Arab-Israeli conflict, Japan called for Israeli withdrawal from occupied territories in order to be perceived as a friend of the Arab nations. Japan was also reluctant to play an active role in the Persian Gulf War of 1991.

Europe

Europe has remained a center of attraction for Japanese tourists as well as for Japanese intellectuals, who regard it as the quintessence of Western culture; but the trade imbalance has also engendered the acrimonious charges of many European nations. In 1991, the prime minister of France, Edith Cresson, remarked that "Japanese are short yellow people who stay up all night thinking of ways to screw the Americans and the Europeans," and that Japan has "an absolute determination to conquer the world."[17] These remarks were especially galling to Japanese Francophiles, who aspire to be loved by the cultured French and are so eager to adopt French culture, fashion, and cuisine.

The French, and the general European, criticism of Japanese trade practices stems from the imbalance of trade between Japan and the European Economic Community (EEC). In 1992, Japan had a favorable balance of trade with the EEC of $31 billion. The European nations, in particular France, have been much more willing to adopt stronger retaliatory measures than the United States has.

The French market has not been as open to Japanese products as other European markets have been, and restrictions on Japanese goods by the French have been more stringent than those imposed by other European nations. As a result, the export of Japanese goods to France in 1992 was only 1.9 percent of Japan's total exports and the import total was 2.3 percent. But the actual dollar value of exports rose from $127 million in 1970 to $6.312 billion in 1992, and imports rose from $22.765 million to $5.412 billion. In addition, direct Japanese investment has increased in recent years.

Among the EEC nations, Japan's trade with Germany is the largest, capturing 6 percent of its export trade, in terms of monetary value, and 4.6 percent of its imports in 1992. The dollar value in 1992 in exports was $20.31 billion, and in imports, $10.739 billion. Germany is Japan's second-largest trading partner. However, trade with the United States, its largest partner, is far greater at 28.2 percent export and 22.4 percent imports. Japan's next-largest trading partner in 1992 in the EEC was the United Kingdom, with 3.6 percent and 2.1 percent. France was the third-largest, followed by the Netherlands, with 2.24 percent and 0.6 percent.

Political and economic relations between Japan and Germany have been good, with few acrimonious comments emanating from either side. Whatever strains there are between the two countries result from the closed nature of the Japanese market. Japanese investment in Germany between 1951 and 1990 came to $4.689 billion, whereas German investment in Japan during that period amounted to $0.95 billion. During the same time period, the largest Japanese investment in Europe was in the United Kingdom, amounting to $22.598 billion; the Netherlands was next, at $12.816 billion. Investment in Luxembourg was $5.607 billion, and in France, $4.156 billion. As for European investments in Japan in the same period, the Netherlands' investment was highest with $1.464 billion, and Switzerland was the next-largest investor, at $1.157 billion.[18]

Relations with the United Kingdom have also gone fairly smoothly, in spite of some vestiges of bitterness about World War II that were manifested during Emperor Hirohito's visit to England and Europe in 1971, as well as during the anniversary of Pearl Harbor. Japan's direct investment in England between 1951–1990 was second only to Japanese investment in the United States. Japanese exports in dollar value rose from below $500 million in both exports and imports in 1970 to $12.287 billion in exports and $4.89 billion in imports in 1992.

4

Economic Developments

The most urgent task facing the Japanese leadership at the end of the war was to revive the economy so that inflation, unemployment, and shortages in all areas could be dealt with. Industrial production was almost at a standstill at the end of the war, and recovery was slow. In 1946, industrial production stood at 30.7 percent of what it had been during 1934–1936.

The food shortage resulted in urban dwellers having to travel to the countryside to exchange whatever they had for food, and the Communists led protest movements over the food shortage. However, the United States provided some relief with shipments of cereal and grain, and after the harvest of 1946, the food shortage eased somewhat.

To deal with the inflation at the war's end, in March 1946 the Shidehara government made the Japanese people deposit their currency in the bank, then froze it, and issued new currency. Each family could withdraw only 500 yen of the new currency. In 1947, the international currency exchange was set at 360 yen per US$1. The Yoshida government established a loan program to facilitate economic recovery and provided funds to the coal, steel, chemical fertilizer, and housing industries, but the issuance of government loans tended to accelerate the rate of inflation. To combat this trend the government decided in July 1947 to stabilize the price of goods at 65 times the prewar level and wages at 28 times that level. But inflation continued to spiral upward, so in June 1948, the government revised its goal of curbing inflation, setting prices at 110 times the prewar level and wages at 57 times that level. As productivity began to rise slowly, the inflation rate also began to decline.

Stabilizing the Postwar Economy

SCAP official William H. Draper returned to Washington and, with the support of foreign policy adviser George Kennan, advocated a policy of easing SCAP controls over Japan in order to foster a freer economic system to hasten the recovery. This was regarded as essential in buttressing the U.S. position in the Cold War. A decision was made by the National Security Council in October 1948 to gradually turn SCAP's authority over to the Japanese government and remove obstacles to Japanese economic recovery. President Truman sent SCAP a nine-point directive on economic policies that were to be followed. The document outlined a program of massive U.S. financial aid, combined with measures designed to remove obstacles to Japanese foreign trade, increase Japanese production, balance the budget, curb inflation, and stabilize the Japanese economy.[1]

In order to implement this policy, a Detroit banker, Joseph Dodge, was dispatched to Tokyo. Dodge was a believer in the laissez-faire, free-market economy. In March 1949, he arrived in Japan as the economic adviser to SCAP. In order to curb the inflationary spiral, Dodge advised the government to balance the budget, end government subsidies, and discontinue the practice of extending loans from the Reconstruction Finance Bank, which had been set up to rebuild the war-ravaged economy. He also advised that the yen be fixed at 360 yen per dollar. Thus, subsidies were eliminated in many areas, government economic regulations were relaxed, and a laissez-faire economic system began to emerge.

Carl S. Shoup of Columbia University accompanied Dodge to Japan to reform the taxation system. Among the recommendations made by the Shoup mission was a progressive income tax system. Its adoption meant a lower income tax for the poor and a higher tax for the rich—as high as 75 percent. This tax system remained in place until 1989, when the ruling Liberal Democratic Party lowered the maximum tax rate to 50 percent and added a 3 percent consumption tax.

These measures checked the inflation, and deflation set in, followed by unemployment. Thus, labor unrest rose and labor disputes and strikes began to break out, especially as the government set out to reduce the workforce in government-run enterprises like the national railroad.

The economy was given a boost by the United States as it turned away from the vindictive policy of making Japan pay for initiating the war and suffering the consequences of defeat. By 1951, the United States had poured more than $2 billion into the Japanese economy. The Japanese economy also received a strong boost from U.S. procurements during the Korean War. By the mid-1950s, the United States had spent about $4 billion in Japan for "special procurements," that is, the purchase of supplies, equipment, services, and recreation for American troops. As a result, during this period the Japanese economy began to grow by 9 percent or more each year. There was, of course, a complex mix of other factors that helped to sustain the initial upswing and thereby kept the economy growing. Industrial production in this period rose from index 100 in 1949 to 240 in 1954.[2]

After SCAP's control over Japan ended in 1952, the Japanese government began to relax the antimonopoly measures introduced during the Occupation.

As the Korean War procurements began to decrease, business interests began to advocate easing the antimonopoly laws, and in 1953, the laws were made more flexible. Thus, the former financial and industrial conglomerates, the *zaibatsu,* began to reemerge. These conglomerates are known as *keiretsu* (enterprise groups). The *keiretsu* consists of a group of firms in different industries that maintain close relationships through cross-shareholding, interlocking directorates, intragroup financial commitments, president's clubs, customer-supplier agreements, and personal and historical ties. There are two types of *keiretsu*: the horizontal, and the vertical. The former, composed of prewar *zaibatsu* complexes like Mitsubishi, Mitsui, and Sumitomo, has at its core a large bank or trading company, and major industrial firms from all the key industries are affiliated with it. The vertical *keiretsu* has a giant producer at the top, like Toyota, Honda, Nissan, Sony, or Matsushita (Panasonic), and a complex of satellite firms that supply it with the necessary parts for its product. Under this arrangement, Toyota, for instance, can assemble its cars by using parts supplied almost entirely by its subsidiaries. Thus, even though major Japanese automobile manufacturers have established plants in the United States, most of their parts are provided by their subsidiaries in Japan. One analyst sees the cooperation and coordination that prevails in the *keiretsu* as a product of the Japanese sociocultural tradition of belonging to a family circle. The system leads to more efficient use of resources (capital, expertise, skilled manpower, information, etc.), and coordination gives the *keiretsu* conglomerates a competitive edge in overseas trade.[3]

The Managed Economy

The laissez-faire policies recommended by Dodge began to be modified after SCAP departed, and the Ministry of International Trade and Industry, or MITI, began to play a greater role in guiding the nation's economic growth. What emerged was a managed economy. The government began to provide subsidies and tax breaks to companies to foster economic growth. Laws were passed to facilitate the growth of the machine and electrical machinery industries. The government encouraged the importation of technology. For example, in the synthetic fiber industry, nylon and polyester manufacturing technology was introduced from abroad. The government imported a General Electric (GE) dynamo and allowed the major Japanese companies to produce their own dynamos by copying the GE model. In addition, American engineering technology was imported in the petrochemical industry, and the production of ethylene, propylene, and butane gas was introduced.

Policies were designed to increase foreign trade. Modern steel plants were built by adopting innovative technology imported from the United States. The shipping industry had been almost completely destroyed in the war, so the government provided loans to the shipbuilding industry to rebuild it. By 1956, Japan had become the world's premier manufacturer of merchant vessels.[4]

In the prewar years, the textile industry constituted the most important sector of Japan's exports. In 1934–1936 textile exports accounted for 57.4 percent of Japan's export value. Following the wartime devastation, the textile sector was among the first in the economy to revive, and by 1950, textiles constituted 48.2 percent of Japan's export value. The growth of other industrial sectors, combined with the drop in the market as developing countries that had formerly provided markets for Japanese textile goods began to develop their own textile industries, caused the textile industry to decline in importance after the 1960s. In 1993, it accounted for only 3 to 4 percent of Japan's total factory output and total exports.

There was a slight recession after the end of the Korean War because of the reduction in U.S. procurements. Exports did not increase, profits dropped, and unemployment rose. But by 1955, the food shortage was no longer a concern because a rich rice harvest of 12.385 million metric tons was harvested, over 3 million tons more than the prewar 1940 harvest. Sales of durable consumer goods gradually increased, and electric washing machines, refrigerators, and TV—referred to as "the three sacred jewels"—came into greater and greater use. Consumer spending grew due to the increased purchasing power of farmers, who prospered with the new land reform program. Factory workers' wages were also increasing, enabling them to purchase more goods. Consumption expenditures per family grew by 36 percent between 1955 and 1960.

The Economic Planning Agency issued a white paper in 1955 stating that the postwar years were over. Generally, the beginning of Japan's high-speed economic growth is dated at 1955, although it was in the 1960s that the economy began to grow at a phenomenal pace. Still, during the latter half of the 1950s, industrial production grew by 9.3 percent per year. Thus, the period from 1955 to 1961 is seen as the takeoff point for postwar Japanese economic growth.

During this period, companies in the steel, shipbuilding, machine and electrical, and petrochemical industries made large capital investments, replacing outdated prewar plants and facilities with modern plants and equipment. Demilitarization resulted in minimal defense spending, which enabled the government to invest money in public works and social welfare programs. Exports began to increase. In 1946, exports amounted to only $103 million, but by 1956, the figure had risen to $2.011 billion. However, until 1965, the balance of trade remained unfavorable. But with increased production and with the opening of the U.S. market and the markets of other countries, a significant increase in exports began to occur in the 1960s.

In the mid-1950s, people saw their time as the most prosperous since the era of Emperor Jimmu, a legendary emperor who was purportedly enthroned in 660 B.C. The Suez Canal crisis caused a slowdown in exports. Nonetheless, the economy revived quickly, and by the early 1960s, people were calling the period the Iwato Boom, the greatest years of prosperity Japan had seen since the Sun Goddess shut herself up behind a stone door to protest her brother Susano-o's misbehavior.

The truly spectacular growth began in the 1960s under the leadership of Prime Minister Ikeda, who set out to implement his income-doubling plan. The groundwork for economic growth had been laid in the early 1950s. However, Ikeda pursued a policy of lowering interest rates and taxes to stimulate economic activities in the private sector and adopted an aggressive policy of capital investment in the infrastructure—building highways, high-speed railways, subways, airports, port facilities, and dams—as well as in the communications system, that is, the telephone and telegraph sectors. Investments were also made in water facilities, industrial land development, housing, and so on.

The bullet train railroad between Tokyo and Osaka was completed in 1964; travel time between the two cities was reduced from 6.5 hours to 4 hours. The freeway between Nagoya and Kobe was completed in 1963. Next, the Tokyo-Nagoya highway was completed to link Tokyo to Kobe. Government expenditures on the infrastructure increased by 40 percent in 1960 over the previous year and increased 30 percent each year after that during the 1960s. Holding the Olympics in Tokyo in 1964 facilitated and accelerated the plan to upgrade the infrastructure. For example, the Tokyo-Osaka high-speed railway was scheduled to be completed in five years, but to be ready for the 1964 Olympics, it was completed in three and one-half years.

Regional governments also invested in public work projects, and local governments were granted subsidies to develop local projects. The government devised a plan to develop fifteen industrial regions nationwide and six secondary industrial zones. Industrial zones were developed first along the Pacific coast strip. New industrial plants, such as steel plants, oil refineries, and petrochemical companies, were constructed along the coast. The plan initially called for the development of such industrial zones in other regions also, but industrial centers ended up being concentrated in the Pacific coast. This, as noted earlier, led to Prime Minister Tanaka's proposal to restructure Japan by spreading the industrial-commercial centers to the outlying regions, but his plan was never adopted.

Prime Minister Ikeda also promoted a more active role for Japan in international trade associations. In 1963, Japan joined the General Agreement on Tariffs and Trade (GATT), and in 1964, it joined the International Monetary Fund (IMF) as well as the Organization for Economic Cooperation and Development (OECD). The yen was accepted in the international currency exchange system. These measures were designed to enable Japan to break into the international market as a major player and to loosen Japanese trade restrictions. In fact, however, liberalization did not take place. Complex rules and minute, stringent, item-by-item inspection of imported goods remained in place, hindering easy access to the Japanese market. Moreover, rigid restrictions on auto and computer imports were enforced.

In order to compete in the international market and, it was contended, to keep Japanese companies from being taken over by giant American companies, government and business interests began to advocate relaxing the antimonopoly laws introduced by SCAP. To foster and strengthen certain industries, it was deemed necessary to allow the emergence of cartel-like groups. The Japanese companies that had been broken up by SCAP in the 1940s began to recombine when the government relaxed restrictions on monopolistic business activities. For example, Mitsubishi Heavy Industries, which had been split up into three companies, recombined as one. The Mitsui and Mitsubishi trading companies began to recombine with companies that had been separated from them by SCAP.

New conglomerates were also formed. Nissan took over Prince Auto Company in 1969, and Yawata Steel and Fuji Steel merged to form Nippon Steel. Three paper companies merged to form a new company, Oji Paper. Also non-*zaibatsu* companies that had emerged in the postwar era and had expanded into giant companies such as Matsushita, Sony, and Honda, became key players in the economic arena. Thus, the emergence of the *keiretsu* came about.

All these measures, in concert with a favorable international market, enabled Japan to expand its economy at a rapid rate. In 1964, the last year of the Ikeda government, the GNP grew at the rate of 13.9 percent. Exports continued to rise in the 1960s. For instance, in 1964, the year Ikeda left office, exports reached $6.673 billion. A positive balance of trade was achieved in 1965, and, except for a couple of years, the trade surplus began to increase steadily. Ikeda's successors followed his policy of expanding the economy, and by the end of the 1960s, exports had risen to $19.363 billion—$490 million over imports.[5]

Japan's Growth Spurt

Truly spectacular growth occurred after this period. By 1965, manufacturing, as well as the economy as a whole, had risen to nearly four times the level reached before the war, while in the same time period the population had only grown 42 percent, from 69 to 98 million. The average family in 1965 consumed 75 percent more goods and services than did its counterpart in the mid-1930s. This consumption rate was the third-largest in the world, after the United States, whose GNP, or total output of goods and services, in the same year came to about $1 trillion; by comparison, the Soviet GNP then was $350 billion.

The Japanese GNP grew on the average of 11.0 percent per year during the 1960s, compared to the 4 percent growth rate in the United States. In 1960, Japan's GNP was seventh-highest in the world, whereas in 1970 its GNP was second-highest among the capitalist nations. Japanese production accounted for 6 percent of the world's production. The U.S., with the world's highest GNP, accounted for 30.2 percent of world production in 1970.[6]

Especially significant growth occurred in the heavy industrial and petrochemical sectors. Advances in the petrochemical industry led to the production of new materials like synthetic rubber, plastic, and synthetic fibers. At this time, the production of electric home appliances, optical instruments, precision and electronic machinery and instruments became a significant component of Japanese industry. Cameras, watches, and television sets soon emerged as major export commodities. These products and heavy industrial goods came to replace textiles as major export items in the 1960s. The increase in auto production was a highly significant development in this period of high-speed economic growth.

The emphasis on industrial expansion resulted in a shift in the working population from the primary sector (agriculture, forestry, and fisheries) to the secondary (mining, construction, and manufacturing) and tertiary (commercial, financial, government, and service) sectors. In 1950, soon after the end of the war, 48.3 percent of the workforce was in the primary sector, 22 percent was in the secondary sector and 29.6 percent had entered the tertiary sector. In 1991, the ratio was 6.7 percent primary, 34.1 percent secondary, and 59.2 percent tertiary.[7]

The general economic growth and the accompanying rise in the standard of living led people to refer to the second half of the 1960s as the greatest economic boom since the days of the god Izanagi (the creator of the Japanese islands and the progenitor of the Sun Goddess)—and this comparison pushed the comparative yardstick even farther back into mythical times.

The Japanese economy continued to grow at a phenomenal rate after 1970, most notably in industrial manufacturing and high technology. The growth was especially spectacular between 1965 and 1974 when industrial production more than doubled.

In October 1973, war in the Middle East broke out, and OPEC began to raise the price of oil drastically. Japan relied on oil imports for 75 percent of its energy requirements. Its heavy reliance on coal had been shifting to oil since the 1950s. Almost all (99.5 percent) of Japan's oil had to be imported, and 88 percent of the imported oil came from the Middle East. Prime Minister Tanaka was informed that Japan had only a forty-nine-day supply of oil but forty-five days' worth had already been allocated to the industrial firms, so only four days of reserve oil supply was generally available.

The price of oil increased from $2 a barrel to $11 a barrel in 1973. Then it went up to $24 in 1979 and $34 by 1981. The oil crisis triggered panic buying by people who feared that shortages would ensue. This, in turn, triggered an inflationary spiral. Faced with this crisis, industrial leaders and government officials at MITI formulated plans to reduce energy use in industrial production, concentrating its use in the high-technology industries. Further, in order to ensure that oil supplies from the Middle East would not be cut off, Japan, as mentioned previously, made pro-Arab statements and called on Israel to abide by the UN resolution of 1967 and return the occupied territories to the Palestinians. This led the Arab nations to classify Japan as a friendly nation.

The policy of cutting back on the use of oil and "rationalizing" (which meant cutting costs by reducing the number of workers) business practices led to readjustments that allowed Japan to cope with the oil crisis. Traditional oil-guzzling smokestack industries were cut back. After the oil crisis, a shift from heavy industries to production of high-tech goods like precision machineries and electronic products came about. The government increased the money supply by issuing government bonds and relaxed its policy of balancing the budget and keeping prices down. These measures helped to pull Japan out of the brief recession resulting from the oil crisis.

Between 1973 and 1979, the amount of energy required to produce motor vehicles was reduced by 25 percent; during the same years, it was reduced by 23 percent in the chemical industry. By 1980, unit energy consumption in the iron and steel industry had been reduced by 27.8 percent since 1975. General dependence on oil for energy needs was reduced from 80.3 percent in 1972, lowering to 61 percent by 1983. The amount of oil for transportation and heating was reduced as well and the oil thus saved was allocated to industries producing export goods. Part of this policy to reduce heavy dependence on oil entailed greater reliance on nuclear energy. After 1983, over 25 percent of Japan's electricity was generated by nuclear plants. The government's plan to continue building additional nuclear plants, however, encountered opposition from the antinuclear movement, which feared nuclear accidents.

As a result of these measures, industrial and high-technology production began to rise and continued to expand. By 1983, industrial production had increased 40 percent over 1974 and continued to increase throughout the 1980s. In 1990, Japan produced over one-fourth of the passenger cars manufactured worldwide, over 9.948 million—and more than the 6.069 million produced in the United States. As car production increased, so did Japanese exports. In fact, the oil crisis had a positive effect on the car market for Japan because Japanese cars were smaller than U.S.-produced cars and were much more fuel efficient. Thus, consumers stopped buying huge gas-guzzling cars in favor of smaller cars, and Japan was able to make significant inroads into the U.S. car market. In 1950, Japan manufactured only 1,593 passenger cars, but following the oil crisis, in 1980 it produced 7.038 million passenger cars, and one decade later, in 1990, it produced 9.948 million.

Increased production meant a greater push to penetrate the foreign automobile markets. In 1990, Japan exported 4.482 million passenger cars. The big market for Japanese automobiles was the United States. The largest number of cars was shipped to the United States in 1986, when the figure reached 2.383 million.

By 1987, Japan had gained 21.3 percent of the U.S. passenger-car market. If the cars manufactured in Japanese automobile factories in the United States are included in this tally, by 1990 about 25 percent of Japanese cars produced were sold in the U.S. market.

Faced with this kind of competition from Japanese automakers, U.S. manufacturers lobbied the U.S. government to pressure the Japanese to adopt a voluntary quota. In 1981, the voluntary export ceiling that Japan set was 1.68 million automobiles. This was raised to 2.3 million in 1985–1991. In 1990, the number of Japanese cars exported to the United States numbered 1.719 million, which came to 18.5 percent of the U.S. auto market. In 1992, the ceiling was set at 1.65 million cars, but the actual export number fell to 1.57 million that year.

The limit placed on exports to the United States was offset by the production of automobiles in the United States by Japanese manufacturers like Honda, Toyota, Nissan, Mazda, and Mitsubishi. Japanese manufacturers other than automakers began establishing plants in the United States as well. Between 1987 and 1992, the number of such companies increased from 774 to 2,070, and the number of American workers employed in these companies rose from 303,000 to 707,000.[8] The practice of establishing plants in the United States and also investing in U.S. enterprises was the result of the high interest rates that prevailed in the United States in the 1980s. Interest rates in the United States rose as high as 18 percent, whereas the rate in Japan was only 3 to 4 percent.

It was not only the success of the automobile industry that made Japan a dominant manufacturing nation in the 1980s. The production of crude steel, which was at 4.8 million metric tons in 1950 and at 93.3 million metric tons in 1970, reached 110.339 million tons in 1990—21 million tons more than U.S. steel production. Pig-iron production, which stood at 2.233 million tons in 1950 and at 68 million tons in 1970, reached 80.229 million tons in 1991. Merchant-ship manufacturing, which reached a high of nearly 17 million tons in 1975, declined to 4.04 million tons in 1988, but then began to recover and reached 7.582 million tons in 1992. This constituted 40.7 percent of world production of merchant ships; South Korea followed, with 25.6 percent. Production of electric home appliances also continued to increase. In 1965, 2.2 million washing machines were produced, and in 1991, 5.587 million units were manufactured. The production of refrigerators increased from 2.3 million units to 5.2 million. Color TV set production increased from 96,000 to 13.4 million in the same period.[9]

The concentration on high technology has resulted in a relative decline in the traditional industries. For example, Japan is no longer the major producer of textile goods or steel. In 1950, textiles accounted for 48.2 percent of Japan's exports, but by 1989, this figure had dropped to 2.5 percent.

Japan also outproduced or challenged the supremacy of other major industrial nations in the manufacture of electronic cameras, radios, quartz watches, television sets, calculators, home videos, videocassette recorders, computers, silicon memory chips, robotics, and genetic engineering. In 1990, Japan exported $2.4 billion worth of radios, $2.071 billion worth of TV sets, and $2.033 billion worth of cameras. For the closest competitor, Germany, the figures were $498 million for radios, $2.199 billion for TVs, and $330 million for cameras. In 1991, Japan produced $11.618 billion worth of machine tools, about 2.5 billion more than Germany, although Germany exported more machine tools than Japan.[10]

Japan also began to use industrial robots to save labor and improve productivity. In 1990, Japan had about 60 percent of the world's industrial robots in use. By 1981, Japan had gained 70 percent of the world market in computer chips, and in mid-1985 the *New York Times* concluded that "Japan has won the computer chip race." This turned out to be a somewhat premature prediction, because by 1993, the United States was beginning to turn the tide.[11]

A study conducted by the Japanese government in 1982 predicted that by the year 2000 Japan would have the world's highest per capita GNP; this was achieved, in fact, by 1990, with a per capita GNP of $25,840, compared to $21,810 for the United States. In 1991, Japan's per capita GNP was $26,920, whereas that of the United States was $22,560. Per capita national income (income from salaries, interests, dividends, profits, etc.) for Japan in 1990 was $19,035, whereas for the United States it was $17,379. However, in 1993, the trend was reversed with the U.S. per capita national income rising to $23,000, whereas it was $19,800 for Japan.

Japan's share of international trade also increased steadily. It was less than 4 percent in 1960 but rose to about 8 percent during 1980–1990. In the prewar period (1934–1936) 57.4 percent of Japanese exports consisted of textile products. In 1992, the figure had dropped 2.5 percent. In 1992, export commodities consisted of 45.2 percent machinery and 17.8 percent automobiles. The United States has remained Japan's major trading partner. In 1991, 29.1 percent of Japanese exports went to the United States, but this dropped slightly in 1992 to 28.2 percent. In 1992, 22.4 percent of Japan's imports came from the United States. Of the dollar value of Japanese exports to the United States, 44.7 percent consisted of machinery and 25.8 percent automobiles.

The balance of trade for Japan, which was mostly unfavorable until 1980, began to shift steadily in its favor; in 1993, exports over imports came to $121.99 billion. As noted earlier, the balance of trade with the United States steadily rose in Japan's favor, reaching $59.3 billion in 1993. The same situation developed in Japan's trade with the European Community, with the balance of trade in Japan's favor reaching $31.194 billion in 1992. A similar balance of trade favoring Japan prevailed in its trade relations with the ASEAN and the Newly Industrializing Economies (NIE) nations. In 1992, the favorable balance with ASEAN was $9.155 billion, and with the Asian NIE, it was $46.470 billion.[12]

The large trade imbalance in Japan's favor has resulted in international pressure on Japan to open its markets more fully and to liberalize the stringent and detailed rules and regulations imposed on import goods. Also, as noted earlier, pressure was applied to strengthen the yen on the international exchange, but despite the rise in the value of the yen, Japanese exports did not decline, but rather continued to increase.

By the early 1990s, however, it appeared that the Japanese economy had peaked, and Japan was beginning to experience some economic difficulties. During the years of high-speed economic growth, the GNP grew at a rate of over 10 percent annually, but that rate had dropped to 0.8 percent in 1992. In fact, the downturn in the Japanese economy was presaged by a drastic drop in the Tokyo stock market, which saw the Nikkei average drop from 39,000 yen in 1989 to 22,000 yen; soon after, it dropped below 20,000 yen. During the years of rapid economic growth, Japanese banks had overextended themselves in making risky loans, overpriced real estate investments, and corporate investments. These practices began to affect the stock market negatively. Also, the Finance Ministry sought to curb overspeculation in stocks and land, and it restricted the money supply and raised interest rates, thus curbing the continuous upward spiral in stock and land prices.

Japan's supremacy in auto production was also challenged by the recovery of the U.S. auto industry. The higher yen made Japanese cars more expensive and contributed to the drop in the number of Japanese cars imported to the United States. Further, in 1993, production of audio and video equipment dropped by 12.7 percent from the previous year, a consecutive double-digit drop. Overall consumer electronics production dropped by 5.9 percent in 1993 compared to 1992. By 1994, Japan began falling behind in consumer electronics because of the emerging information highway and the merging of the computer and consumer-electronics industries. The open, creative software industry of the United States had surpassed Japan's proprietary computer operating systems by 1994.

Until about 1990, Japan was regarded as having surpassed the United States in the economic realm in terms of efficiency, productivity, and technological innovation, but by 1994, the situation had been reversed. In 1992, U.S. factory productivity increased 4.3 percent over 1991, whereas Japan's dropped by 5 percent. Japan was behind the United States by 17 percent in labor productivity in 1990. The average American worker produced $49,600 worth of goods and services per year; in comparison, a Japanese worker produced $38,200. Japan was behind the United States in the use of computers, using 9 for every 100 workers, compared to 34.5 per 100 in the United States.[13]

Explaining Japan's Economic Growth

Numerous explanations have been offered for Japan's success in strengthening and expanding its shattered economy after the end of World War II. It is interesting to note, in any case, that Japan's economic growth was not a sudden development in the postwar era. Since the early Meiji years, the Japanese economy had undergone steady and significant growth. For example, between World Wars I and II, Japanese manufacturing output grew 600 percent, compared to only about 66 percent growth in the United States during that period.

Perhaps the most significant factor in Japan's economic recovery was the support the United States provided in rebuilding Japan's economy. When the United States decided to foster Japan's recovery, it provided financial and technical assistance. Also the outbreak of the Korean War, as noted earlier, gave the Japanese economy a boost because of the huge special procurements designated by the United States to purchase supplies, equipment, and numerous services in Japan. These procurements totaled $4 billion.

Undoubtedly, the U.S. policy that benefited Japan most significantly was the fact that the United States provided Japan with a wide-open market for its products. An authority on the Japanese economy, Chalmers Johnson, writes:

> The American approach to Japan after the war was to declare that Japan was of great strategic importance and very little economic importance. It is for this reason that we allowed Japan to maintain protection of its domestic markets much longer than any European country, to maintain an undervalued currency much longer, why we transferred huge amounts of technology to Japan at bargain basement prices, and also gave Japan virtually unlimited access to the world's largest market, namely, the American market, in a way that we didn't do for anybody else.[14]

In addition to opening its markets to Japanese goods, the United States persuaded other noncommunist nations to open their markets to Japan and also sponsored Japan's membership in GATT in 1955. Furthermore, thanks to SCAP's imposition of the no-war clause in the Japanese Constitution, Japan was relieved of investing huge sums of money in defense expenditures and could invest in rebuilding its economy instead. In order to take advantage of the markets opened to it, Japan had to make the best use of the technical, social, human, institutional, and intellectual resources available.

One reason given by different authorities for Japan's success is the Japanese mastery of management technology (i.e., the science of manufacturing goods efficiently); other experts credit the Japanese social system and mores; the astute planning by government agencies; the close cooperation between government and big business; the dual structure of the economy, in which small businesses absorb the negative costs; or the complex web of obstacles that keeps foreign competition out. Some ascribe Japan's success to "cartels, regulations, subsidies, graft, barriers against imports and foreign investors, a rigged capital market."[15] Other important qualities that can be cited as having contributed to Japan's success in rebuilding its economy are cooperation between labor and management; a well-educated, skilled, disciplined, and hardworking labor force; the work ethic; and the communitarian spirit.

The managerial class played a significant role by making long-range plans, continuously adopting and improving on modern technology to make its plants more efficient. The fact that most of the country's old plants had been destroyed by the war provided Japanese business companies with the opportunity to start from scratch. Management moved swiftly to build modern industrial facilities and adopt advanced and innovative technology from abroad. Capital investment in new equipment was facilitated by the high rate of savings. In the early 1960s, at the outset of the period of rapid growth, about 40 percent of the gross national expenditure was used each year for the replacement and expansion of capital stock. A small portion of the funds came from abroad, but 96 percent of the corporate investment funds came from domestic sources. In 1990, savings per household averaged $71,016 (compared with $28,125 in the United States). Savings are encouraged by the Japanese tax system, which does not tax interest on savings and does not allow tax exemptions on interest payments—the reverse of the situation in the United States.

Japanese manufacturers paid serious attention to perfecting the quality of the goods produced. In the late 1940s, W. Edwards Deming, an American pioneer in the field of quality control, failed to get American manufacturers to adopt his suggestions—but the Japanese turned to him for assistance. He advised them on quality control, and his ideas have been incorporated in the production system. Since 1951, the Deming Prize has been awarded in Japan to firms with outstanding achievement in production and quality control. Most major companies organized quality-control teams in the workforce and encouraged them to devise ways to improve efficiency and productivity in the workplace. In a recent survey of twenty-three industrial countries on product quality, Japan ranked first.

Investment in research and development has also been stressed by Japanese corporations. In the early 1980s, Japan spent 6 percent of its total sales on research and development, in contrast to the 1 percent spent in this area by the United States. These investments have resulted in greater reliance on automation and in higher productivity per worker. Frequently, concepts or instruments conceived or invented in the United States that are not of interest to U.S. industrial firms are adopted by Japanese firms.

The effort to improve productivity and quality has permitted Japanese business firms to adjust constantly to world economic developments. For instance, in the immediate postwar years, textile production constituted an important component of Japan's economy; then, when the industry faced stiff tariff barriers and foreign competition, Japanese industrialists moved on to producing consumer electronic products.

Government agencies, especially the Ministry of International Trade and Industry, and the business sector have cooperated closely in charting the course of economic developments. MITI does not have absolute control over the economy, however. Analysts who downplay MITI's role note that Japanese automobile manufacturers ignored its advice to pool their resources to produce a low-cost "people's car." And there are instances in which its policies failed. But in the 1970s, MITI restructured the shipbuilding industry to cope with the surplus capacity in world shipbuilding. The government also assisted nascent industries, such as the auto industry in the postwar years, by imposing high tariffs and a web of complex rules and regulations that discourage foreign manufacturers from penetrating the Japanese market. It also regulated use of foreign currency to purchase technology and raw materials abroad. Therefore, despite the fact that MITI's influence over private entrepreneurs, who have been going their own way as their resources have expanded, has diminished somewhat, it still remains an important force in charting the course of the Japanese economy. Japan inclines toward a managed economy rather than the free-market system prevalent in the United States.

Japanese management is also credited with long-term planning and a willingness to accept low levels of profits in the short run. Unlike U.S. executives, Japanese business leaders are not the victims of constant pressure to increase profits and dividends because they are secure in their positions, given the assurance of lifetime employment. In addition, much of the funding for capital investment is borrowed from banks, which are more concerned with interest payments than with stock dividends. Moreover, as noted later on, many of the industrial and financial conglomerates are built around banks, which constitute the core of the *keiretsu*. Thus, they are not subjected to constant pressure by stockholders to maximize dividends. Furthermore, two-thirds of the shares of major companies are not traded on the stock exchange, so these companies are not dependent on daily stock fluctuations. Management can therefore engage in long-term planning and concentrate on maximizing market shares rather than on maximizing profits, as U.S. management is compelled to do.[16] Finally, if some stockholders are inclined to raise troublesome questions at stockholders' meetings, the company in question may well rely on a core of "bullies" known as *sokaiya*—corporate extortionists—who are linked to the Mafia-like *yakuza* to keep them in line.[17]

Most Japanese executives have a strong sense of public service. In contrast to U.S. businesspeople, who tend to regard property rights as sacred, Japanese businesspeople consider property rights to be secondary to social needs and regard business companies as public entities that must meet social needs. This difference in attitude is reflected in the compensation received by top executives in the two countries. In 1982, the head of Toyota received $1.3 million in salary, in addition to other compensations, whereas the chairman of Ford received $7.313 million in salary and stock options, at a time when the U.S. auto industry was being pressured by Japanese car exports. In 1990, a typical Japanese executive salary was only six times that of the average employee, while in the United States the ratio was 93 to 1.[18]

Conflict between labor and management was prevalent until the onset of high-speed economic growth in the 1960s, when labor unrest abated. After this, the perception emerged that Japanese management's labor policy is benevolent and paternalistic. This perception sustains generally harmonious relations between management and workers and fosters a sense of group cohesion and commonality of interest. The managerial staff, the office workers, and the laborers in the plant all identify with the company, which is organized like an extended family. In the major companies, there had been the assurance of permanent or lifetime employment until the recession of the early 1990s, when some cracks began to appear in this system. When personnel reduction has to be made, however, the major firms usually do not dismiss the employees outright but send them to work in subsidiary firms, keep them on half-pay, or assist them in starting their own businesses.

The workers are well-educated and well-trained and are governed by a strong work ethic. They are loyal and dedicated to the company and have a sense of belonging to the company rather than merely working for it. Thus, they take pride in their jobs. They are also willing to sacrifice for the success of their company and to work long hours at an intense pace. The payoffs are fewer labor disputes and higher productivity. In addition, workers do not resist the increasing trend toward automation, because in the large companies they are retrained and kept on the payroll.

Perhaps it is not so much the paternalistic benevolence of management that keeps laborers working hard as it is the general attitude toward work that has persisted in Japan since the feudal days, or earlier. The values and attitudes that have traditionally prevailed, such as obedience, submissiveness, conformity, nonassertiveness, avoidance of conflicts, self-denial, and acceptance of a hierarchical order, have eased management's job in dealing with the workforce—a much easier job for Japanese managers than it is for their Western counterparts.

Working in a modern plant may not be anything like laboring in the textile plants of Meiji Japan, but it is still strenuous work. According to Robert Dore, a sociologist specializing in Japanese society, a job at Toyota "as a regular worker is indeed rather more like joining the army in America than going to work for General Motors."[19] But the benefits of being a regular worker for a major manufacturing firm are much greater than those granted to temporary workers or workers in smaller companies: Regular workers are paid well, have job security, and receive generous bonuses when the company makes high profits.

It is noteworthy that labor unions in Japan are far less militant than those in other countries. As discussed later in this chapter, they consist of enterprise unions or company-based unions rather than groups whose membership cuts across the industry. Thus, the Japanese unions identify closely with the company rather than with fellow machinists or welders in other companies, and they avoid making exorbitant demands or staging lengthy strikes that might damage the company. The days lost in labor disputes in Japan in the 1980s came to about

3.7 percent of the days lost in such disputes in the U.S. The identification of the union leaders with the company is strengthened further by the fact that many aspire to rise into the management circle in the company. Younger workers, however, appear not to be as interested in becoming union members. Union membership has been declining since 1970. In 1970, 35.4 percent of the workers were in unions. By 1992, the percentage had dropped to 24.4 percent.[20]

There is a strong sense of community and cohesiveness among the managerial and office staff members because of close personal contact among the business staff. The elite companies pick graduates of top universities, who are then assured of lifetime employment. They become much more solidly part of the "family" than is true of factory workers. They give themselves over to the company, leaving almost no time for their own families. Their superiors look after their interests in a paternalistic manner, even to the point of watching over their personal lives. After hours, staff members are expected to go out together and socialize until late at night—yet another necessary part of developing a sense of family or a community of interests. As Jared Taylor, who grew up in Japan, has noted, "Many Japanese have been happy to let the company arrange their weekends, their hobbies, their vacations, their marriages—in short their lives."[21] Individual ambition must be stifled in favor of group interest as well as the hierarchical order of things. An employee's status is fixed by seniority in this hierarchy. Even the wife of an employee is ranked according to her husband's status, much like the status ranking among military personnel in Western nations.

In short, the paternalistic "total embrace" of the employees by the company and its executives, which would be stifling to an individualistic Western worker, is accepted by Japanese employees, whose social tradition has conditioned them to accept a communitarian and holistic lifestyle.

This kind of communitarianism entails working toward consensus in decisionmaking. For instance, lower-echelon staff members are often asked to prepare proposals or working papers that are then passed around for study by the managerial staff. Eventually, a consensus is arrived at. Thus, the decision becomes a joint one that presumably everyone can support. On the other hand, the process may also diffuse responsibility so that no one person can be blamed if anything goes wrong. (In a grave crisis, however, the chief executive officer takes the responsibility, whether he is personally responsible or not. Such was the case in August, 1985, when the crash of a Japanese airline plane resulted in the death of over 500 people. The president of the airline resigned.)

Lifetime employment, a common practice in large companies, though not in smaller firms, has been cited as one of the reasons for the success of Japanese management. However, although this practice ensures the loyalty of employees to the company, it also has a negative side in that it entails the retention of deadwood, employees who, as they attain seniority, are given meaningless jobs. It also results in a lack of flexibility in personnel utilization and, for the employees, destroys the opportunity to move on to better jobs. Employees are stuck with particular jobs whether they like them or not.

In the early 1990s recession, some adjustment in the lifetime employment practice began to occur. The move toward "corporate labor-adjustment," as it was called, became noticeable in autumn 1992, when the recession following the collapse of the "bubble economy" of the late 1980s finally hit home. During 1993, 783 companies, or nearly one-half of the 1,664 companies listed on the Tokyo Stock Exchange, eliminated 88,423 jobs. Some companies began to lower the retirement age from sixty to fifty-six, and some workers were being encouraged to take early retirement. Part-time workers, often housewives, who do not have the benefit of lifetime employment, were being released. There have also been some plant closings. For example, in 1993, Nissan announced its plan to close the Zama plant, affecting 2,500 workers.[22]

Big business firms cooperate not only with the government but also with each other. As noted above, conglomerate complexes, the *keiretsu*, work as a networking mechanism for in-group cooperation and coordination of business planning and action. Conglomerate members confer with one another and coordinate their efforts in the use of resources, technology, overseas trade, and so on. What prevails is a closed system—an exclusive club in which only the members derive benefits and privileges. Because Japan as a nation is already a closed society (insofar as it does not really admit outsiders readily into the family that is Japan), the *keiretsu* can be seen as a closed system within another closed system. In the intertwining relationships of business interests, favors are mutually exchanged. In 1991, it was revealed that the top four brokerages expended over $1 billion to compensate big investors for their losses. This affair also revealed the shady relationship that exists between business and financial circles and the *yakuza*. Taking care of members of the privileged circle means, of course, that the little investors and the public-at-large get shortchanged.

The additional factor that makes it difficult for outsiders, for foreign firms in particular, to break into the closed system is the old-boy network of personal relationships, involving not only members of the conglomerates favoring each other but also similar personal bonds that extend between influential bureaucrats, especially from MITI and the Finance Ministry, and top company officials. These bonds are cemented by the conglomerate firms providing positions for top bureaucrats after their retirement. Thus, personal contacts between the firm and members of the bureaucracy are established to ensure that favorable government decisions are made on the firm's behalf. Some American companies are starting to take advantage of this system of networking and are beginning to employ retired bureaucrats as advisers to lobby on their behalf, as the Japanese firms in the United States do.

Normally, the subsidiary firms of a vertical *keiretsu* toe the line and submit to the demands of the company at the top. If an official in the subsidiary firm challenges the top firm, he will find himself removed from his position. This was demonstrated in 1991, when the chairman of a parts supplier to Nissan was fired when he objected to Nissan's interference in his firm's management policies. He then protested publicly against Nissan's action and became the first insider to expose the system, which treats suppliers as docile subsidiaries.

Not all Japanese manufacturing plants are modern, efficient, gigantic complexes, however. Japan has a dual economy, a two-tier system in which only about 30 percent of the companies are highly productive major corporations that utilize advanced technology. Seventy percent are smaller, less efficient companies and family businesses. In the mid-1980s, 60 percent of Japanese workers held jobs in plants that employed fewer than 100 workers, and only 13 percent worked in companies employing more than 1,000 workers. Although the labor shortage prior to the oil crisis improved the pay of both the temporary workers in the major companies and second-tier workers, compared to the regular workers in the major firms, temporary and second-tier employees continue to receive less pay, lack job security, and do not receive the large bonuses of first-tier workers. Their working conditions are poorer, and they have lower prestige. In the late 1980s, workers in small companies were paid about 70 percent of the wages of workers in first-tier companies. In plants that employ fewer than 30 workers, and in family-run shops, workers earned 50 to 60 percent of the wages paid to major company workers.

The major companies lower production costs by making use of the smaller satellite and subcontracting companies. In the mid-1980s, 70 percent of the production costs of Nissan Motors was absorbed by work done by subcontractors. The latter are at the mercy of the big companies, serving as buffers to cushion their costs and losses. In an economic recession, when it becomes necessary to reduce production costs, the major companies cut to the bone the price they will pay subcontracting firms. As a result, it is the small companies that go bankrupt. In 1981, 17,600 small firms went under. Thus, the concern for the common good applies only to the "core family" and not to people outside that realm. Toyota and Nissan must prosper and survive—even if the adjunct companies go under. Of course, when times are good and the labor market is in the workers' favor, workers can shift to better jobs because lifetime employment is not the norm in these jobs. To cope with this situation, small plant owners have begun to rely more on automation.

Some analysts assert that concentration of high-tech production in a handful of elite companies poses the danger of an economic collapse. For example, 50 percent of the almost $100 billion in exports to the United States consists of goods produced by twenty companies in the electronics and auto industries, making the well-being of the Japanese economy largely dependent on the success of these twenty companies. Moreover, 13 percent of the 67 million Japanese workers are in the electronic and auto industry. The other 87 percent are in the secondary and tertiary economic domains in wholesale and retail businesses that are incapable of competing with their U.S. counterparts. These companies are able to survive only through government assistance, provided in the form of lower taxes and artificially rigged high prices for their products. In effect, the 13 percent of the workers in the electronics and auto industries are subsidizing the other 87 percent. Therefore, when the top twenty companies began to fall behind in international trade, the Japanese economy as a whole began to slow down.[23]

Other analysts believe that the most important reason for the phenomenal growth of the Japanese economy has much less to do with the ingenuity of management than with the work ethic, the same force that has propelled Japanese economic growth since the early Meiji area. Jared Taylor maintains that "the single most important ingredient in Japan's success is the Japanese attitude toward work. . . . The individual worker brings to his job a set of attitudes and expectations that make him the perfect company man." These attitudes are conformity, group loyalty, and a sense of national uniqueness.[24]

A survey of salaried workers revealed that "work is the most important thing in their life." Peer pressure spurs the individual to work hard, for shirkers are ostracized. Management, by making the company the most important thing in the workers' lives, effectively utilizes these traditional qualities. Some observers have contended that the idea of homogeneity, as used by prewar militarists to emphasize the uniqueness of the Japanese nation, is now being employed by big business interests to "convince the Japanese that they must work hard, train, save, do all sorts of things to protect the image of the nation in order to confront the outside world."[25]

For office, or salaried, workers, adherence to a rigid work ethic means putting in long hours and a six- or seven-day workweek. Before 1990, Japanese business company workers put in 2,111 working hours per person per year, or two to three hundred hours more than the number put in per person by workers in the West. There has been growing concern about overwork that results in physical breakdown and death, particularly among middle-management executives who may put in twelve to sixteen hours a day at work, working six or seven days per week. It was estimated in 1992 as many as 10,000 Japanese worked themselves to death every year. Hence, a movement to cut the working hours to 1,800 per year by 1995 was started in 1992, with the standard workweek to be reduced to forty from forty-four. But office workers seem to be reluctant to take paid holidays. Junior staff workers are especially reluctant to take time off if their superiors do not do so. Also, workers in small and medium companies work longer hours; because of the growing labor shortage, the move to reduce the workweek in big companies is not taking place in the smaller firms. The government's effort to encourage workers to take more leisure time has not been very successful because the Japanese work ethic leads people to see work as an end in itself. One middle-level manager who died of overwork used to go to sleep only after setting three alarm clocks and wearing a wristwatch with an alarm to make sure he would not be late for work. Those who take time off are seen as shirkers and are often passed over for promotion.

It is not only the work ethic that has made the Japanese successful competitors in the international market. It is also their concern for quality and meticulous attention to minute details. These traits are revealed, for instance, in the way strawberry growers wrap each individual berry with protective tissue paper and in the apple farmers' practice of nurturing and pampering every single fruit. In short, the spirit of the artisan who strives for perfection seems to survive in Japanese industrial workers. As Frank Gibney, a longtime American resident of Japan, has observed, "In the search for quality, the modern Japanese workers perpetuate the same feeling of respect for the craftsman which makes Japan one of the few countries in the world to honor her artisans and skilled performers with the designation of Living National Treasure."[26]

The Labor Movement

It was SCAP's policy to free labor from the fetters imposed by the prewar and wartime Japanese government. Accordingly, a U.S. government directive of November 3, 1945, required "the Japanese to remove, as rapidly as possible, wartime controls over labor and reinstate protective labor legislation."[27] SCAP oversaw the drafting and enactment of the Trade Union Law in 1945. The law guaranteed the right of workers (except for the police and firefighters) to organize and join unions in both the private and public sectors, engage in collective bargaining, and to strike. In 1947, the Labor Standards Law was adopted, broadening the protective legislation provided in the Factory Law of 1911. The Labor Standards Law set minimum standards for wages, hours, insurance, injury compensation, and unemployment benefits. The provisions exceeded the U.S. Fair Labor Standards Act in coverage. For example, the new Japanese law required employers to give workers who were to be dismissed thirty days notice.[28]

As a result of the liberal labor union policies supported by SCAP, a massive move to organize labor unions commenced. At the war's end Japan had no labor unions, but less than one year later, in June 1946, there were 12,006 unions and 3.679 million members.[29] The Sodomei (Japan General Federation of Labor), which was linked to the Socialist Party, was organized in fall 1945. The Communists then organized the Sanbetsu (National Congress of Industrial Unions).

Contrary to SCAP's expectations, the unions, led by Communists, made political activism a key component of their program. The initial object of the Sanbetsu was to control the means of production. The two major union organizations joined forces, with the goal of overthrowing the Yoshida government. In 1964, they organized a "struggle committee" and staged numerous strikes. Led by the Communist leader Tokuda, the unions managed to force the government to back down on its policy of reducing the number of workers in the national railroad and merchant-shipping industries in mid-1946.[30] Encouraged by this victory, Sanbetsu staged a series of strikes against a number of private companies, opposing reductions in the workforce and demanding raises for workers. Among the unions' targets were the electric power companies. The Japanese officials tried to convince SCAP to ban strikes in "critical" industries, but their proposal was rejected because "from every point of view, the strike ban proposal was repugnant to SCAP's mission."[31] The electric power workers gained concessions from the power companies guaranteeing them living wages, plus additional pay based on performance. This settlement became the model for other unions.

In January 1947, the union leaders, led by Tokuda, planned to stage a general strike on February 1. Tokuda's objective was political: He wanted to drive the Yoshida government out of office. The economic component in the plan was the continued demand for higher wages for workers. Theodore Cohen, who served as chief of SCAP's Labor Division, notes, "Bad as economic conditions were, vigorous as the labor movement was, and unnecessarily irritating and inept as the government had been in labor relations, the general strike movement of 1947 was still the conscious, purposeful work of Tokuda Kyuichi, his collaborators, and the Communist Party machine of Japan."[32] Even though faced with the threat of a general strike, General MacArthur was reluctant to act as a strikebreaker. However, when rational arguments failed to persuade the Tokuda-led labor leaders to back down, the general issued a ban the day before the strike was to start. Tokuda, failing to get support to defy the strike ban, backed down. But he and the Sanbetsu attempted to keep the momentum for the general strike going by calling the effort not just a strike for workers' economic betterment but a strike to overthrow the feudal system representing the special interests of the *zaibatsu*. The union alliance also organized a movement to get the workers throughout the country to engage in absenteeism to advance their political agenda. The radical unionists then organized the Zenroren (National Labor Liaison Council). Early in 1948, some members of the Sanbetsu, chagrined at the Communist leadership's manipulation of the unions for political ends, split from the Communist Party and formed the Mindo (Democratization League), then linked up with the left-wing Socialists. The Sodomei group, uneasy about the growing political radicalism, ceased cooperating with the Sanbetsu in June 1948.

In order to deal with the rising militancy of the workers, business leaders organized the Japan Federation of Employers' Association (Nikkeiren) in 1948. Soon after forming the association, the business leaders had an opportunity to demonstrate their willingness to take a strong stand against labor. The Toho Movie Company labor dispute took place from April to October 1948. Toho officials were known as staunch anticommunists from the prewar years, and in order to cleanse the company of Communists and communist sympathizers, they set out to dismiss about 1,000 workers, among whom were a number of prominent directors and actors. The workers fought back by occupying the studio and staging a sit-in, but the movie company got the police and American troops to evict the protesters.[33]

Because of the militant labor tactics adopted by the Communist-led unions, SCAP and the Japanese officials moved to revise the Trade Union Law of 1945 in order to curb the militant groups. In 1949, the Yoshida government revised the law and prohibited public-enterprise workers from striking. In addition, another law was passed that denied civil servants the right to strike or engage in collective bargaining. The new law had provisions that prohibited acts of violence during labor disputes; prohibited management personnel from joining unions or from putting union officials on the company payroll; and prohibited automatic extension of labor agreements. It also provided for the right of management to dismiss workers involved in labor disputes without the approval of the labor relations commissions (which consisted of labor, management, and public-interest representatives).[34]

In May 1949, the government announced its decision to reduce the number of workers in government-run enterprises by 290,000 people. As the first step, the government submitted to the national railroad workers' union its plan to dismiss 95,000 railroad workers and proceeded to dismiss 37,000 of them. This move triggered union protests. A few days later, the body of the first president of the National Railways, Shimomura Sadanori, was found; he had been run over by a train. The pathologist ruled it a suicide, but government officials implied that he had been murdered by union activists. Following the announcement by the National Railways that the second phase of worker reduction had begun, a runaway electric train crashed into a house, killing six people. The authorities arrested a number of Communist Party members as perpetrators of the incident. One month later, a train derailed because a section of the tracks had been removed, and three trainmen died in the accident.

These incidents cast the opponents of the government's rationalization policy in a bad light and put a damper on the union movement's bid for public support. Worker participation in strikes and labor disputes dropped, and union membership began to decline. Membership in the Sanbetsu had dropped from 1.68 million to 0.76 million by late 1949. Overall, union membership dropped from a high of 6.65 million in mid-1949 to 5.77 million one year later.[35]

In 1950, the Yoshida government dissolved the Communist-led Zenroren as part of the Red Purge program initiated by SCAP and the Japanese government. In 1950, another union federation, the Sohyo (General Council of Japanese Trade Unions), was organized. It was regarded as a moderate group willing to cooperate with occupation authorities, but it fell under the domination of left-wing Socialists and began to take active political positions, such as opposing the 1951

U.S.-Japan Mutual Security Treaty. In 1952, the Sohyo declared its goal to overthrow the Yoshida government and establish a Socialist government.

Government response was swift. In 1952, to curb the political activities of the unions, the Yoshida government passed the Subversive Activities Prevention Law. Yoshida then began procedures to pass a law preventing general strikes. This move led to massive protest demonstrations on May Day that year. During the course of 1952 and 1953, the Sohyo took the leadership in staging strikes and making income-doubling demands. The strikes by workers in the coal and electric power industries prompted the Yoshida government to enact the Strike Regulation Act in 1953, outlawing work stoppages in these industries.[36]

In the 1960s, when the economy entered the period of high-speed growth under Ikeda, labor militancy began to abate. Real wages rose by 150 percent in 10 years, and unemployment dropped below 1 percent. Rural dwellers moved into the urban areas and found temporary employment or worked in small- and medium-size factories and businesses. Thus, a two-tier system developed in which workers in the modern, major companies were paid higher wages and had job security and other fringe benefits, whereas workers in the smaller companies that subcontracted work from the big companies were paid lower wages and did not have job security or other benefits. Rather than joining forces with the militant labor unions, the workers in the second-tier group tended to look to the secular Buddhist activist organization, the Soka Gakkai, for psychological support.

Labor launched one major offensive before entering a period of cooperation with the government. This was during the Mitsui Miike coal mine workers' clash with the mine operators. In 1953, the union had staged a strike and gained concessions from the company that granted the union more say on working conditions in the mines. These workers were perceived as having succeeded in building "a powerful union on the base of a local working-class culture."[37] Faced with the decline in coal as a source of energy as oil became the major source of industrial power, in early 1959, Mitsui Mine officials announced their plan to reduce the workforce and asked for the voluntary retirement of 6,000 workers. The union rejected this request. In August 1959, the mining company reduced its request for voluntary retirement to 4,580, but this, too, was rejected. As a result, the company set out to dismiss 1,200 workers on its own initiative. The union challenged this action. The company then effected a lockout of the workers in early 1960, whereupon the union launched a strike. The Miike strike coincided with public protest against the Mutual Security Treaty, so the two movements combined, hoping to arouse public fervor against the government and capitalist forces. The union leaders, heavily influenced by Marxist thinking, saw the mining company's move as an attempt to crush the union.[38]

Some workers soon began to defect from the militant, inflexible stand being pursued by the union leaders and formed a rival union, consisting of about one-fourth of the Miike miners' union membership. When members of the rival union tried to enter the mines to return to work, they clashed with the preexist-ing union's workers. The company brought in some thugs to protect the strike-breakers; over one hundred strikers were injured, and one worker was killed. The struggle continued into the summer, with strikers' clashes with the police result-ing in further injuries. The Sohyo regarded the Miike labor struggle as part of the protest against the Mutual Security Treaty, which was designed to combat the re-vival of fascism under Prime Minister Kishi. The Sohyo spent a large sum of money to send 290,000 members to support the strikers and man the picket line, but the tide began to turn against the strikers.

The number of workers leaving the original union to join the rival union grew steadily, and the original strike leaders were forced to agree to arbitration by the labor relations commission. They agreed to regard company-initiated dismissals as voluntary retirements. This was seen as a defeat of militant unionism and as a decline in the fervor of political activism and class struggle that had character-ized the labor union movement since the mid-1940s. Thereafter, the Sohyo de-cided to concentrate on economic goals and began to stage "spring offensives" to win wage increases to match the wages of European workers.[39]

In the 1960s, the workers began to focus on furthering the economic gains of the company where they were employed because company success meant higher wages for workers. It was to the advantage of Japanese trade unions, which were not horizontally linked unions but rather enterprise-based or com-pany unions, to have strong, successful companies. Thus, the trend toward co-operation rather than confrontation came to characterize labor-management relations. The left-leaning and militant Sohyo watched its membership decline as a rival organization, the Domei (Japan Confederation of Labor), was formed in a 1964 merger between the right-leaning Sodomei and the Zenro (National Labor Union Federation), creating a union with a membership of 1.5 million. The Domei affiliated itself with the Democratic Socialist Party.[40]

The policy of cooperation became more firmly entrenched during the oil cri-sis of 1973–1974. The unions accepted the management policy of "rationaliza-tion" to ride out the crisis, that is, the policy of reducing the workforce and tight-ening up the production process. To increase efficiency and productivity, many companies adopted the quality control system that the American innovator W. Edwards Deming had introduced. In many companies, the workers themselves formed quality control circles and adopted measures to increase productivity, cut labor time, and reduce the number of workers needed to perform a given task.[41] After the oil crisis, the spring offensive sponsored by the Sohyo failed to gain the kind of worker support it had formerly engendered before the oil crisis.

In 1976, labor unions led by the Electrical Workers' Federation (Denki Roren) and the Metal Workers' Federation (Tekko Roren) set out to organize an anti-communist labor front and formed the Trade Union Council for Policy Promotion. They were then joined by other unions, and in 1982, they formed the All Japan Council of Private Sector Labor Organizations (Zenmin Rokyo). To counter this group, the Communist-led Sohyo organized the Conference of Labor Unions in order to promote a united-front program. But this effort failed to gain popular worker support; its affiliation with the Communists weakened its position because of the emergence of Gorbachev and his revisionist stance.

In 1987, the Zenmin Rokyo leaders initiated a plan to turn their organization into a national federation that included all the organized workers of both the private and the public sectors. To this end, in 1988, Domei and the Independent Federation of Unions (Churitsu Roren) disbanded and formed the Rengo (Japan Trade Union Confederation). The Shinsanbetsu (New Sanbetsu) and the Sohyo joined the confederation, and by 1991, its membership came to 7.615 million, or 61 percent of all union membership.[42] Through the 1970s, 1980s, and into the 1990s, labor adhered to a policy of cooperation with the business and industrial community and advanced Japan's economic expansion in the world market. Very few serious labor disputes occurred in this period. The overall rate of unionization had dropped from a high of 35.5 percent in 1970 to 24.5 percent by 1991.[43]

Agriculture

In 1950, a few years after the war's end, 48.3 percent of the workforce was engaged in agriculture. By 1960, this figure had lowered to 30.2 percent. As a result of the rapid turn toward industrialization, however, in 1992 only 6.4 percent of the workforce was working in the primary sector (farming, fishing, and forestry), compared to 34.1 percent in the secondary sector (manufacturing, mining, and construction) and 59.5 percent in the tertiary (service) sector. Agriculture accounted for only 1.8 percent of the gross domestic product, compared to 9 percent in 1960. Even though there were fewer workers on the farms, agricultural production, nonetheless, increased.

Traditionally, rice was the staple in the Japanese diet; about 59 percent of the total caloric intake came from rice. Rice, therefore, was the chief agricultural product. Yet in the prewar years, about 20 percent of the rice required by the country had to be imported. However, with improved farming methods and greater use of chemical fertilizers, farm production increased. In 1935, the yield per hectare (2.47 acres) was 2.71 metric tons. By 1969, the yield had risen to 4.5 metric tons, and in 1991, to 5.86 metric tons. In 1935, Japan's total rice production was 8,619,000 metric tons; in 1967, it was 14,453,000 metric tons. At the same time, the dietary pattern of the people changed, by the mid-1980s, and rice comprised only 28 percent of the Japanese food intake. As a result, by 1968 Japan began producing a rice surplus. There has also been tremendous growth in the fishing industry, with the annual haul, excluding whaling, increasing from 3.374 million metric tons in 1950 to 9.978 million tons in 1992. Whaling continued despite the criticism of environmentalists, and the catch in whaling increased significantly compared to the prewar years.

The agrarian population and number of households declined steadily as the urban centers drew more and more people, especially young people, away from the villages. In 1964, there were 5.667 million farm households, but by 1992, the number was down to 2.888 million. Of these, only 15.6 percent, or 451,000 households, were engaged in full-time farming, 15.5 percent were engaged mainly in farming, and 68.9 percent were engaged primarily in other jobs. The farm household population, which numbered 37.670 million in 1950, was down to 13.423 million by 1992. Only 10.9 percent of the total land area was arable. In 1992, 92.8 percent of the farm households worked plots less than 3 hectares in size, and 57.6 percent farmed less than 1 hectare. In 1989, one hectare of rice-growing land cost about $83,000.

The government moved to reduce the amount of surplus rice produced by encouraging land use for nonrice production, but the policy did not result in any significant decrease in rice production. The price of rice is not determined by the law of supply and demand but is fixed by the government, which purchases rice from the farmers at a price higher than the world market and sells it to wholesale dealers. This policy has kept the price of rice artificially high. It was seven times the price of rice in the world market in 1992.

The government stores the surplus rice, and until the 1990s, a large surplus was stored in government warehouses. In 1978, the government had 6 million metric tons of rice in storage, about one-half the annual rice production. Per capita rice consumption declined from 118 kg (1 kg equals 2.2 pounds) in 1960 to 95.1 kg in 1970, then went to 69.9 kg in 1991. As early as 1968, there was a surplus of 2.4 million metric tons, 20 percent more than demand.

Rice producers have been protected from external competition with a virtual ban on rice imports. (In 1994, the ban was relaxed somewhat when a poor rice harvest in 1993 resulted in shortages). The farm bloc has vigorously opposed any move to relax the restrictions on rice imports, and rice has become symbolic of Japanese barriers against foreign imports. The farm interests seek to create a mystique about rice to keep from opening up the Japanese market. They say that rice is a source of Japanese culture, the Japanese mind, and the Japanese way of thinking.

Rice has remained the principal crop raised, though the percentage declined from 47.4 percent in 1950 to 25.5 percent in 1991. The production of vegetables has increased from 9.1 percent of agricultural output in 1960 to 24.2 percent in 1991. Government price support ensures that the farm household income stays higher than that of the rest of the nation. Disregarding the shift in the purchasing value of the yen, the yen income of farm households rose by 16.7 times from 1960 to 1991. In comparison, the worker household income rose by 13.4 times in the same period. In 1980, the annual income per farm household was 7.6 percent above the national per household income. In 1991, the farm household income was about 3.7 percent more than the average worker household income. The special measures to support the farmers, in combination with import restrictions, has kept food prices high. In 1992, food purchases accounted for 23.6 percent of consumer expenditures, compared to about 19 percent in the United States. Despite the surplus in rice, the production levels of wheat, barley, soybeans, and other farm products do not meet the consumers' demand. In 1990, Japan was only 67 percent self-sufficient in food production. In 1992, 16 percent of Japan's total imports consisted of foodstuffs.[44]

The Early 1990s: Recession

The Japanese economic engine began to slow down in the late 1980s, and in the early 1990s, it appeared to enter a period of recession and stagnation. The bubble had burst: "The sun also sets," people said. Japan no longer appeared invincible, and the United States began to regain its former supremacy. One analyst concludes that Japan's success until 1990 depended on "hard work, good management and productive investment," in addition to the adoption of "technological advances already pioneered abroad." Since the mid-1970s, "exports benefited from . . . a low value of the yen and sleepy competitors that underestimated Japanese products." But these advantages are no longer present: "There aren't many major foreign technological advances left to borrow." The value of the yen has risen, and "U.S. companies have awakened to Japanese competition."[45]

The banks, (which form the linchpin of the *keiretsu),* had invested heavily in speculative real estate ventures and found themselves in a bind when the stock market and real estate market began their collapse, that is, when the economy began its slide in 1989. In 1992, it was estimated that Japanese banks had loaned 70 percent of their entire loan portfolio, collateralized by real estate property. It was estimated that in 1992 the banks were saddled with 30 trillion yen (or about $300 billion) in nonperforming loans on which no interest was being paid.[46] The boom years when the economy often grew by over 10 percent had expired, and growth in the 90s had sunk to 1 to 2 percent. Many of the "go-go" companies, as they were called, began to see the bottom line drop into the red. For example, Nissan net losses rose to $835 billion in fiscal year 1993, which ended in March 1994.[47] Still, some analysts believe that it is premature to pronounce that the era of Japanese economic ascendancy is over. So long as there is a world market open to Japanese goods and demand exists, Japanese manufacturers will find ways to supply that market. James Fallows believes that counting the Japanese out is premature. Since the end of the war, American observers have declared the decline of the Japanese as an economic force half a dozen times.[48]

5

Social Conditions

Many of the social problems that beset Japan before World War II were alleviated by the reforms introduced by the U.S. occupation authorities and subsequent policies of the Japanese government, by growing social consciousness, and by economic developments in the postwar years. For example, living standards improved so much that the growth in per capita national income reached a figure higher than that of the United States by 1990. The per capita national income in 1955 was only slightly over $500, whereas by 1990, it had risen to $19,035. The improvement in the standard of living is reflected in the change in the Japanese self-perception. In the early 1990s, close to 90 percent of the Japanese people considered themselves members of the middle class.

Material improvements in living conditions are reflected in higher life expectancies, as noted further on in the chapter. At the same time, the death rate dropped almost one-third from the prewar years. These changes resulted, of course, in a larger population, even though the birth rate continued to drop.

Greater affluence in the high-tech age has produced a society that enjoys all the modern mechanical, electric, and electronic machinery and gadgets that make life more convenient. The 1970s has been labeled the time of the "three-Cs," when cars, color TV, and coolers ruled the consumer world. This affluence has also produced a more harried, pressure-ridden lifestyle, with people driven to obtain all the "necessities" and keep up with the "Tanakas." Thus, there is pressure to overachieve and overwork. The rate of people ruining their health by overwork to the point of death has become a serious social concern.

Social pressures emanating from different sources may account for the fairly high rate of suicides in Japan, especially among the older generation. Perhaps these pressures also account for sporadic outbursts of antisocial behavior, such as bullying among students, which can result in the suicides of the harassed victim. The unleashing of nerve gas in the Tokyo subways in March 1995 may have been the result of social pressure as well. The perpetrators belonged to a sector of the population that follows gurus, who promise salvation by combating the malevolent forces responsible for people's social and psychological uncertainties. Many still worship and pay homage to numerous bodhisattvas, or Buddhist deities, who aid people in distress; the Kannon (Goddess of Mercy) and the Jizo (protector of children) are two such deities.

However, economic growth and the rise in the standard of living do not mean that no material problems confront the Japanese in the 1990s. The society at large is burdened with problems of overcrowding, environmental pollution, and an aging population that requires growing welfare care, among other serious unresolved social issues.

In the realm of social relations, the reforms introduced by the U.S. occupation authorities have resulted in the legal and political enhancement of the position of women as well as that of other groups formerly discriminated against. But legal changes do not mean the realization of equality. As will be discussed in this chapter, traditional social, economic, and political discrimination still besets women, the *burakumin* (people formerly treated as outcaste members), and non-Japanese residents like the Koreans, Chinese, and recent immigrants from other Asian countries. Thus the proverbial island mentality—the belief in Japanese uniqueness, which leads people to regard non-Japanese as outsiders—remains strong and results in social, legal, and political discrimination against people who have lived in Japan for several generations.

The extended family system has been replaced by the nuclear family, though a sense of family ties stays firmly in place. Individualism seems to be in the ascendancy, but traditional social ties and cohesion still govern people's behavior. Social conduct based on the traditional concepts of *giri* (moral obligation) and *ninjo* (human sentiment or compassion) continues to undergird Japanese behavior. This code of conduct was evident during the great Kobe earthquake of January 1995, when thousands died and hundreds of thousands became homeless. Reflecting their belief in these traditional values, the *yakuza* gang in the Kobe region was the first group to extend a helping hand to the victims of the earthquake. Meanwhile, government bureaucrats remained entwined in red tape, not even allowing aid from the outside world to enter the country, treating aid goods like import commodities required to meet rigid standards set by the government. In a crisis, then, the traditional Japanese values and mode of thinking surface, in a way belying the outward manifestation of the craze for Western things and ways. Freedom, equality, and individualism give way to traditional values such as *giri, ninjo*, propriety, communal and family interests, hierachical order, self-restraint, and discipline.

Population

The population of Japan in 1945 was 72.147 million. By 1992, the Japanese population had risen to 124.450 million, and it is expected to peak at 130.44 million in the year 2011. The population density per square kilometer (1 square kilometer equals 0.386 square miles) had risen from 195.8 in 1945 to 332.9 by 1991.[1]

The general improvements in Japan's material situation—better diet, medical care, and sanitation— resulted in the attainment of the highest life expectancies in the world. In 1947, life expectancy for women was 53.96 years, and for men, 50.06. By 1994, it had risen to 82.51 years for women and 76.25 for men. This rise in life expectancy has resulted in an increase in the number of people over age 65. In 1992, about 13 percent of the population was age 65 or older. It is projected that by the year 2000 the population over age 65 will rise to 17 percent, and by 2025, to 25.8 percent. The crude death rate dropped from 14.6 per thousand in 1947 to 6.2 in 1987, and it has edged up somewhat since then to 6.7 in 1991. The infant mortality rate, which was 124.2 per thousand live births in 1930–1934 was 13.1 in 1970 and dropped further, to 4.4 per thousand, in 1991. By comparison, in 1988, the infant mortality rate in the United States was 9.9.

Because of the low death rate and longer life expectancy, the population has continued to increase despite the drop in the birth rate. The birth rate has continued to decline since the end of World War II. In 1947, the birth rate per thousand was 34.3; by 1991, it had dropped to 9.9. The natural increase in population—birth rate minus death rate—dropped from 19.7 per thousand in 1947 to 3.2 in 1991. The fertility rate, that is, the average number of children a woman gives birth to in her lifetime, was 1.53 in 1991. This caused concern among some Japanese demographers because it is believed that the overall population begins to drop when the figure falls below 2.09. If the current rate at which the birth rate is declining continues, it is believed that in thirty years the Japanese population will drop by 20 percent from the 1991 level. The reason for the decline in birth rate is that more women are working and more are marrying later. The average age of marriage for women was 25.9 in 1991, whereas it was 24.2 in 1970.

Women who marry have traditionally been expected to leave their jobs and return to housekeeping and child rearing. In 1992, a child-care leave law went into effect. Companies with more than thirty employees are required to allow the mother or father to take one year's leave from work to care for newborn babies. They are not paid while on leave, however.[2] Another factor explaining the drop in the birth rate is the legalization of abortion in 1947. In 1990, doctors performed 456,797 abortions.

General Conditions

The phenomenal economic growth naturally resulted in a rise in the Japanese standard of living. The per capita gross domestic product, which was $9068 in 1980, had risen to $23,801 by 1990. Per capita gross national product, which includes production figures from overseas investments, was $25,840 in 1990 and $26,920 in 1991. By comparison, in the United States, it was $22,560 in 1991. The per capita national income increased from $284 in 1958 to $1336 in 1969, going up to $19,035 in 1990. In 1990, the comparable figure for the United States was $17,379.[3] Household savings in Japan were among the highest in the world. In 1980, 17.9 percent of the household disposable income was in savings. But with the increasing tendency toward greater consumption, the percentage dropped to 14.1 percent by 1989. Still, the per household savings averaged $71,016 (compared to $28,125 in United States), with 7.3 percent of Japanese household disposable income in savings.

The public's sense of well-being is reflected in the perception of class standing. In 1990, 89 percent of the people considered themselves to be in the lower to upper middle class. The highest number of people, 53.1 percent, considered themselves to be in the center of the middle class. Only 7.2 percent considered themselves as belonging to the lower class and 0.7 percent thought they were upper class.

The sense of general well-being that prevailed within the Japanese populace around 1990 was confirmed by the United Nations Human Development Report of 1992. Japan was ranked Number One in human development.[4] In terms of the quality of life, however, Japan was far behind the other major economic powers in such areas as housing, roads, sewage, sanitation facilities, and so on. The steady increase in population size has created overcrowding, housing shortages, congestion, and pollution, among other problems.

Even so, the affluence of the society is seen in the phenomenal increase in the number of automobiles and household appliances in use. By 1991, 79.5 percent of households had a passenger car, 99.3 percent had a color television set, 99.4 percent had a washing machine, 98.8 percent had a refrigerator, and 68.1 percent had an air conditioner.

A nation's well-being used to be measured in terms of daily caloric food consumption, on the assumption that a higher intake—especially of meat and animal fat—reflected a healthier society. Thus, Japan's low life expectancy in the pre–World War II years was regarded as the product of a diet low in meat and fat. People ate large amounts of rice then, and little else. The average Japanese consumption per day was 13 grams (1 gram equals 0.035 ounces) of protein, 1 gram of which was animal protein.

The caloric intake per person per day in 1934–1938 was 2,020, whereas in 1991 it was 2,622. In the 1930s, a high percentage of food consisted of cereal (71.8 percent), whereas cereal consumption had dropped to 38.7 percent by 1991. Animal food consumption was at 3.0 percent then, whereas in 1991, it had risen to 20.4 percent. Fats and oil constituted 1.1 percent of the daily consumption in the 1930s; the figure had reached 13.5 percent by 1991. Daily consumption of milk and milk products amounted to 9.0 grams per day per person in 1934–1938, whereas it came to 231.7 grams in 1991. Consumption of eggs was 6.3 grams in the 1930s and had risen to 47.2 grams by 1991. Meat consumption was at 6.1 grams in the 1930s; in 1991, it was 79.1 grams.

It is a standard rule that the poorer the nation's economic condition, the higher the percentage of expenditures people have to allot to food. In 1945, Engel's coefficient (the ratio of expenditures on foodstuffs to the total expenditures) for Japan's urban households was 63 percent, and in 1950, it was still rather high at 57.4 percent. By 1970, the figure was down to 32.2 percent, and by 1992, it was 23.7 percent. Thus, despite the improvement in the amount and quality of food, less of the family income was being spent on food by 1990.

The Japanese consumption of approximately 2,500 calories a day, in combination with a low meat and fat diet, is regarded as having contributed to the increase in life expectancy. The low incidence of heart disease in Japan is also seen as a product of this diet. In 1990, there were only 135 deaths per hundred thousand from heart disease, compared to 302 per hundred thousand in the United States. But the general increase in protein intake is believed to be responsible for taller youngsters. Between 1960 and 1980, the average height of seventeen-year-old boys increased by 1.7 inches.

The increase in household income and the general economic prosperity have resulted in more money being spent on leisure activities and travel. In 1965, the average family spent 17.2 percent of family expenditures on leisure activities. By 1991, the figure had risen to 24.2 percent. In 1990, 9 million Japanese tourists traveled abroad; 3.1 million of them traveled to the United States. If business travel is included, the number of Japanese who traveled abroad reached 11 million in 1990.

Cost of Living

With the rapid growth in the economy, the price of goods skyrocketed. A government survey conducted in November 1991 indicated that consumer prices in Tokyo were 27 percent higher than in New York. In 1994, gasoline cost $4.25 per gallon. Around 1990, one pound (1 pound equals 0.45 kilograms) of rice cost over $1.80; an ordinary cut of beef, about $13 per pound; a top-grade cut of beef, over $80 per pound; a cup of coffee and piece of pie in a fancy restaurant, $12. One pound of apples cost $1.40, and a pound of strawberries, $4.50. If someone wanted to bring an extravagant gift when making a visit in 1990, that person would have paid $115 for a muskmelon; $16 for a single cherry; $210 for a bottle of Remy Martin XO; $3,800 for a case of six bottles of Ronanee Conti; and $400 for a box of matsutake mushrooms.

Before the recession of the early 1990s, there was a great deal of conspicuous consumption. For stepping out on the town, an elegant man might have worn his Chester Barrie jacket from London, his $22,900 Swiss Corum wristwatch, and his Gianni Rossi shoes, at $270 a pair. Then he might have climbed into his BMW 7501, a vehicle worth $104,000. His wife might have joined him, carrying her $800 Louis Vuitton bag on her arm.

In the 1980s, Japanese buyers boosted the price of paintings at art auctions abroad. Every year, the Mitsukoshi Department Store sold twenty to thirty paintings priced at more than $1 million apiece in the age of high-speed economic growth and conspicuous consumption. In Japan, retail stores are under the control of manufacturers and the wholesale distribution system, therefore prices at the retail level are high. In the late 1980s, retail prices in Japan on the average were 4.21 times higher than wholesale prices, in contrast to the United States, where retail prices were only twice as high as wholesale prices.

With the economic downturn in the early 1990s, conspicuous consumption and purchases of expensive name-brand goods began to ease off somewhat. The sale of superexpensive imported luxury goods began to decline, and consumers began to purchase more domestic products. Also, luxury items began to be discounted in many stores. But discounting in certain areas is strictly controlled. In 1994, an airline ticket agent offered half-price airline tickets because of the sky-high cost of domestic air fares. At the time, it cost about $400 for a round trip ticket from Tokyo to Sapporo, a few hundred miles away. For the offense of discounting the tickets, the agent was forced to close down his business.[5]

Housing

The general overcrowding has been aggravated by the concentration of the population in major urban areas. In 1990, close to 60 percent of the population was concentrated in four major metropolitan areas—around Tokyo, Osaka, and Nagoya, and in Kita Kyushu. The population of the Tokyo metropolitan region rose from 13 million in 1950 to close to 32 million in 1990. The population shift from rural areas to the urban centers meant loss of residents, especially young people, in rural areas. The population size in northern Japan and Shikoku Island began to drop as early as 1950.

The urban sprawl has resulted in aesthetically unattractive landscapes. The eastern coastal region from Tokyo all the way to Hiroshima has turned into a continuous urban strip. One British scholar teaching in Japan observed:

> Tokyo is admittedly an urban planner's nightmare. . . . Ignore the skyscrapers of the central districts . . . and downtown Tokyo is a patchwork of bath houses, *pachinko* [pinball] parlors, stand bars and tenements, in competition with factories, timberyards, offices and school playgrounds for the precious space. Motorways weave overhead to add to the noise and neon. It is rarely pretty, but Tokyo is undeniably alive in contrast to some European and American inner cities.

The uncontrolled urban sprawl into the suburban areas "without the slightest aesthetic pretense," he further remarked, "has caused tourist information offices' pictures of Japan largely to disappear."[6]

   The concentration of the population in a few urban centers has resulted in serious housing problems. The situation is especially acute in Tokyo Prefecture, where in 1992, close to 12 million people were crowded together in cramped houses and apartments. There were 5,444 persons per square kilometer, compared to 337 in Hiroshima. Houses and apartments in Tokyo sell or rent for exorbitant prices. Residential area land prices in large cities rose by 200 times between 1955 and 1990. The best residential property in Tokyo cost $82,520 per square meter in 1990. A 3.3 meter square plot of land in a Tokyo suburb, which cost $.39 in 1927, cost $92,000 in 1990, increasing by 236,000 times. In metropolitan Tokyo, the cost of housing in 1991 was 8.99 times a property owner's annual income, compared to the national average of 5.7 times. (That year, in the United States it was 3.4 times.) The cost of a family-size apartment was over $516,000. Residential land prices in Tokyo in 1990 were estimated to be 89 times higher than those in New York. And commercial space was costlier still. One square meter of commercial space in Tokyo cost $251,000 in 1990. Thus, a 280-square-meter structure would have cost $51.45 million.

   Prior to the downturn in the economy, property prices nationally grew by over 10 percent annually, fueled by real estate speculators, banks, and investors. In 1990, prices rose by 13 percent in residential areas and by 14 percent in commercial areas. At its peak of value in 1989, Japan's land mass, the size of California, was valued by the real estate industry at $13.986 trillion, four times the land value of the United States, with a land mass 24.5 times larger than Japan's. But with the economic downturn in 1991, the inflation in land prices slowed to 2.7 percent in residential areas and to 3.4 percent in commercial areas. And what was called "the greatest speculative binge of the twentieth century" ended by 1990. By 1992, one-third of the speculative investments had evaporated. However, this did not result in significantly lower housing costs for people.

   Despite the heavy concentration of the population in urban areas, the sewage and sanitation systems have not been modernized sufficiently, and there is very little modern plumbing. Only about 9 percent of housing had flush toilets in the late 1980s, and by 1990, only 50 percent of urban dwellings were connected to the sewage system. Most homes have no central heating or hot-water systems. Because the housing shortage is acute in city centers, people spill over into the outskirts and then have to spend hours every day commuting in overcrowded buses, electric trains, subways, and cars. In 1985, about 40 percent of the salaried workers commuting to Tokyo from the outskirts had to travel for 90 to 120 minutes to get to their workplace.

   Given the cost of land and housing, it is not unreasonable for the average Japanese person to feel financially pinched despite the low unemployment rate (2.1 percent in 1990), the high average per capita income, and the high rate of savings per household. Naturally, there are pockets of poverty where many urban dwellers live in cramped, substandard housing with inadequate sanitation facilities.

Environmental Problems

The price of industrialization has been industrial pollution. One of the most widely publicized such cases occurred in 1953 when a chemical plant poisoned the sea waters off the coast of northwestern Kyushu in Minamata Bay with methyl mercury. The mercury-contaminated fish were then consumed by local people in the region. Consequently, many people were paralyzed or suffered loss of vision, speech defects, and muscular disorders. A large number of babies were born with symptoms akin to cerebral palsy. It was not before 1959 that the cause was identified as mercury poisoning, and in 1963, the source was finally identified as a nitrogen plant, but neither the plant owners nor the government took any action until public furor and legal action taken against the company compelled them to respond. One thousand people died as a result of the mercury poisoning, and thousands more continued to suffer physical difficulties into the 1990s.[7]

Other cases of chemical pollution began to surface in different areas after that. In Niigata, a port city on the Japan Sea, cases of mercury poisoning similar to those in Minamata broke out. In Toyama in central Japan, residents suffered from cadmium poisoning, which caused splintering of bone tissue, disfigurement, and severe pain. Residents have suffered from asthma and emphysema caused by industrial pollution from smokestacks in Yokkaichi in central Japan and in Kawasaki, near Tokyo. PCBs (polychlorinated biphenyls) in fish have been discovered; fish caught in Ise Bay were made inedible by oil dumped in the sea. Also, lakes have been found to be contaminated by nitrates and phosphates that have flowed in from industrial plants.

Over time, public opinion was aroused, and demands for pollution control and environmental protection grew in intensity. Business and industrial interests opposed control and initially managed to have government pollution regulations weakened. Finally in 1970, the Sato government enacted environmental laws and established the Environmental Agency. In the same year, auto emission standards were established by the Transportation Ministry. The air in Tokyo, which was so polluted that policemen wore masks to cover the nose and mouth, became clean enough to inhale.

Still, environmental issues have continued to concern people. Critics have charged that pollution control legislation by the central government could be made more stringent. Many local governments, however, have adopted stricter control measures and dealt with pollution and other environmental problems fairly effectively. However, disposal of industrial waste has remained a problem because of the lack of disposal land space.

International environmentalists such as Greenpeace have criticized Japan's whaling industry. In 1972, the UN Conference on the Human Environment passed a resolution imposing a ten-year moratorium on commercial whaling. Japanese authorities decided not to abide by the resolution and continued to allow commercial whaling. The rationale was that the Japanese needed whale meat, a traditional part of the Japanese diet, for food. The younger generation, nevertheless, is moving public opinion toward ending commercial whaling.

The other major environmental issue is the preservation of the natural environment. Urban sprawl has been transforming the natural environment into a concrete and asphalt jungle. Moreover, the general lack of concern about preserving the natural environment is seen in the conversion of scarce land into golf courses. In 1992, there were 1,700 golf courses, the combined area of which exceeded the land mass of Tokyo. At that time, 300 more courses were under construction, and 2,700 more were in the planning stage. All of these courses together will number 4,700. Great Britain, where the game originated, has only 1,200.

The heavy use of herbicides and chemicals also concerns environmentalists. In order to keep the golf courses from reverting to their natural state, vast quantities of such compounds are sprayed on the greens. In addition, twenty percent of the world's herbicidal chemical spraying occurs in Japan, which has only 0.15 percent of the world's farmland.

Welfare Programs

Caring for Japan's growing population of elderly people has placed an increasingly heavy strain on the national budget. In 1955, people 65 and over composed 5.3 percent of the population. By 1992, the figure had risen to about 13 percent, and it is expected to increase to 23 percent sometime after 2010. The imbalance between the percentages of young and old people is expected to put a strain on the Japanese social security system. In the next thirty years, the number of pensioners is expected to triple, whereas the working population contributing to the pension fund will continue to shrink. By 2020, it is expected that every two workers will be supporting one pensioner. In 1992, the ratio was five to one.[8]

Japan has a comprehensive social welfare and medical insurance program, although the amount of coverage per person is limited. The idea of providing comprehensive social security coverage stems from Article 25 of the Japanese Constitution, which provides for the right of all people to maintain "minimum standards of wholesome and cultural living" and, more specifically, that "the State shall use its endeavors for the promotion and extension of social welfare and security, and of public health." Accordingly, in October 1950, the Advisory Council on Social Security, a consultative body to the prime minister, presented a recommendation for a social security plan. Since then, social security and welfare measures, as well as public health and medical care programs, have been improved and expanded. In 1961, a universal national insurance system and a pension system were introduced, providing the basis for the gradual implementation of a comprehensive social security plan for all Japanese citizens. Although the welfare pension and health care payments may not be sufficient to meet all the needs of recipients, the amount being paid out by the government and other insurance programs has been increasing steadily, causing premiums to rise.

Social welfare benefits cover the elderly, the physically or mentally handicapped, single mothers and their dependents, and those suffering from diseases difficult to cure. The benefits include pensions, stipends, and home-care helpers. The major portion of the welfare cost has been devoted to the elderly. In 1991, about 60 percent of the budget was given over to the elderly.

Health and Medicine

The steady improvement in people's health in the postwar years clearly is the product of advances in medical science, such as the discovery and use of antibiotics, better health care in general, and a better diet.

The American occupation authorities contributed greatly to the improvement in medicine and hygiene. Smallpox, diphtheria, typhoid fever, and tuberculosis were still prevalent when the Occupation started. SCAP initiated a massive inoculation and vaccination program, and within three years, cholera was eliminated, smallpox was curbed, diphtheria was reduced by 86 percent, tuberculosis by 79 percent, and typhoid fever was practically eliminated. It is estimated that 2 million lives were saved in the first two years of occupation by these health measures. Life expectancy during the Occupation had risen to 60.8 for men and 64.8 for women by 1951.

The Japanese government also provides its citizens with medical insurance, a practice that started with the Health Insurance Law of 1927. The program was expanded in the postwar years, and by 1961, all Japanese citizens were covered by a health insurance and pension plan. There are two types of health insurance. The first is employee health insurance, consisting of a government insurance plan and a nongovernment, employer plan. The second is a national health insurance system, managed by municipalities and national health insurance associations. Every Japanese citizen is covered by some health insurance program. About 70 percent of the Japanese populace is covered by employer health insurance plans; the rest of the population is covered by community health insurance guaranteed by the government. Premiums for employer insurance plans cost from 6 to 9 percent of a worker's monthly pay, and the employer pays an average of 3.5 percent of the cost. Employees also pay 10 percent of medical bills, though no more than $550 in any given month.

Health care for the elderly has become comprehensive. In the late 1980s, a hospitalized elderly patient paid a basic fee of about $3 each day, or slightly over $90 per month. Even if a 65-year-old patient has open-heart surgery, which costs over $30,000, that individual will pay only about $90. If the patient is 70 years or older, or 65 and severely handicapped, the national health insurance covers the entire cost, whether the affliction is a cold or cancer.[9]

Because the cost of national health care continued to rise rapidly, the government increased the employed beneficiary's share of medical cost payments to 10 percent (30 percent for dependents). In 1990, the national medical care expenditure came to 6 percent of the national income. But the per capita annual medical cost in Japan in 1992 was $1,171, less than one-half of the $2,566 per capita cost in the United States.

However, universal coverage and the low cost of medical care to the patient have led to frequent visits to the doctor and hospital for minor ailments. The average Japanese person visits a doctor 15 times a year, compared to about 5 times in the United States. Doctors, not surprisingly, are swamped with patients. One dermatologist reported that he usually saw 60 patients in 4 hours, an average of 1 every 4 minutes. Doctors in a clinic said they saw 64 patients a day, allotting an average of 5 minutes per patient. This means that doctors can give most patients only a cursory examination, and frequently patients with serious ailments have to wait for a long time before receiving proper care. Since fees are covered by health care plans, many patients seek to go to the best hospitals and specialists. In order to be treated by the best specialists or surgeons, wealthy patients offer large under-the-table payments to secure immediate care. A Japanese doctor admitted, "It's a bribe, but it's the way things are done."[10]

Japanese doctors provide little information to patients about their medical condition, make injections frequently, and freely prescribe many types of pills, whose efficacy often has not been proven. Doctors are not required to provide patients with full details about the diagnosis. Several years ago, the Supreme Court held that doctors were not required to tell patients if they were suffering from cancer.

Still, medical and health care has improved significantly compared to the pre–World War II years, as can be seen in the longer life expectancy and lower death rates. The chief causes of death in the immediate postwar years were tuberculosis and pneumonia, but deaths from these illnesses dropped drastically, thanks to modern medicine. For example, in 1950, deaths due to tuberculosis numbered 1,464 per million, but the death rate had dropped in 1991 to 27 per million. The major causes of death in 1991 were cancer, heart disease, cerebral apoplexy (stroke), pneumonia, and bronchitis. These accounted for 71 percent of all deaths.[11]

There are two major public pension systems: the national pension plan (covering agricultural workers, the self-employed, and others); and the employees' pension insurance plan, which covers most salaried workers. In addition, there are four other public pension programs for specific groups, such as civil servants. The pension payments for retirees have been increasing but still remain relatively low. In 1991, employees' pension insurance came to only 41.3 percent of the average wage. This is somewhat lower than the 47.6 percent in the United States, although it is higher than Germany's 34.4 percent.[12] A large number of people are covered by the pension plans.

The problem for retirees becomes acute when they are compelled to retire before age 60. In 1992, the retirement age in 29 percent of the companies surveyed by the Ministry of Labor was between 55 and 59. In 66.4 percent of the firms, it was age 60. Thus, over 95 percent of the firms had retirement ages between 55 and 60. Even though many workers are required to retire before age 60, the government's social security payments do not start until age 60. The privileged executives in first-tier companies are provided with nominal jobs in the company or sent to work at satellite firms to tide them over. However, retirees from second-tier companies generally find themselves cut loose without adequate pension or retirement benefits and therefore have to find postretirement jobs to supplement their limited retirement income. The need to save for life after retirement undoubtedly accounts for the comparatively high household savings in Japan.

In the 1970s, the government and private employers increased their expenditures on pension, social welfare, and medical care programs. Government expenditures in these programs increased tenfold from 1970 to 1986. In 1987, 55.1 percent of health expenditures were covered either by the public or private sectors.

Social Problems

Because of overcrowding, as well as the intense pressure to study hard, work hard, and live up to one's personal and professional expectations, the social tension in Japanese society, which has always been present, has intensified in recent years. Suicides (albeit traditionally regarded as an acceptable way out of a dilemma) have been increasing—especially among people over 65 years of age. The total number of suicides in 1991 was 19,875, amounting to 16.4 suicides per thousand, or 2.4 percent of the death rate. In the United States, the number was 12.1 per thousand. In 1991, the Japanese suicide rate for people in their twenties was 12.7 per thousand. For people in their fifties, the rate was 27.4, and for those over 65, it rose to 37.4. The suicide rate for men was much higher than for women. For men in their fifties, the rate was 38.7 per thousand, whereas for women, it was 16.4. For those over 65, the rates were 43.3 for men and 33.4 for women.

The reason for the higher suicide rate for men may be the traditional early retirement age and the absence of a meaningful life after retirement. The traditional concept of *inkyo* (a secluded existence), which has a more negative connotation than the Western concept of retirement, may persist in society, giving the elderly a sense of simply marking time until death. Many retired people, especially civil servants, "lapse into depression and even commit suicide. These men have spent their working lives in a conservative, authoritarian world where everything is done by the book." After they retire, contrary to their expectations, society does not appreciate them. They are not wanted even as husbands or fathers.[13]

Social Unrest and Crime

The stereotypical image of the docile, conformist Japanese person governed by a sense of social harmony gets shattered from time to time. The protest movements of the 1960s and 1970s, as discussed in Chapter 6 on education, certainly challenged this stereotype.

A case in point is the growing unrest among the young, manifested in an increase in juvenile delinquency. Violence in the schools had become a problem by the 1970s and 1980s, although the situation had improved by the late 1980s. In 1987, the number of arrests in school had declined 73 percent from 1981. However, petty crimes committed by youngsters increased from 58,000 in 1975 to 136,000 in 1988. Overall, the number of juveniles arrested for crimes hit a peak of 304,088 (16 per thousand in 1985), but the number had dropped to 236,224 (13 per thousand) by 1991. Adult crimes, which hit a high of 32.2 per thousand in 1965, were down to 25.5 in 1991.

Incidences of violent crimes in Japan are low compared to many other countries. People can walk alone in the streets of Tokyo late at night without fear of being molested. Firearms are stringently controlled. For example, in 1983, there were only 66 cases in which murders with handguns were committed, compared to 15,000 in the United States. In 1991, firearms were used in only 74 murders and 22 robberies. In 1990, there were 1,261 cases of homicide (or 1 per thousand), compared to 23,438, or 9.4 per thousand in the United States. The number of robberies committed in 1990 amounted to 1.3 per thousand, compared to 233 per thousand in the United States. Drug use has traditionally remained low compared to other societies. In 1991, there were 271 arrests for the use of narcotics and 126 for opium. Arrests for the use of stimulant drugs numbered 16,330 in 1991.[14]

The *Yakuza*

A darker side of this image of Japan as a land safe from crime and violence is reflected in the existence of the *yakuza*. The *yakuza*, a group of gangsters involved in organized crime, have existed since the pre-Meiji years and in the modern era have been involved in gambling, drugs, petty crime, and prostitution.

Running houses of prostitution was not made illegal until after World War II, in 1956, but even after that, prostitution continued to be a business operation of the *yakuza*. Those who were forced into the business were not only Japanese women; young women from abroad were imported to Japan for that purpose as well. Frequently, young women from Southeast Asia are lured to Japan by promises of lucrative jobs, such as employment in bars as hostesses. One young Filipino woman recalled, "I came to Japan to work as a bar hostess, but instead I spend half my time working as a hostess and half my time as a prostitute." She was forced to engage in prostitution to pay the loan she incurred to travel to Japan.[15]

Some of these women incur large debts (they also send money to their families at home) and become overburdened and unable to pay off the debt, which leaves them enslaved indefinitely. They are kept in locked rooms and forced to serve the clients. Those who refuse to serve as prostitutes are tortured, or in some cases, killed. The director of a shelter for maltreated women reported in 1991 that 90 percent of the women who came to her had been forced into prostitution.

> Women who refuse are tortured with cigarettes and knives in front of other workers at the club; many jump off balconies to escape the infamous "monkey cage," the locked rooms in which they must cater to clients. Some women are cremated before an autopsy can be performed. One Filipino woman was reported as having died of hepatitis but a post-mortem conducted in the Philippines revealed that she died after she was sadistically beaten, burned and stabbed in the thigh and vagina.

However, not all *yakuza* are inhumane monsters. One Filipino woman was helped to return to the Philippines by a *yakuza* visitor who heard her story, got her a passport, and paid her way back home.[16]

The *yakuza* do not hesitate to commit acts of violence against those they deem their foes. In May 1992, the filmmaker Itami Juzo was attacked—his face, neck, and hand were slashed repeatedly—for making a satirical movie on how to fend off *yakuza* extortion schemes.[17]

The number of gang members peaked at 184,000 in 1963 but began dropping after a strenuous police crackdown was launched. However, in 1990, it was estimated that there were still over 86,000 gang members in 2,800 separate groups of gangs. In 1992, the police reported that there were 86,000 *yakuza* belonging to 3,300 different groups, with most affiliated with three major gangs. Their aggregate income is estimated at $10 billion a year, although it is believed it could be several times higher. The biggest syndicate, known as Yamaguchi-gumi, is centered in Kobe and has about 22,000 members. Like other gangs, it has close ties with construction companies and controls much of the construction business.[18] The second largest *yakuza* group, the Inagawa-kai, has in its network over 300 organizations. This *yakuza* has ties with Sagawa Kyubin, the express delivery company that was involved in the political scandal involving Prime Minister Takeshita and LDP party boss Kanemaru Shin.

In the late 1980s, the *yakuza* gangs have progressed from petty crime to extorting huge sums of money from large business firms. In 1990, it was reported that 41 percent of 3,000 major firms—1,900 of which were listed in the Tokyo Stock Exchange—were asked to donate to the gangs. The National Police Agency reported that one-third of all Japanese corporations give in to such threats from the *yakuza* and pay extortion money. Some have paid as much as $8 million. The police reported that there were 20,806 cases of corporate shakedowns in 1989.

The *yakuza* also engineer all sorts of lucrative behind-the-scenes deals by working with business firms associated with them. For example, in 1991, the Inagawa-kai obtained $35.7 million in loans from a construction company through the mediation of Sagawa Kyubin. And two of the largest brokerage companies provided loans totaling $257 million to Ishii Susumu, the head of Inagawa-kai, so that he could corner shares in a large railway conglomerate. Ishii then made another deal with a leading construction contractor.[19]

Yakuza gang leaders have established ties with the political establishment. One radical right-wing activist contends that "almost all politicians have relations with the *yakuza*."[20] One of the *yakuza* leadership's links to the political world from the early postwar years until the mid-1970s was Kodama Yoshio, an ultranationalist whose political career dated from the prewar years. Kodama had run an intelligence network for the Japanese military in China. He also made a fortune by establishing exploitative business deals there. After World War II, he began to play a role in domestic politics from behind the scenes. He established close ties with *yakuza* gang leaders and sought to arrange the cooperation of separate gangs to combat what he regarded as a threat from left-wing Communists. He also built up close relations with conservative political leaders, helped strengthen the Liberal Party by backing it financially, and in 1954, assisted Hatoyama in his bid to become prime minister. He was a close ally of two LDP leaders, Kono Ichiro and Ohno Banboku. Ohno also had close ties with *yakuza* gang leaders. In a *yakuza* meeting in 1963, Ohno publicly praised the *yakuza* society for its adherence to the chivalric ideal of *giri* and *ninjo*. In the early 1970s, Kodama served as the middleman for Lockheed's bribery of government officials like Prime Minister Tanaka Kakuei. Kodama passed millions of dollars of Lockheed money to key government officials.

Links to the *yakuza* have also been maintained by other conservative political leaders. In 1963, former premier Kishi put up bail for a Yamaguchi-gumi boss convicted of murder. The *yakuza* gangs' role in helping Takeshita quash the public protest against him by the Kominto is just another example of the political role that *yakuza* gangs play. With their access to enormous amounts of money, *yakuza* leaders have been instrumental in raising campaign funds for their political allies.[21]

Traditionally, the police have looked the other way concerning *yakuza* activities. In the immediate postwar years, they used the *yakuza* as a shadow police force to curb left-wing activities. One observer remarks that in earlier times the *yakuza* had been regarded as a social disease but that they had grown into an economic disease as they moved into the arenas of big business and high-level politics. With the outbreak of numerous scandals involving big business firms and politicians, the police could no longer ignore *yakuza* activities. As the police stepped up efforts to curb them, the *yakuza* began complaining that their constitutional rights were being violated. One gang boss protested that "the intention of the police is to create a police state."[22]

There is a subculture of motorcycle gangs, known as *bosozoku* (meaning reckless gang). Many of these gang members are preparing to be admitted to the *yakuza*. They roar around on flashy motorcycles without mufflers to let people know "they don't give a damn" about the rules of propriety and courtesy. In the early 1990s, there were about 70,000 of these Japanese Hell's Angels.

Social Discrimination

Japan's insularity of outlook—an outlook that tends to be confined to narrow national concerns without taking into account the broader international perspective—has often been criticized by the international community. Although some Japanese stress the need to become more internationally minded, for the most part the society remains introspective and adheres to ethnocentricity, emphasizing the Japanese people's uniqueness and homogeneity. Antonin Raymond, an American architect who has lived in Japan for fifty years, concludes that "The Japanese think—no, they know—that they are a chosen people, more so than the Jews. They are chosen to dominate the world; not dominate physically so much as being above every other nation."[23] The comments quoted earlier by French Prime Minister Cresson are more critical in judgment, but they reflect a similar view of the Japanese. Karl van Wolferen concludes that "the pervasive sense of being victimized, the sense of being at once unique and misunderstood, and the absence of leadership all combine to perpetuate Japanese isolation in the world. The isolation is further aggravated by the seemingly insurmountable difficulty of fitting Japan into a larger, 'legal' international framework."[24]

The Japanese propensity to perceiving things in a hierarchical order inclines the Japanese to rank the Western nations, especially the United States, at the top internationally in terms of political, economic, and social importance, and to place the underdeveloped nations lower down on the scale. Japan's defeat in the war resulted in a shattering of self-confidence and ushered in an age of uncertainty in Japan. However, Japan's success economically has brought about a "recovery of nerves": The desire to be Number One has returned.

However, this recovery of nerves has not resulted in the sort of self-confidence that would freely open the nation of Japan to the world. Americans and Europeans living in Japan express irritation and frustration at the fact that, regardless of how long they live in Japan and how well they learn the language, they are ultimately not really accepted in the Japanese community. They remain *gaijin* (outsiders). In fact, if a *gaijin* becomes too well-versed in things Japanese—particularly in the language—the Japanese begin to feel ill at ease with that person. Such a person threatens the faith that only the Japanese can truly understand the Japanese mind and soul. According to Jared Taylor, "Their language is vital to their image of themselves and is an essential ingredient in their sense of uniqueness."[25]

The area most difficult for outsiders to penetrate is that of the traditional arts. One young American who apprenticed with a prominent pottery family was at first regarded as a cute bungler. He commented, "But when I got good, I was a threat." Ultimately, he was no longer welcome in the studio and was forced out.[26] *Gaijin* are discriminated against even in institutions that are presumably more internationally minded. An American professor at a Japanese university asserts that "basic attitudes toward foreign instructors have not changed in one hundred years." Foreigners are virtually denied permanent appointments, and business firms seldom hire foreigners for management positions.[27]

The belief in the homogeneity of the Japanese people, which is a myth most Japanese accept, was also responsible for the unwillingness of the Japanese to accept refugees, for example, the Vietnamese fleeing their country following the Communist victory. In the mid-1970s, when thousands of Vietnamese were fleeing their land in boats, only a few hundred were admitted—reluctantly—by Japan, when other nations were admitting thousands. In 1985, the Japanese government finally agreed to accept 10,000 Vietnamese refugees, but even so, the public did not welcome them with open arms. A public opinion poll taken at that time showed that a majority of Japanese people objected to allowing Vietnamese refugees into Japan.[28] Those interviewed argued their objection in terms of the need to preserve the homogeneity of the Japanese people. One Japanese critic lamented, "The glorification of homogeneity implies an intolerance of that which is alien."[29]

A foreigner born of non-Japanese parents cannot easily become a Japanese citizen even if born in Japan. One is born Japanese and cannot become Japanese. As one resident in Japan observed, "I have found that the Japanese do not tend to think that 'all men are brothers' but that 'all Japanese are brothers.'"[30] A strong sense of "we" and "they" pervades the Japanese mentality. Within the society itself, outsiders or strangers are treated as "nonpersons." For the most part, then, the Japanese are courteous and polite to acquaintances and people in their own circle but not to strangers. Therefore, when a crowd of people is fighting to get on the train or enter subway cars, they push, shove, elbow, and jostle, with little consideration for the convenience of others, who are strangers to them.

Of course, the clannish, parochial outlook of the Japanese is not unique to that nation. One longtime student of Japan divides the world into two types: clubs, and missions. "France and China, for example, are missions: if you conform, if you learn the language and adopt their customs, the people accept you entirely.... Britain and Japan, on the other hand, are clubs: you can be accepted and belong to them as corresponding associates, but you are never really a standing member.... In fact, for foreigners it is more difficult socially in England than it is in Japan."[31]

Koreans in Japan

The parochial outlook and sense of hierarchy that govern Japanese thinking lead to an essentially racist mentality. Thus non-Japanese are frequently treated in an inhumane fashion. The Korean residents of Japan, for instance, are still treated as outsiders, despite the fact that most have been born in Japan. Many of their forefathers were brought to Japan against their will and were forced to work in mining and on construction projects. Many were drafted to work as laborers in the war zones during World War II.

Tens of thousands of Korean women were forced to serve as comfort women for the Japanese troops. Some estimates run as high as 100,000. They were kidnapped by the Japanese police or were led to believe that they were being recruited to work in a factory, then sent to work in government-run brothels. Many were "broken in" by beatings, rapes, and other brutal treatment.[32] Accounts of the conscription and enforced service of these women were revealed by Korean scholars, as well as by a Japanese man who had served as a policeman in Korea. The latter related that he and his fellow policemen combed through rural Korean villages seizing women between the ages of eighteen and thirty-five. He said he had seized about 2,000 women.[33] But the Japanese authorities would not acknowledge the fact, or asserted that these women had been volunteers in the war effort. In 1992, Japanese government officials finally acknowledged the practice when scholars studying public documents were able to verify the fact.

In 1990, some of the women, who had remained silent because they felt ashamed and disgraced, began to demand that the Japanese government compensate them for their enslavement and then filed lawsuits. However, the Japanese government refused to compensate them for fear that Japan would be overwhelmed by demands for compensation from other victims of Japanese military activities. Finally, in August 1993, the Japanese authorities acknowledged that women from at least six Asian countries had been forced into sexual slavery by the Japanese army. Some historians estimate that as many as 200,000 young Asian women, from China, Southeast Asia, and the South Pacific were forced to serve in brothels between 1932, following the Japanese takeover of Manchuria, until the end of the Pacific War.[34]

Between 1940 and 1945 during the war, about 1 million Koreans were brought to Japan to work as virtual slaves; at the end of the war, there were close to 2.4 million Koreans in Japan proper. Many managed to return to Korea, but in 1989, there were 682,000 Koreans still in Japan. It is estimated that as many as 240,000 Koreans were conscripted to serve in the army or work as civilian laborers on military bases overseas. Forty-three thousand of the Koreans who had been forced to serve the Japanese forces were sent to Sakhalin Island, then under Japanese control. In the 1980s, they and their offspring—a total of about 60,000 Koreans—still remained there, unable to return to their homeland.[35]

The Koreans in Japan are not accepted as part of the "homogeneous" Japanese nation and continue to suffer discrimination socially, economically, and politically. A Korean born in Japan does not automatically become a Japanese citizen but must adopt a Japanese name and then undergo the process of naturalization. Koreans were required to be fingerprinted even if they were born in Japan. In 1990, the Japanese government agreed to drop this requirement, not for all Koreans, but only for the grandchildren of those who were registered as residents as of 1971. Finally, during Prime Minister Kaifu's visit to Korea in 1991, the Japanese government agreed to drop the fingerprint requirement for all Koreans as of 1992. The Diet finally passed a bill in 1992 that ended the practice of fingerprinting permanent foreign residents.

This did not mean, of course, that numerous other obstacles that plagued the Koreans and other non-Japanese residents were eliminated. As of the 1990s, they are still subject to arrest if they do not have alien registration cards and face criminal prosecution if they fail to report changes in address or employment to the government within two weeks.[36] There is virtually no intermarriage between the Japanese and the Koreans. If a Korean manages to get a job with a business firm by adopting a Japanese name, he is likely to be fired as soon as his identity is revealed. In general, Koreans are paid 30 percent less than Japanese for comparable jobs. Also, all non-Japanese are barred from holding government jobs. In 1991, because of the shortage of workers, the Osaka municipal government sought to drop the nationality clause that bars foreign nationals from holding certain municipal jobs. There were about 110,000 Koreans in Osaka then, and the aim was to employ them in these jobs. The Osaka city government had to abandon its plan because the Ministry of Home Affairs of the central government objected.[37]

About 100,000 Koreans were living in the two cities of Hiroshima and Nagasaki (many were brought there from their homeland to work as forced laborers) when the atomic bombs were dropped on those cities. About 20,000 Koreans in Hiroshima and 2,000 in Nagasaki were killed in the bombings. In other words, 1 out of 7 who died in Hiroshima was Korean. But the Koreans' request that a monument commemorating the Korean dead be erected in the

Peace Park in Hiroshima was denied because the officials claimed there was no room. Moreover, until 1978 the Japanese government did not extend the kind of medical care to Korean bomb victims that was provided for Japanese victims.

One longtime American resident of Japan noted, "No minority in the world (no minority that I know anything about) is treated more badly by a majority than the Koreans and the Chinese by the Japanese. And it makes the black-white thing in America look like kindergarten in some ways because it is so pervasive and so insidious and it's an absolute blanket condemnation."[38] In 1989, there were about 137,000 Chinese residents in Japan. They also suffer similar legal and social discrimination.

The Ainu

Another indigenous people are the Ainu, who patiently endured a life of isolation and discrimination in the northern island of Hokkaido. They number only about 24,000. They, too, have been fighting an uphill battle to gain recognition of their rights, such as fishing rights and the use of the Ainu language for instruction in their schools.[39]

The Ainu, descendants of the early inhabitants of Japan, were slowly driven off the main island over the years and eventually settled in Hokkaido. Accounts of the campaign to conquer the Ainu appear in historical records as early as the eighth century. The office of the shogun was originally established to subdue the "barbarians," meaning the Ainu. In the Tokugawa period, for instance, the Tokugawa shogun granted trading rights to one of the northern feudal lords. The feudal domain gradually tightened its economic control over the island, reducing the native Ainu to a condition of semislavery and compelling them to harvest marine products.

When the Meiji government was established in 1868, it brought Hokkaido under the central government's direct administration and set out to foster Japanese settlements and develop the island's economy. The Ainu lost their land and their hunting and fishing rights. In order to Japanize the Ainu, the government banned traditional Ainu practices and forced Ainu children to learn Japanese in the school system. In the post–World War II years, a movement among the Ainu to preserve their culture, language, and way of life emerged. The leadership of the Ainu Association of Hokkaido has requested the Japanese government to guarantee the basic rights of the Ainu people and respect their cultural and ethnic identity.

Recent Immigrants

A recent development in the Japanese economy may lead to more openness about admitting Asian immigrants into Japanese society. The labor shortage has resulted in the government's willingness to admit more people from Southeast and South Asia into the country to engage in menial and backbreaking work, work that many Japanese youngsters are not willing to undertake. In addition, there has been an increase in the number of illegal immigrants. It is estimated that in 1991 there were about 100,000 to 300,000 unskilled workers from other Asian countries who had entered Japan illegally.[40] They are often subjected to a host of abuses and unfair treatment. Many women are induced to come to Japan from other Asian nations with promises of attractive jobs, but they are frequently compelled to work as hostesses in bars or as prostitutes. Some estimates held that in 1991 there were as many as 300,000 Asian women fooled into going to Japan to work, with 93 percent of them forced to serve as prostitutes. As noted earlier, many of them are held in captivity, locked in monkey cages, and forced to cater to customers. Those who refuse are brutally tortured or murdered by the *yakuza* lords who run the sex racket.[41]

A recent phenomenon, which is somewhat inexplicable in light of the Japanese bias against interracial marriages, is the importing of young women from Southeast and South Asia to marry young farmers in the rural areas. Young Japanese women refuse to marry farmers in these remote villages, preferring to seek their fortune in the more glamorous urban centers like Tokyo. Marital arrangements are made by marriage brokers; it is estimated there are more than 700 such brokers. In 1989, approximately 17,800 interracial marriages took place. In some cases, the brokers deceive the young women, promising them white-collar jobs, and then force them into unwanted marriages. The brokers who arrange these marriages charge the women an average fee of $20,000. Unsavory as the practice of the brokers is, if interracial marriage continues and becomes more widespread, perhaps the narrow ethnocentrism that prevails in Japan might gradually change. A more cosmopolitan outlook might emerge because the intermarriages are taking place within the most provincial segment of society.[42]

Currently, however, discrimination against the non-Japanese persists. It is virtually impossible for foreigners to gain Japanese citizenship. Until 1992, foreigners were fingerprinted. In the courts, foreigners, especially Asians, have been treated more harshly than Japanese. A lawyer defending a foreigner for shoplifting was outraged that his client was sentenced to one year in prison, whereas Japanese offenders were usually released for the same offense with just a warning. He investigated the record of sentences imposed on Japanese and foreigners in shoplifting cases in a Tokyo District Court between 1985 and 1988, discovering that 63 percent of Japanese shoplifters were given suspended sentences, whereas only 24 percent of non-Japanese shoplifters were given a similarly lenient sentence. In 1989, a Chinese student stole $23 worth of lipstick from a store. She was held in custody for two months during the trial and was sentenced to ten months in prison. Although the sentence was suspended, she was deported. In another such case, a Chinese man spent six months in prison for making $5 worth of telephone calls by using a doctored telephone card that he did not know had been altered.[43]

The *Burakumin*

The belief that homogeneity is the distinctive characteristic of the Japanese people has not only resulted in treating all non-Japanese as outsiders. It has also caused discrimination against people who are Japanese but are regarded as being different, a view reinforced by the myth that such Japanese people are actually descendants of Koreans. The discrimination against them has persisted for centuries. This unlucky segment of the population is the outcaste group formerly identified by demeaning terms such as *eta* (great filth) or *hinin* (nonhuman). Today they are called *burakumin* (hamlet people). There may be 2 to 3 million people who fall into this category.

Despite public denial of discrimination by business and political leaders, discrimination against the *burakumin* continues. The Buraku Liberation League is carrying on a difficult struggle against discrimination with only limited resources. In discrimination against the *burakumin,* the "we-they" mentality spreads its insidious influence in the job market, in social relations, and in marital arrangements.

The origin of the class of people who came to be regarded as beyond the pale is not clear. Some believe that they were not Japanese but had come from Korea as immigrants or prisoners of war in the distant past, sometime between the fourth and seventh centuries. Others believe that they were discriminated against because of their occupation, that is, they engaged in "unclean" work, such as disposing of dead people and animals. Further, people who worked with parts of animals, for example, tanners and leather workers, were also viewed as unclean. In addition, butchering and consumption of animal flesh were regarded as unclean activities, in part as a by-product of Buddhist influence.

In the Tokugawa era (1603–1867), when the shogunate established rigid social class distinctions, two subclasses, the *eta* and the *hinin,* were placed below the four major classes of samurai, peasants, artisans, and merchants. The *eta* were people who had inherited their status and were involved in unclean work. Initially, the *hinin* were people who had been designated "nonhuman" because they had broken the law or violated some serious social taboo. Their status was not hereditary at first, but soon they were relegated to hereditary outcaste status. Often, entertainers, beggars, vagrants, and people with abhorrent diseases became classified as *eta* or *hinin.* They were called *senmin* (vulgar people) in contrast to *ryomin* (good people). They were restricted in the occupations they could pursue, confined to segregated living sections, and barred from having social relations with nonoutcaste or intermarrying with the "good people." They were restricted to wearing certain clothing and were banned from entering nonoutcaste shrines and temples. Given such impediments to pursuing a mean-ingful occupation, some turned to gambling and began to form gangs to protect their interests and turf. In fact, the origin of some of the modern *yakuza* can be traced to Tokugawa-era *yakuza*, who resembled the Italian mafia with their tightly knit *oyabun-kobun* (boss-follower) relations. Another ganglike group that emerged was the *tekiya*, who ran an operation that controlled the business of peddling and running street corner stalls. Outcaste members tended to be drawn to this group also.[44]

Under the Meiji government, legal class distinctions were eliminated in 1871, and the outcaste people, in theory at least, were accorded legal equality. But they were classified as "new commoners" in the family register. Thus, employers and schools could easily identify them as outcastes because in any application for jobs or school admissions, applicants had to submit a copy of their family regis-ter. Social and economic discrimination continued without any improvement in outcaste status. Members of the outcastes were held to be dirty, vulgar, smelly, untrustworthy, and dangerous. They were locked out of factory and office jobs. Many were forced to sell their daughters to the brothels. One person recalled, "My older sister has practically no education. At the age when she should have been finishing the 6th grade she was sent out as a geisha [to a brothel]. Discrimination was a fact of life. We were insulted as cow-killers and four-legged animals. No one would hire us."[45]

In the Taisho period (1912–1926), the outcaste members sought to fight for their rights and organized the Suiheisha (Levelers' Association). They failed to make any headway, especially because of the upsurge of nationalism and mili-tarism in the 1930s.

After the war, the practice of identifying outcaste members as new common-ers was dropped, and according to the new constitution, equality was to be ac-corded to all Japanese. Still, discrimination and practices based on bias and prej-udice persisted. In 1987, the government reported that there were 4,603 *buraku* districts with a total population of 1,155,733. However, these figures include only government-designated districts, and unofficial estimates indicate that there are as many as 6,000 districts, with a total population of 3 million.[46] The heaviest concentration of such districts is in western Japan, especially in the Kyoto-Osaka areas. Since 1969, the government has provided funds designated for Area Improvement to improve housing in these districts, so the housing situation has improved, but discriminatory practices in education, employment, and mar-riage have not ended. The Buraku Liberation League has therefore continued its fight to gain equal rights and fair treatment. For example, the practice of track-ing down the background of job applicants and marriage candidates to ascertain whether they are members of the *buraku* community continues. There are nu-merous private detective agencies that specialize in tracking down *burakumin* applying for jobs. In 1975, a "*buraku* list" giving locations of *buraku* districts throughout Japan was uncovered. Nine lists were acquired by more than two hundred companies to identify *burakumin* job applicants. Discrimination is organized to the point that "there are even computer databanks with lists of burakumin names so people can investigate prospective employees and spouses."[47] Investigators also obtain illegal access to family registers to check the background of job applicants and marriage prospects.

It is not only the business companies that discriminate against the *burakumin*; even religious organizations do so. A number of Buddhist sects in the past engaged in the practice of giving discriminatory posthumous names to the *burakumin*, identifying them on the tombstone with such words as *kaku* (leather) and *boku* slaves. These words were not removed from some tombstones until the late 1980s.[48] A *burakumin* educator visiting the United States in 1991 reported,

> We face discrimination at work, in school, and in marriage. . . . We are ten times more likely to be on welfare than the general population. We are twice as prone to illness. Half of all burakumin live in public housing. . . . Our children drop out of school at a high rate. As a people we have been vilified, shunned and segregated.[49]

In 1983, the Buraku Liberation League of Osaka received 189 reports of incidents of discrimination, and in 1989, it received 323 such reports. These incidents involved malicious letters and phone calls, as well as such graffiti messages as "Kill Burakumin" and "Send them to the gas chambers."[50] Hate messages are also sent over computer networks.

The average *buraku* family income is only about 60 percent of the national average. Those who are successful in the entertainment or business world conceal their *burakumin* background. "The only visibly wealthy buraku people are gangsters, one of the few professions which does not seem to discriminate. The preeminence of buraku people within the yakuza . . . does little to improve the minority's image."[51]

Those who have sought to conceal their background, or "pass," live in constant fear of being exposed. About thirty such people commit suicide every year. Most of them are women who were rejected by their fiancés after their *burakumin* status was uncovered.

The Urban Poor

As Japan's economy grew and the nation emerged as a world economic power, the Japanese standard of living in general improved, and the entire nation seemed to be wallowing in luxury and conspicuous consumption. Nevertheless, pockets of poverty and homeless people could still be found in the major cities. These features of Japanese life tend to escape the attention of the media and society at large but occasionally they come to the surface. For example, in early 1994, the story of a homeless person in Tokyo, whose diary recording his daily struggle was discovered upon his death, hit the airwaves. Rather than taking steps to provide for such people's needs to prevent further occurrences of death in the streets, the Tokyo authorities instead cleared the street where the man had died to ensure that others would not find refuge there. The tendency to pretend that the homeless, the beggars, and the vagrants do not exist still seems to prevail.

Among the "festering sores," or poverty-stricken districts, are San'ya in Tokyo and Kamagasaki in Osaka. San'ya, a one-half-mile square area (1.3 square kilometers), became the center of the homeless and poor after the war. SCAP had designated the region a temporary dwelling zone for those who had lost their homes because of the air raids and other ravages of war. It became a place of refuge for the homeless, the unemployed, the down-and-out, and the poor. The inhabitants of San'ya are likely to be drunks, vagrants, prostitutes, gamblers, and jobless day laborers looking for work. Also, those who are discriminated against—the Koreans, Chinese, Okinawans, Ainu, and *burakumin*—tend to seek refuge and day jobs there. The *yakuza* gangs have their home bases there, too. Subcontractors go to San'ya to hire day workers for construction work and public works projects. In 1994, as many as ten thousand laborers line up every morning hoping to get hired for the day. The populace of San'ya sleeps in flophouses or on the streets. Homeless people who are old may go without food for days. Many in San'ya are aging and are "ravaged by diseases, including tuberculosis and cirrhosis, and mental disorders."[52] Many are partially disabled World War II veterans. One social worker noted, "Men who fought in the jungles of Southeast Asia or were prisoners of war are now camped out on the pavements of Tokyo."[53]

There are many homeless people who sleep in the underground passages of Tokyo's rail and subway stations. One reporter toured these areas after midnight and found hundreds of homeless people, many sleeping in cardboard boxes. Police regularly come along and dump the boxes in sanitation trucks. They round up the homeless in the parks, destroy their shelters and meager possessions, and drive them away, which turns them into vagrants. The only concern of the police seems to be to clear the streets and parks, not to worry about the fate of the homeless. The number of homeless people who died in the streets of Tokyo rose from 103 in 1990 to 218 in 1992.[54]

There are similar homeless people struggling to survive in other major cities as well. In 1990, residents of the skid row district in Kamagasaki in Osaka rioted against the police. As one protester complained, "the police treat us like garbage." Like people in San'ya, Kamagasaki residents also live in cheap flophouses smelling of urine and alcohol. They line up every day to try to get work with construction firms, whose recruiters are *yakuza* members. In 1990, *yakuza* gangs had about forty-five storefront offices running gambling joints and managing extortion schemes and prostitution rings. Kamagasaki residents charge that some of the police are under the pay of the *yakuza*. The district is the home base of motorcycle gangs, the *bosozoku*, whose members hope to be recruited into the *yakuza* gang.[55]

The Status of Women

The 1946 Japanese Constitution embodies the principle of equality between the sexes. Article 14 states, "All of the people are equal under the law and there shall be no discrimination in political, economic or social relations, because of race, creed, sex, social status or family origin." Article 24 reads, "Marriage shall be based only on the mutual consent of both sexes and it shall be maintained through mutual cooperation with the equal rights of husband and wife as a basis. With regard to choice of spouse, property rights, inheritance, choice of domicile, divorce and other matters pertaining to marriage and the family, laws shall be enacted from the standpoint of individual dignity and the essential equality of the sexes."

Although the new Japanese Constitution and the reforms introduced by SCAP strengthened the legal rights of women, their social, political, and economic condition either did not improve or improved very slowly.

The vast majority of women are most likely to be engaged in jobs as office workers or workers in the service industries. Very few are in career- or administrative-track positions. In 1990, 58.0 percent of the office workers, 51.3 percent of the service industry employees, and 42 percent of technicians and other specialists were women. A large number of part-time workers or temporary workers are female. In 1993, 70 percent of part-time workers (those who work less than thirty-five hours a week) were women.[56]

Discrimination against women is most glaringly evident in the corporate world. According to Jared Taylor, "The male supremacy that lurks in the background on campus is a sacred institution at the office, and women soon learn their place."[57] Indeed, it was well-nigh impossible for women to get on the track that leads to higher executive positions, although by the 1980s, some women had managed to land administrative positions. But the vast majority of female workers still find the path to the top blocked by the glass ceiling. Most female college graduates are hired as office workers and are expected to serve tea to the male office staff and do errands for them. A woman who became the first bureau chief of the state radio broadcasting system in 1991 recalled that when she started out at the Japan Broadcasting Association (NHK), "my first job of the day was to wash the glasses left by male reporters."[58]

Even well-educated, well-trained women are regarded as temporary workers who will, or are expected to, leave their jobs as soon as they get married. In the 1970s, a female college graduate who had majored in journalism took a job with an advertising company. She was assigned to a menial position, so she asked for an assignment commensurate with her education. The president told her, "You know, for women, the happiest job in the world is to be a wife and mother. Women should not be so tough and aggressive as men."[59]

For the most part, then, whereas men are given positions of responsibility, women are assigned to clerical jobs. The emergence of women in administrative or executive positions has occurred at a snail's pace. Even a well-known "progressive" firm keeps women off the career-management track. In the 1980s, one woman who asked for leave from her position as secretary to the chairman to get an M.B.A. from Harvard was told not to return to the company because there would no longer be any place for her when she returned with her degree. After she got her degree, she got a job with an American firm—like so many other women who feel frustrated with their positions in Japanese firms. In 1985, about 150,000 women worked for American or European firms in Japan.[60]

In the 1980s when the economy was booming and the need for well-educated, highly trained workers increased, women began to make some gains. For example, Toshiba corporation hired fewer than 100 women college graduates in 1984, but in 1989, the company hired more than 200. It also dropped the separate pay scale for men and women in 1984.[61]

In May 1985, the Diet passed the Equal Employment Opportunity Law and then enacted it in 1986. Although the law prohibits discrimination in the job market on the basis of gender, women's groups were unhappy that the bill contained no provision for penalizing companies that do not comply with the law. The director of the Federation of Employers' Association decried the bill, saying that it would undermine the lifetime employment system because women employees would marry and quit their jobs. Others were convinced that the resolutely male-oriented society would pay little heed to the law.

However, together with the economic boom of the 1980s, the law may have contributed to the employment of more women in managerial-track positions. Before the law was enacted, there were 140,000 women working in some type of managerial position. In a six-year period, that is, by 1992, the number had risen to 190,000. In 1986, 2.6 percent of middle-management positions were held by women. By 1993, this had risen to 3.6 percent. Another survey reports that 7 percent of corporate managers were women. Various surveys present conflicting figures because they use different definitions of "administrative position." A different report stated that in 1988 37 percent of the workforce consisted of women, though only 48,600 of the 16.2 million, or 0.3 percent, of working women were in some sort of administrative position. Earlier in 1981, a Ministry of Labor survey found that 45 percent of companies said they did not promote women to supervisory positions. In 1991, the ministry reported that the number of women in administrative, managerial positions amounted to 8.2 percent. In contrast, in the United States, the figure was 41.7 percent. Japanese banks have been especially slow to entrust key positions to women. In 1993, less than 1 percent of branch bank managers were women.[62]

The economic slowdown of the early 1990s adversely affected opportunities for women to gain employment and enter the administrative track. A Labor Ministry survey of 1,000 companies in 1993 revealed that more than one-half of the companies indicated plans to cut back on hiring women. This was because they could then keep on hiring male students, who generally remain longer with the company and make virtually no demands for child-care leave. In 1993, one major bank reduced the number of management-track recruits to 390 from 475 in the previous year. The number of women on that track was reduced from 10 to 5. The employment of female college graduates in 1993 dropped by 23.7 percent, compared to the previous year, whereas male employment dropped by only 5.1 percent. In 1992, among the top business firms, Mitsubishi hired only 4 women, compared to 213 men. Another major firm, C. Itoh, hired 5 women and 198 men, and Nissho Iwai hired 3 women and 127 men. In all cases, 10 percent of the applicants were women. During the spring graduation period of 1994, a Labor Ministry survey indicated a 39.9 percent drop from the previous year in the number of women students who found employment. For male students, the decline was 28.8 percent. With the economic slowdown, companies also began to lay off part-time workers, most of whom were women.[63]

Prior to the law of 1986, many Japanese firms made it clear that they would not consider applications from female college graduates. The director of the Japanese Federation of Employers' Association justified the policy of preventing women from entering the executive track by saying that "generally, women lack loyalty to the groups to which they belong. They are extremely egotistical and individualistic."[64] This kind of attitude reflected on the number of women hired for administrative positions, which continued to remain small. Employers preferred submissive, docile women workers to do routine, menial work at low pay.

Historically, a large number of women have been employed in factories. Since the Meiji period, young women workers labored in textile mills, silk filatures (factories where silk is reeled), and small plants. In 1914, 86 percent of all women workers were laboring in textile mills. Fewer women were employed then in heavy industrial plants, but in recent years as mechanization and computers were introduced in the factories more women have entered the industrial labor force. In 1990, 37.9 percent of the workers in major industries were women.[65]

Taking into account the labor output of housewives working on household affairs and on family farms, women easily contribute 50 percent of Japan's labor output. During the period of rapid economic growth in 1965–1975, more women left the family household to take temporary, part-time, and full-time jobs. The fact that housework became less time-consuming with the widespread use of electrical and mechanical home appliances made it possible for more housewives to take advantage of job opportunities that opened up during the boom years. In the 1980s, 90 percent of part-time workers were housewives.[66] Business companies preferred to hire temporary women workers because they could pay them low wages and drop them from the workforce when their labor was not needed. The companies thus avoided the encumbrance of lifetime employees.

The gap in pay between the average male and female worker has been slow in narrowing. In the 1980s, on the average, women's pay was about 53 percent of men's. By 1990, the gap had narrowed to about 60 percent. In 1993, the average working man earned $4,180 a month, whereas his female counterpart earned $2,118.[67] In 1994, female employees of three companies affiliated with the Sumitomo Bank discovered that a woman with twenty-five years' experience was making on the average only one-half the pay of a man with a similar experience. Women over forty years old have rarely advanced up the corporate ladder as high as men who are only three years out of college.[68]

Pay differences when workers start their jobs in their youth are not as large as later in their lives. For example, in 1993, the wages of twenty- to twenty-four-year-old female workers were about 88 percent of the males that age. By age fifty, the difference had dropped to below 60 percent. One woman who had worked for thirty-three years complained that "I was 52 and getting paid as much as 20-year-old men."[69]

The inequality in pay is rationalized by male executives who claim that women are only temporary workers. The Equal Employment Opportunity Law has not resulted in either equal opportunity or equal pay for women. A Labor Ministry official explains that the law merely requires "endeavors" for equal opportunities: "We don't enforce rigid equality systems. Japan is a free country. We have to work to raise public awareness of the issue first."[70]

In conducting business negotiations, foreign businessmen are warned not to include women in the negotiating group. As one American who was sent to Japan to do business in the early 1980s remarked, "Would you send a black to do business in South Africa, or a Jew to work in Saudi Arabia? They would actually be better off than a woman in Japan. . . . If a company sends a woman to Tokyo, it is setting her up for failure and frustration."[71] Nevertheless, this may not always be the case. Women who worked as negotiators for the office of the United States Trade Representative found that being a female negotiator often proved to work in their favor because the Japanese negotiators "may be thrown off balance . . . and feel extremely uncomfortable with female negotiators."[72]

The government's record is no better than that of business firms in providing equal job opportunities for women, even though it has the responsibility for reducing discrimination. There are few women in the upper ranks of the central government. Not until 1989 was a woman, Moriyama Mayumi, appointed to a cabinet position. She filled the office of chief cabinet secretary, the equivalent to the U.S. president's chief of staff. However, her tenure was brief; she was removed from her post in the cabinet reshuffling of late 1990. At the same time, another woman was appointed a state minister as director general of the Agency for Science and Technology. In 1991, Moriyama observed: "In the past five or six years, women's rights and the growing role of women in Japan have been the biggest change . . . and will continue to be. . . . But in Japan, politics is the last bastion of men, and women now are beginning to enter that world too."[73] In 1993, Prime Minister Hosokawa appointed three women to his cabinet. As noted earlier, in 1989, a woman, Doi Takako, was chosen to head the Social Democratic Party, as the first woman to head a major political party. But she resigned her post in June 1991, taking responsibility for her party's poor showing in local elections.

Women have not made many inroads in increasing membership in the Diet, especially in the more powerful lower house. In the 1946 election, the first since women were granted the franchise, 39 women won seats in the Diet. But the number dropped drastically after that. In most elections the number of seats won by women hovered below 10, rising occasionally above 10. In 1991, women occupied 34 of the 252 seats in the upper house and 6 of the 512 seats in the lower house. At the local level, women made greater progress. In the local elections of April 1991, women won 657 of the 11,397 seats in city assemblies and 431 of the 20,579 seats in town and village assemblies.[74] Although this is only about 3 percent of the seats nationally, it is an improvement over the 1.1 percent of the early 1980s. In addition, in 1991, a woman won in city mayoral elections for the first time in the city of Ashiya near Osaka, and a woman was named deputy governor of Tokyo in 1993.

The situation in the academic community has not been much better. In 1980, there was only one female professor at the University of Tokyo. Because education for women is often regarded as a superfluous ornament, the best universities still cater predominantly to male students. By 1992, more female high-school graduates (40.8 percent) went on to college, as did 37.0 percent of men, but a large percentage of those female graduates entered junior college. In the early 1980s, only 22 percent of four-year college students were women, but 88 percent of junior college students were women. Even in the culinary field, women are frequently blocked out. Although men would not be caught dead in the kitchen at home, of the 55,000 sushi makers employed in sushi bars in 1985, only 15 were women.

Only a small number of women are in professional fields. In 1983, 6.4 percent of scientists, 2.4 percent of engineers, 9.3 percent of lawyers were women. In 1990, women made up only 6.1 percent of Japan's lawyers and 2.9 percent of its certified public accountants. But there are indications that more women are entering the professional fields. In 1979, there were 14,000 women engineers, but by 1990, there were 62,000.[75]

A woman's place is in the home, many Japanese men (and many women) would argue. The social dictum is that every woman should stay home and take care of her husband so that he can go out and do a good job. One union leader contended that he fights for higher wages for men so that the wives can stay home and not have to take part-time jobs to supplement the family income.[76]

Women have been conditioned to believe that they must marry and become keepers of the house. A career woman remarks that a typical young woman will go to junior college or technical school and learn to do office work, then marry and give up her job. After that, she takes on the task of keeping things running smoothly for her husband and takes charge of their home. With this system, economic security, social and familial harmony, and personal stability are all woven together.[77]

Some surveys indicate that most women are content with their role as housewives, although the younger generation tends to be less satisfied. And those who believe that women need not marry and become housewives have been increasing. In a 1990 survey, 52 percent of respondents said that it was acceptable for women not to marry. Further, the steady drop in the number of children being born is attributed in part to wives' desire not to be tied down at home as housekeepers. Both men and women are marrying at a later age. One-third of women and two-thirds of men in the 1990s do not marry until they are in their thirties. The belief that women should stop working after they marry is also weakening. In 1990, 60 percent of women left their job to get married. But many return to the workplace after their children grow up.[78]

Some surveys have indicated that wives are happy to have their husbands spend as little time as possible at home, where he gets underfoot. The wife takes charge of household affairs, the family finances, the children's upbringing and education. Men spend little time at home, work until late at night, and spend their weekends on the golf course. It is argued that housewives are content because they have full authority at home, but everyone understands that the ultimate authority rests with the husband. If a husband is having an affair with another woman, a marriage counselor is likely to advise the wife, "For the sake of your baby's happiness you should hold on and try to win back the heart of your husband. Treat him more kindly. Perhaps you could set out the table more beautifully for him and take more care of him."[79] The traditional ideal wife is the *yamato nadeshiko* (small pink flower). A popular film star who has played the role of the perfect wife presented her as "gentle on the surface, supportive of her man to the last." She is the counterpart of women in the samurai age; she "takes care of the home while her man fights hard in the outside world." But contemporary Japanese women are becoming more intolerant of undeserving husbands and the divorce rate is rising.[80]

As noted, the Japanese Constitution provides for equal rights for women, and the 1979 Civil Code reform increased the wife's share of inheritance from one-third to one-half. Upon marriage, a wife is usually registered in the family register under the husband's family name. Employers usually insist that women employees, even professional women, use their husband's family name at their jobs. Some women have been fighting to use their own family name and are seeking to change the law to retain their maiden surname in the family register.[81]

Given the better education and rising consciousness of younger women, the current generation is less inclined to be content with egotistical husbands. "Men want servants and slaves," they charge; and even though divorced women are treated as failures with flawed personalities, more women are leaving their husbands. Hence, unlike the prewar years, most of the divorce proceedings have been initiated by women. The number of divorces in Japan, however, remains low. In 1970, the rate was 0.93 per thousand population, reaching a high of 1.51 in 1983. In 1990, it was 1.28 (compared to 4.8 in the United States in 1987.)[82] Usually, a wife gets no alimony, although in over 50 percent of the cases she gets custody of the children. In 1990, in 71.4 percent of the divorce cases, the wife got custody. Granting the wife the right of child custody is a significant change from the prewar years, when the children always remained by law with the husband's family. But even in the 1990s, the children of divorced parents remain registered in the husband's family register.

The plight of the young wife has become less stressful in many cases, specifically because the former practice in which three generations lived under one roof is now less common and the nuclear family has become more prevalent. There were an average of 3.19 persons per household in 1987. In the past, a young woman married to the eldest son had to be subservient not only to her husband but also to her husband's father and mother.

Abortion was made legal in 1949. A 1983 survey indicated that 500,000 abortions, or one for every three births, were performed that year. Two out of three women had had at least one abortion. Abortions, as well as other methods of birth control, have reduced the birth rate significantly. In 1930, the birth rate per thousand was 32.4, whereas by 1989, it was down to 10.1. The average number of children born to an average Japanese woman before the age of fifty fell steadily from the early 1950s, when it was 3; by 1991, it had dropped to 1.53.[83] This has concerned government leaders because a rate of 2.08 is needed to maintain a stable population size. As a result, the government is proposing a program of subsidies for each preschool child. This has led some women's organizations to protest the government's plan because, they say, it is reminiscent of the prewar government's program that honored families with eight children or more.

As the average number of children per family has declined, the burden of child care has lessened. And with modern household appliances at her disposal, the average housewife has more leisure time than her prewar counterpart. Thus, she has more time to devote to the supervision of her children—especially her sons' education. The prewar practice of arranged marriages has also become less common, although a fairly high percentage of marriages are still arranged by parents.

6
Education

In the immediate postwar years, the American authorities under SCAP sought to decentralize the educational system and weaken the nearly total control over the education system that the Ministry of Education had exercised since the Meiji years. The occupation authorities set out to remove militaristic and ultra-nationalistic elements from the schools. They began by purging ultranationalistic teachers and instituted a program of textbook revision. They put in place curricular and institutional changes to foster democracy and academic freedom, to provide students with a chance to develop their personalities fully, and to give the society an opportunity to "create a culture, general and rich in individuality."[1]

Postwar Developments

Among the changes introduced by SCAP were the elimination of the multi-track and elitist structure of the educational system and its replacement with a single-track, egalitarian system. The occupation authorities introduced a new curriculum that reduced the number of subjects taught in the schools by 50 percent at all levels. The object was to eliminate elitism, introduce a comprehensive curriculum for students interested in either vocational or academic pursuits, and provide a more practical education for the 90 percent or more who would not attend college. Mathematics courses were made less difficult and social studies courses were introduced. Courses in history, geography, civics, morals, and economics were deemphasized, and greater emphasis was placed on the arts and the natural sciences. Also, more elective courses were introduced at the junior and senior high-school levels. For the curriculum during the first two years of college, the reformers pushed for the adoption of a liberal education system over a more specialized, professionally oriented approach.

Policymaking for the educational system was to be lodged in the hands of elected local school boards and the centralized control exercised by the prewar government through the Ministry of Education was to end. However, this policy never became firmly established, and the Ministry of Education's control over educational institutions from kindergarten to college was reestablished soon after the occupation authorities left Japan.

Critics of local control contended that local school boards became embroiled in ideological squabbles between left- and right-wingers when the teachers' union became dominated by Marxist ideologues. Furthermore, financial exigencies led local boards to turn to prefectural governments for support, which were closely linked to the central government.

As a result, the process of centralization gained force, and the Ministry of Education, which now controls the bulk of the finances and has authority over the prefectural superintendents of schools, weakened the concept of local control introduced by SCAP. In 1956, elected school boards were replaced by board members appointed by prefectural governors and mayors, and prefectural committees were established to oversee the educational programs in the prefectures.

The ministry reasserted its control over the curriculum and educational objectives. It regained the authority to determine the nature of the curriculum for all the elementary schools, junior high schools, and senior high schools. The Ministry of Education provides each local board of education with an approved list of textbooks, from which the latter can select titles for use in its schools. The ministry accredits all textbooks in the public schools, specifies the subjects to be taught, and stringently regulates the curriculum. Teachers are denied the right to select public-school textbooks, which is in the province of the local school board. The ministry reintroduced the morals instruction, Japanese history, geography, and Chinese literary texts that had been dropped by SCAP.

The ministry refused to accept any input from the teachers in the school system. When some teachers expressed an interest in participating in the formulation of the curriculum, the mindset of ministry bureaucrats was summarized by a ministry official who asserted, "the curriculum is none of their business."[2]

Teachers thus have no flexibility regarding what they teach or how they teach the subject. As one teacher remarks, "The Ministry lays out guidelines for what each teacher has to teach during the first year. You have to teach music, you have to teach Japanese. A precise direction is given and we have to follow it." Teachers cannot take into consideration the individual needs of the students. All students are to be taught the same subject at the same rate, regardless of differences in ability or interest. This practice is justified, say the authorities, because the system is based on the principle of complete equality. If teachers grouped their students according to their abilities, the defenders of the system contend, they would get in trouble because parents do not want their children labeled as "slow learners."[3]

The ministry officials also justify centralized control on the basis of the principle of equality. The Japanese Constitution states that "All people shall have the right to an equal education corresponding to their ability." Thus, the government, via the ministry, is equalizing education by enforcing uniform standards nationwide. Nonetheless, this puts a great deal of pressure on slow learners because the instructional level is established for the high academic group.[4]

The return of centralized control over the school system reflects the conservative government leaders' reaction to the growing political activism of the teachers' union. The union became increasingly militant in opposing the government's foreign policy after the conclusion of the peace treaty in 1951 and the official end of U.S. occupation. The union followed the political line of the left-wing Socialist and Communist Parties and the Marxist-leaning union Sohyo, all of which were critical of the government's adherence to the U.S. Cold War foreign policy line and its anticommunist power stance.

The teachers' union was acutely sensitive to any indication that Japan might rearm or become involved in an international conflict with the Communist powers. The union promulgated the slogan "Do not send the students to the battlefield ever again." It also played a key role in opposing the security pact that accompanied the peace treaty. In 1954, the Yoshida government proposed legislation that would restrict political activities by teachers in the public schools. The Socialist and Communist Parties vehemently opposed the legislation but the government managed to pass it. However, the legislation did not prevent the union from continuing to play an active role in opposing what critics of the government regarded as the adoption of a reverse course policy, that is, undoing the SCAP reforms.

In 1956, the Hatoyama government tried to pass legislation to control the educational content of school curriculums, hoping to ensure that leftist political indoctrination was not taking place. The government therefore sought legal backing for its plan to examine and, in effect, censor public-school texts. The legislation passed the lower house of the Diet but was rejected by the upper house. Then, the system of textbook certification by the Ministry of Education came into effect. Critics of the system say that in certifying textbooks the Education Ministry bureaucrats seek to foster nationalistic sentiments in the students. They assert that the ministry's recommendation that the public schools hoist the national flag and have the students sing the national anthem on special occasions is symbolic of this trend. In addition, the mythical origin of Japan is beginning to be mentioned again in history lessons.

In their approach to certifying textbooks, ministry officials tend to ensure that controversial subjects are not dealt with and Japan's wartime activities are downplayed. For example, Chinese authorities became upset when the Education Ministry sought to change the phrase "invasion of China" to "advance into China." As a result, schoolchildren grow up with a distorted view of World War II. A recent newspaper article quoted a high-school teacher who said his students were surprised to learn that there had been a war with the United States. The first thing they wanted to know was who won the war.[5]

Professor Ienaga Saburo, who wrote a textbook that was rejected for certification, challenged the constitutionality of the government's practice of certification in 1965. The Education Ministry had asked Ienaga to rewrite portions of the high-school history textbooks that he had written. For example, he was asked to revise his account of the Nanjing Massacre of 1937, which dealt with atrocities committed by the Japanese troops, as well as his account of the Japanese army's use of thousands of Chinese for human experiments for several years. Ministry officials asked him to change the word "invasion" when discussing Japanese aggression in Asia. The Ministry also wanted Ienaga to change his reference to "anti-Japanese resistance" by the Koreans following Japan's annexation of that country in 1910, requesting that he to change the phrase to read "difficulties in obtaining the Korean people's cooperation."[6] The case dragged on in the courts until 1993. In 1994, the Tokyo Higher Court held that the Ministry of Education had the right to certify textbooks but that it had illegally ordered Ienaga to make changes and deletions. The court ordered that Ienaga be compensated with the sum of $2,800. The government failed to appeal the decision by the deadline, so in effect Ienaga won his case.

In 1956, the Ministry of Education advised the prefectural educational committees to introduce a system for teacher efficiency rating. Accordingly, the educational committee of Ehime Prefecture adopted such a system. In 1958, the Ministry of Education mandated that all the prefectures adopt a similar system. The teachers' union, with the support of Sohyo, opposed this move vigorously and sought the public's backing. To counter this effort, the government enforced the implementation of this system by firing school principals who did not comply with the practice and got the practice adopted. In the 1960s, as the era of high-speed economic growth commenced and people became "economic animals" more interested in personal rather than economic issues, public support for militant political activism tended to abate and membership in the teachers' union began to drop as well. In Gifu Prefecture, membership in the union dropped from 12,000 in 1959 to 2,000 in 1964.[7]

The Nature and Quality of Japanese Education

The traditional belief in the importance of education and in the need for a child to plug away at the learning process from the kindergarten years until entering college has remained strongly embedded in the minds of both parents and children. There is no stinting when it comes to education.

In 1989, 13.7 percent of the national administrative expenditures in Japan were devoted to education. Japanese students attend school 5.5 days a week and 240 days a year, compared to 180 days in the United States. In 1992, the government decided to reduce the number of days schoolchildren have to attend classes on Saturday (when students attend class for one-half day) and decreed that schools should close on one Saturday each month. Some critics believed that this would weaken the moral fiber of Japanese children and make them lazy. Some were concerned that children would not know what to do with the extra free time. Others thought that many would simply be sent to the *juku* (cram school) on Saturdays when school was not in session. The period of compulsory education was extended to nine years by SCAP, so youngsters attend school for three years more than during the prewar years. The number of those who continue on to high school has steadily increased. In 1954, the percentage of junior high graduates going on to senior high exceeded 50 percent for the first time. By 1992, the proportion had risen to 95.9 percent. Of senior high students, 38.9 percent advanced to junior colleges or universities. In 1956, the percentages were 51.3 and 16, respectively. By 1990, the percentage of female students exceeded the percentage of male students continuing on to college. In 1965, the percentage of women going on to college was about one-half that of men. In 1992, 40.8 percent of women went on to college, whereas only 37.0 percent of men did. However, many of the women students were enrolled in junior colleges.[8]

As economic growth became the goal of the society, five-year technical high schools were established. In 1962, 19 such schools were founded and by 1971, there were 63 of them. The number of students going on to special technical schools after graduating from senior high school increased steadily as well. In 1991, 29.6 percent of senior high graduates entered technical colleges. More college students began to enroll in technical and science courses in the 1960s.[9]

Although the number of students going on to institutions of higher learning steadily increased, the phenomenon of young people dropping out of school also began to increase. Between 1975 and 1988, the number of youngsters refusing to go to school had quadrupled. In 1991, 2.1 percent of senior high school students dropped out before graduation. The number of students who dropped out of elementary and junior high schools in 1990 had increased 3.5 times by 1978. Some observers ascribe this change to a less conformist tendency developing among young people, and others decry this tendency as "a change in personality of youths toward immature, self-centered persons who are languid and unemotional." Some say the cause is the amount of time youngsters spend playing computer games. Others think the growing dropout rate and misconduct by students result from excessive emphasis on cramming to pass entrance exams to enter prestigious institutions.[10]

For many students, the goal of education has not been learning for the sake of learning but rather entry into the elite schools and upward mobility in the social, economic, and political hierarchy. The ambition of some upwardly mobile middle-class parents is to get their children, especially their sons, into the right kindergarten, then an elite school, and finally into the highest bastion of all, an elite university, preferably the University of Tokyo, which virtually guarantees entry into the bureaucracy or an elite private company.

To get into the right school and move on from one level to the next requires almost incessant cramming, if the entrance examinations are to be passed at each step of the way. Thus, students from most middle-class and upper-class families are sent to the *juku* after classes in the regular school are over. The process starts during kindergarten. Jared Taylor, who started his education in a school in Japan, wrote in 1983,

> In Japan there are many high-powered kindergartens that have competitive entrance examinations. The rat race starts at age five. Some kindergartens have such a backlog of applicants that only a few children have a chance even to take the exam, much less be admitted. For the very best in preschool education, parents are advised to put in an application for their child as soon as he is born.[11]

In 1992, close to 4.4 million students were enrolled in 50,000 to 60,000 *juku*. This represents 18.6 percent of elementary schoolchildren and 52.2 percent of students in the middle school. Some parents send prekindergarten children to a cram school. One of the most prestigious cram schools teaches two- and three-year-olds. The *jukus* are expensive, so only the wealthy can afford to send their children to them. In 1992, the average fee for elementary schoolchildren was $160 a month and was $175 for junior high students. The charges for tutoring at an elite *juku* are much higher.

The job of most mothers in these families is to see to it that their sons prepare night and day so that they will stay on the right track. And, indeed, some "education mamas" put their sons through "education hell." It is common for schoolchildren to start their day at 6 A.M. and end it at midnight. One mother says, "I know I am cutting down on my son's play hours. He's sacrificing two years of his adolescence. If he had more leisure, I'm sure he'd be a more lively boy now. But look at what he is gaining in the long run." A teacher critical of the *juku* system says, "Jukus are raising a generation of kids who can only pass entrance exams. But the most important educational purpose is giving children the ability to live in society. That's being left out."[12]

Some students cram at the *juku* till nine and ten at night, then go home and do their homework, not getting to bed until midnight. Then, as one observer notes, they sleep in class, because what they are being taught in school may not be geared toward preparing them for the entrance exams. Children who attend *jukus* have no time for sports, music, hobbies, or other recreational activities. They are also sent to the *juku* during spring and summer vacations.[13]

Entrance examinations are given independently by each university so most students take several entrance exams. Some take as many as five or six. If they are applying to universities in Tokyo, they have to travel there and stay for several days because the exams last for two full days. On exam day, as many as 3,000 students cram into the exam hall and rack their brains. About two weeks later, the results are posted. Those who see their names on the list scream with delight; those who have failed cry and go home, or take other exams, or spend the next year attending prep schools to take the exam again the following year.

The educational system and career opportunities have been tightly linked ever since the Meiji years, when the crowning glory of a young man's life was to enter the Imperial University of Tokyo and advance into the elite bureaucratic system after graduation. Thus the system produces workaholics who may end up working themselves to death.

Because education below the college level is geared toward training students to pass the next series of entrance examinations, memorization of facts and information is vital. Thus, rote memory is emphasized, rather than analysis or creative thinking. Students are taught to master what is known rather than to engage in creative thinking. Deviation from the standardized course of study prescribed by the Ministry of Education is discouraged. Students are not encouraged to develop innovative or creative ideas; in fact, they are discouraged from doing so. Further, they are taught that there is only one right way to solve a given problem. One teacher noted, "There may be 36 ways to solve a mathematics problem, but we don't have time to let them see more than one. So we produce children who can solve every problem with one method."[14] Jared Taylor recalled, "My brother, who went to the same school [as me] and was always good at math, once amused himself by solving test problems in imaginative ways of his own devising. He never did it again. His answers were right, but his methods were wrong, so he lost credit for the problems. The way we arrived at the solution was as important as the right answer."[15]

In teaching the English language, emphasis is on direct translation and memorization of grammar and vocabulary. Little oral English is taught, so although virtually every high-school graduate has studied English for six years, few speak English very well.

Benjamin Duke, an American scholar who has studied the Japanese educational system, concludes,

> What is absent in far too many Japanese classrooms is the searching and probing for the spark of creativity, innovativeness, and originality. Too few Japanese teachers recognize, stimulate and reward the creative response, the imaginative thought, the original idea that may deviate from the planned lesson. . . . The Japanese teacher should become more aware of the differences between instruction and education. Instruction implies the dissemination of knowledge. Education is the development of independent thinking, the molding of character, and the formation of personality.

The school is more than preparation for examination leading eventually to industry. It signifies the overall enrichment and fulfillment of life.[16]

Teachers who attempt innovative teaching on their own are likely to get in trouble. "Two teachers of social studies in Fukuoka Prefecture high school who carried on education of their own contrivance in order to cultivate the students' independent and critical thinking were fired by the Education Board."[17] The teacher's job, then, is to teach from approved textbooks and instill in the students information and knowledge that will help them to pass entrance examinations and enable them to get into "name" schools. And the students' job is to listen and learn what they are told. In sum, "the teacher conveys knowledge, the students accept knowledge. That's it."[18] Teachers who are critical of the Japanese educational system say that Japan places too much emphasis on the name value of schools; there is too much emphasis on grades, and the educational system exercises excessive control over students.

The school system thus instills in students the age-old principle of emulating their masters, converted in modern times to doing as they are told by their teachers. A student who deviates from the orthodox way of doing things is deviating from the group. And one of the objectives of Japanese education is not to develop individuality but to teach students to think as members of a group. This kind of education may produce more expert technicians than creative thinkers. Ezaki Reona (1925–), who won the Nobel Prize in physics in 1973, asserted that Japanese society was not conducive to originality. Twelve years before he won the Nobel Prize, Ezaki left Japan for the United States to engage in research at IBM's research center. He observed that in Japan the best college graduates go into manufacturing, the next-best into product development, and the rest into research; in the United States, it is the other way around. He also said, "Americans are motivated to make the unknown known. The Japanese are highly motivated to make the known work and function better."[19] This undoubtedly accounts for the Japanese success in adopting and improving the discoveries and inventions made by other nations.

As noted in the discussion of Japanese economic growth, discoveries and ideas originating abroad are adopted, improved, and developed in Japan. The most striking example of this in the industrial realm was the adoption of quality control measures formulated by W. Edwards Deming. In science and technology, a similar scenario occurs. A treatment for brain tumors that entails bombarding the tumor with neutron beams was discovered in America, but the process was not perfected. A Japanese doctor trained in America took the idea back to Japan and improved the technique, which resulted in a 50 percent survival rate of patients with brain tumors that normally proved fatal.[20]

A Japanese economic analyst, Omae Kenichi, writes, "The current Japanese education system requires the students to memorize without question and regurgitate what they had memorized. . . . Bill Gates [of Microsoft], Steve Jobs [founder of Apple], and Jim Manzi and Michael Kapor [of Lotus] are people who cannot be fitted in a mold. They are the kind of people that the [Japanese] Ministry of Education would flunk time and time again."[21]

Some observers believe that the Japanese educational system is designed to serve specific objectives: It is designed to serve the long-range interests of the economy and the nation by developing academically and technically competent blue- and white-collar workers and a stable, orderly, and harmonious society. The object of education from the Meiji era was to produce capable and willing workers for the nation's offices and factories.[22] Benjamin Duke contends that the Japanese worker's attitude is formed in the schools. Socialization there stresses cooperation with the group (group training starts in the first grade), emphasis on harmony in the group, and loyalty to the group. The schools also teach the value of perseverance, endurance, and trying hard, and they develop the spirit of "gambare" (doing one's best).[23] These attitudes are acquired and then carried into the workplace.

High-school graduates are expected to possess competence in math, science, reading, writing, and social studies. They are expected to have acquired the ability to read blueprints, music notes, and English materials of medium-level difficulty and to be able to understand graphs and charts.

Japanese leaders have also come to the conclusion that excessive emphasis on memorization in the school system is not conducive to creative thinking. In 1984, a council on educational reform was appointed by the prime minister. The report that the council submitted in 1987 emphasized the necessity of taking into consideration students' individuality and needs and fostering independent thinking. The report called for more flexibility in the curriculum. The council also criticized both the tradition of relating the student's ability to the kind of college the student attended, as well as the assumption that products of prestigious colleges are, ipso facto, first-rate minds.[24]

The Japanese educational system, some observers believe, is not preparing students for the high-tech information age. "With its strict emphasis on uniformity and single-minded focus on the preparation of students for standardised testing, the post-war educational system has spawned two generations of diligent, highly literate workers. It has also quashed independent thinking and given graduates few of the analytical skills necessary to excel in knowledge-based industry."[25] The need to produce students prepared to meet the demands of knowledge-intensive technology is not being met.

There is some evidence, however, that the school system does not inhibit analytical and creative thinking as extensively as some critics believe. In 1970, when a UN-sponsored group administered identical tests to schoolchildren ten and fourteen years of age in nineteen countries, the Japanese students received the highest scores in both age groups. It is equally important that the tests did not screen for facts and information alone but required understanding and application of the information the students possessed.

Discipline in the Schools

Despite the post–World War II liberalization of the educational system, the age-old practice of enforcing rules rigidly and instituting Spartan discipline in the students prevails. A host of rules is imposed on students. They range from rigid dress codes to the color of the bicycles the students may ride to school to strict enforcement of school hours. This occasionally results in tragedy. In 1990, a young girl was crushed to death when a teacher lowered a heavy metal gate as some students were trying to rush into the school compound at the last minute. Infliction of corporal punishment remains a common practice. Sometimes excessively harsh measures are resorted to, such as beating students with a board or kicking them for minor infractions of school regulations. In 1980, the head of a sailing school designed to rehabilitate autistic children beat an autistic student to death, and in 1982, he committed a similar act of "involuntary manslaughter." The defense lawyers argued that the principal should be acquitted because corporal punishment, which is a legal practice, is indispensable in treating autistic children. The beatings, they asserted, should be construed as an exercise of the parents' right to punish children as granted in the Civil Code. After all, the parents had chosen to send the child to the school. The school thus had de facto authorization to punish children there, they contended.[26] In 1991, two students in a private school died of heat and asphyxiation when they were locked in a suffocatingly hot shed for forty-five hours by the principal for violating the school's no-smoking rule. One Japanese critic of Japanese society observed, "The old military spirit of Spartan discipline and rules is alive and well today in sports and in schools."[27]

Some schools prohibit students from stopping anywhere on the way to and from school or from carrying sunglasses or magazines to school. Students may not enter restrooms as a group and are not allowed to spend more than seven minutes there. In certain schools, students may raise only their right or left hand to get the teacher's attention, and the hand must be raised at a prescribed 45- or 70-degree angle. In some schools, girls may ride only white bicycles to school, and boys, only black ones. In many schools, students are not allowed to ride bicycles to school at all.

Almost all private schools and some public schools require students to wear uniforms; the exact length and style are rigidly prescribed. In some schools, girls must wear white socks no more than 5 cm (about 2 inches) above the ankles. Teachers measure the uniforms and socks with a ruler. The color of hair ribbons that girls may use is prescribed in many schools. Likewise, hair style is rigidly prescribed; schoolgirls cannot perm or curl their hair or use hair mousse. Those with naturally curly or wavy hair often get in trouble. In one school, teachers wet down the hair to see if the hair is naturally curly or not. Violators have their hair cut on the spot. In many schools, boys are required to have closely cropped hair.

Students are punished harshly for infractions of school rules. In one case, seven teachers buried two eighth-graders in sand up to their necks and left them there for about thirty minutes for alleged blackmailing of other students. One girl student, age thirteen, was slapped, punished, and kicked by twelve teachers for riding a motorcycle for a few hours one day during her summer vacation. It is alleged she was then beaten every day by her homeroom teacher for the next six months and ended up as an outpatient in a mental hospital. Another thirteen-year-old girl was kicked in the face by her homeroom teacher, a soccer coach, for being three minutes late for lunch. The first kick killed a tooth nerve; the second one dislocated her jaw. The Asahi *Shimbun* reported that in junior high schools in Aichi Prefecture corporal punishment was being practiced almost on a daily basis.[28]

The corollary to all this is that some students have resorted to beating up teachers. In 1983, there were 2,125 incidents of violence in private and public schools and 929 cases in which students assaulted teachers. In 1982, violence against teachers occurred in 775 public junior and senior high schools. In 1990, the number of schools where such incidents occurred dropped to 538. The number of public junior and senior high schools where general acts of violence occurred in 1982 came to 1,803; in 1990, 1,685. In January 1993, a lower-class junior high student was killed by bullying students in Yamagata Prefecture. In 1985, there were about 150,000 cases of students bullying other students in the elementary and junior high schools. The number of such cases dropped to 22,156 in 1990 because of tighter supervision by the teachers.[29]

College Years

After having crammed and worked continuously in order to enter college, the Japanese youth finally enters college—and the studying virtually comes to a standstill. One student remarked, "We work so hard to get into college, and when we get out, we can expect a life without any vacations . . . so we want a four-year moratorium."[30] And the professors do not expect students to study, either. Class attendance is not taken and the professor himself may cut classes as often as he pleases. At the end of the class term, students cram by reading the assigned books and studying notes from the professor's lectures (taken and sold by enterprising students), then take the final exam.

An American professor, who taught for several years at major Japanese universities as a visiting professor in the 1980s, listed the following characteristics of the Japanese university system: Student class attendance of 10 percent to 35 percent is common, except for mandatory-attendance courses, primarily in languages; the rate of class cancellations by professors is 10 percent to 50 percent with the latter figure more common in highly rated national universities; As or Bs constitute 90 percent of the grades (as in some American institutions of higher learning); midterm grades are substituted for final grades if the student misses or cuts the final exam; there is widespread cheating during in-class examinations.[31]

A female American student slaved away to pass the entrance exam to enter Tokyo University to pursue graduate studies. She passed the exam and was admitted. She later recalled, "Once I was in my reaction was, 'My God, is this all it is? Is this what people are killing themselves for?' An American graduate school would have given me an education that was ten times better." All she had to do for her classwork was just show up. Period. She attended a class taught by a famous professor. He turned the class over to a student to speak on any subject he liked. "The famous professor slept through every class. He might as well have been a piece of furniture."[32] If anything, the undergraduate school at the University of Tokyo is worse, she said.

An educator remarked that attending the nation's top universities "means only that you worked very hard in your third year of high school and have a good job guaranteed when you get out, not that you will actually learn anything useful." University is where students make friends and establish contacts. "At the university, the human network you develop is much more important than the education you receive."[33] Instead of continuing their life as cramming bookworms, university students get involved in some sort of extracurricular activity. They may focus on sports; literary magazines; political, social, or recreational clubs; cultural activities; hobbies; or whatever else is of interest. Such activities are seen as useful in developing their social skills. One major company official commented, "In Japanese colleges many students spend four years without doing much of anything. . . . We don't require them to submit grades."[34] The potential employer looks for the prestige of the school and the extracurricular activities the student engaged in. "Students from top-ranked universities [such as Tokyo, Waseda, and Keio] are granted almost automatic admission to the top levels of the country's legal, governmental, scientific and business echelons."[35]

Student Activism of the 1950s and 1960s

Since hitting the books does not occupy that much time, if students are interested in social or political issues, they have all the time they need to engage in protest demonstrations. And that activity came to characterize college life for many students, especially students attending colleges and universities in Tokyo during the 1950s and 1960s. Political activism among college students was triggered by the anti-U.S., antiestablishment activities initiated by the Communist and Socialist leaders. The students were influenced most extensively by the Communists. Since the 1950s, the Minshuseinen Domei (Democratic Youth League), a youth group whose ties to the Communist Party extend back to 1923, played a prominent role among radical activist students. In 1948, the Communist Party organized a national student organization, the Zengakuren. This organization represented every major university, as well as college students, and it took the leadership in protesting and demonstrating against the government and what the Communist Party regarded as its pro-American, anticommunist policies.

The Zengakuren soon began to support the antimainstream faction of the Communist Party, which disagreed with the mainstream faction leaders' focus on an anti-American, patriotic struggle and also objected to its lack of emphasis in fighting the revival of the reactionary forces in Japan. The Zengakuren activists embraced Leon Trotsky's theory of permanent revolution and favored staging a violent revolution. They contended that the main object of their struggle should be to fight against Japanese capitalism; an attack on American imperialism should be secondary.[36] The mainstream faction also tended to side with China against the Soviet Union in the growing split between the two Communist powers. Even before the anti–Mutual Security Treaty demonstrations of the 1960s were staged factional strife had begun to splinter the Zengakuren. Even so, the Zengakuren played a key role in rallying public opinion against the Mutual Security Treaty. The group led the demonstrations against James Hagerty at Haneda Airport when he arrived to arrange for the projected visit of President Eisenhower. From 1967 on, students began to launch protests against the Vietnam War at airports and naval bases.

Even after the Zengakuren split into factions, its members continued to stage protest demonstrations against the United States and in objection to Japanese political and economic interests. Opposition to the Vietnam War provided them with an issue useful in arousing anti-American, anticapitalist fervor. Then they turned their rapiers on the "feudalistic" university system.

Radical student activism was undoubtedly fired up by student activism in Europe and in the United States. Moreover, the great Cultural Revolution in China, during which anyone suspected of bourgeois, capitalistic, or feudal tendencies was harassed, browbeaten, and condemned, seems to have influenced the behavior of some Japanese student groups. Student radicals complained that Japanese universities were being run like personal fiefdoms by professors at the top of the hierachical pyramid—professors who might mouth liberal ideas but behaved like autocratic feudal barons, jealously guarding their privileged bailiwicks.

Student demonstrations started with protests against tuition increases in the mid-1960s in a number of Tokyo universities. The demonstrations at the University of Tokyo received the most attention, but they took place throughout the country. All in all, 115 universities were confronted with student protests, demonstrations, and riots in 1968. The protest movement was led by a radical student organization, the All Student Joint Struggle Council (Zengaku Kyoto Kaigi, known as Zenkyoto). One segment of the student activists sought to change the management of institutions of higher education by turning them into self-governing institutions consisting of the faculty, staff, and students. The more radical faction regarded universities as instruments for imperialistic control and aimed for their dissolution. Many students regarded themselves as part of the hard core of the revolutionary movement, which had been abandoned by the left-wing parties. In some cases, the objectives of the student protestors were not clear. They carried out their struggle simply "for the sake of the struggle." The protesters staged massive strikes, built barricades, and occupied key buildings. Often, professors were given the hotbox treatment and were subjected to kangaroo courts run by militant students who yelled and screamed at them to confess their sins. A number of professors renowned for their liberal principles were subjected to such treatment, including the president of the University of Tokyo.

The trouble at the University of Tokyo, an institution where only the crème de la crème was admitted and the elite of elite professors was entrenched, started in June 1968 over the internship admissions process at the medical school. The controversy soon spread throughout the university and culminated in a general student strike. In November, the president of the university resigned. Even after the students accepted the concessions offered by university authorities, radical students of the Zenkyoto refused to leave the main university hall that they had occupied. In January 1969, the university authorities requested the government to remove the occupants. A task force of 8,000 men moved in to remove and arrest over 600 students. The troubles abated after that, but the university was unable to administer the annual spring entrance exam in 1969. Since one of the objectives of the radical students was to eliminate the stringent entrance exam system, they considered this a victory. They also launched campaigns to block the scheduled entrance exams in other universities.

At some universities, for example at Waseda University, student radicals fell into power struggles among themselves. Acts of violence were committed against rival student groups.

After student attacks on the universities abated, the radical student organizations turned their attention to anti–Vietnam War protests. They arranged demonstrations against the entry of the U.S. aircraft carrier *Enterprise* into Japanese waters because it had nuclear weapons on board. In addition, they staged demonstrations and obstructed the construction of the Narita Airport. In 1970, during protests against the renewal of the Mutual Security Treaty, student radicals threw Molotov cocktails at the police.

After 1970, the number of student supporters of the Zenkyoto declined, but the radicals continued their struggle and began committing acts of violence more frequently. They attacked business headquarters and offices. Some began to commit violence indiscriminately, sending explosives through the mail, attacking government officials, police, and ordinary citizens. In 1970, conflicts among radical student factions resulted in the killing of one student. This, in turn, brought about the lynching of ten rival members. In opposing the construction of the Narita Airport, 25,000 people were mobilized and violent clashes occurred with the police. Firebombs were thrown over arguments concerning the reversion of Okinawa to Japan. A bomb mailed to the home of a Tokyo district police chief resulted in the death of the chief's wife and in serious injury to his son. The wife of the hotel manager of a Karuizawa resort was kidnapped, and gunfire was exchanged with the police. Internecine conflict within a Red Army–like group resulted in the lynching of twelve members. In 1972, three radical youths joined the Palestine liberation movement, traveled to the Tel Aviv Airport, and fired automatic handguns indiscriminately, killing 26 people.

This frenzy of violence and extremism peaked in the early 1970s. After that, the era of high-speed economic growth began to turn most students into "economic animals." They settled down to the routine of completing their education, then joining the suit-and-tie contingent in the prim and proper business world.[37]

7

Intellectual and Cultural Developments

The defeat in the war inflicted a crushing blow on the Japanese people's weltanschauung. All the beliefs and values they had been taught since childhood were shattered. Primary among these vanished concepts were the uniqueness, superiority, and invincibility of Japan; the godlike sanctity of the benevolent, holy emperor living high above the clouds; the importance of self-denial and self-sacrifice for the good of the nation; the honor of dying for the glory of Japan and of the emperor. Gone were social hierarchy and gender discrimination as a natural order of things. One could now question the wisdom and superiority of the ruling elite and the almighty power of the military, the government officials, and the police. The virtue in being obedient, submissive, and deferential to them had also disappeared. The Japanese people were reduced to ground zero in their moral, intellectual, and spiritual life. What counted was to stay alive, find enough food to prevent starvation, find a place to live, and rely upon the aid and friendship of people directly around them—their family, relatives, and friends. They had been led to believe that the Americans were "foreign devils," but found out instead that they were decent human beings, many of whom gave chewing gum and chocolate candy bars to children.

The intellectual and spiritual climate at the end of the war was depicted by the writer Sakaguchi Ango in his essay "On Degeneration" ("Darakuron"), penned in 1946. He wrote therein:

> The social atmosphere changed in half a year. "To serve as the shield to protect His Majesty against evil we set out to war." "I shall not regret dying at the feet of His Majesty." Young people died like petals of flowers blown away by the wind. Some of the same youngsters survived and have become black marketeers. "I do not wish to live for 100 years but . . . I make my pledge to you who are bound to depart to serve as

His Majesty's shield." Thus did the brave women send off their men. But in a half a year bowing before their husbands' graves will become a mere formality. Soon their hearts will be filled with the image of another man. It is not that people had changed. Human beings have always been this way. What has changed is merely the veneer of the social atmosphere. . . . The brave kamikaze warriors are mere mirages. Does history of mankind start when one becomes a black marketeer? The notion that widows will become dedicated disciples is also a simple fantasy. Does not the history of humanity start when people begin to embrace new images? And the Emperor too is a simple mirage. The true history of the Emperor probably begins when he has turned into a simple human being. . . . We do not undergo a moral collapse simply because we lost the war. We degenerate because we are human beings. We degenerate because we are alive. Human beings probably can never escape from moral collapse. This is because the spirit of human beings is incapable of withstanding hardship and suffering like a steel edifice. Human beings are pitiful and weak, and foolish. We are too weak to transcend the path to moral collapse. . . . And like human beings Japan too has degenerated. By collapsing down the path all the way down we must discover our inner selves, and save ourselves. To be saved by political means is only a surface phenomenon, not worthy of a second thought.[1]

American Influence

Soon the intellectual and cultural vacuum began to be filled with American pop culture, Western liberalism, and Marxist ideology, which were humanistic impulses that had been crushed underfoot by the prewar and wartime militarism. A new age of "enlightenment and civilization" was beginning to dawn. Now freedom, democracy, individual rights, justice, equality, openness, and the idea of "doing your own thing" began to fill the air. Books and magazines that had been banned began to reappear. There was an onslaught of new pop culture, ushering in American and Japanese movies, jazz, pop music, striptease shows, "pan pan" girls (streetwalkers), pinball machines, rock music, Coca-Cola, hot dogs, professional sports, American television shows, garish advertisements, Japanized English words, and fashionable apparel. Whatever came into vogue in the United States appeared instantly in Japan.

Murakami Haruki, a contemporary popular writer, recalls that in the 1960s when he was a teenager he was fascinated with American culture. "American culture was so vibrant back then, and I was very influenced by its music, television shows, cars, clothes, everything. . . . Alone in my room I would listen to American jazz and rock-and-roll, watch American television shows and read American novels."[2] The cause for the frenzied turn to pop culture and things Western, primarily American, can be attributed to the exposure to American ways and culture in the occupation era. At no time in the history of Japan has there been so much direct contact with Americans. A large number of American troops remained in the country for more than two decades. Thousands of

American businessmen, students, scholars, missionaries, government officials, and professional people have resided in Japan. For every year in the 1980s, close to 250,000 Americans traveled to Japan. In turn, millions of Japanese travelled to the United States. In 1990, 3.1 million Japanese tourists journeyed to the United States. In addition, thousands of Japanese students and scholars came to study in the United States.

The craze for Western things has continued without letup. The affluent Japanese favor Western over Japanese products to show their sophistication. Highbrow intellectuals, as well as their lowbrow imitators, interject English words into almost every sentence they write. Flipping through a "middlebrow" monthly journal, a reader finds Japanized English words interspersed every-where. Perusal of an article on current affairs greets the reader with words and phrases like "supeedo o seebu site kure" (please save some speed [time]), "risukii na bijinesu" (risky business), "ruuru" (rule), "inputto-suru" (to input), "shisu-temu mo aru" (there is a system), "beesu ni naru" (became the base), "paburikku saabanto" (public servant), "guroobaru ekonomi" (global economy), "entaatein-mento no sekai" (entertainment world), "benchaa supiritto" (venture spirit), "ri-idaashippu o toru" (gain readership), "opereeshonzu risaachi" (operations re-search), "ekonomikku animaru" (economic animal), "nashonaru intaresuto" (national interest), and so forth. As one Japanese observer remarked, "There reigns a veritable babel of confusion in the Japanese language today as a result of this uncalled for adoption of English words, to the utter despair of purists and conservatives. . . . To a Western observer this craze for English words may appear to be another instance of Japanese imbecility."[3]

Labels, signs, trademarks, brand names, and control knobs on electric appli-ances are frequently in English. An advertisement for an apartment may read, "The *manshon* (mansion) is *hai kurasu* (high class) and *gojasu* (gorgeous)." "This must be very tiring for the Japanese because very few really understand English," remarked an American resident in Japan. "English ultimately loses all meaning and becomes nothing but a decorative pattern."[4] In high culture, too, the model is Western culture. In art classes, students learn to paint and sculpt in the Western style. Music instructors, largely ignoring Japanese music, teach stu-dents to play Western musical instruments and learn Western classical music. Suzuki Shinichi (1898–) won international renown for his innovative way of teaching children how to play the violin, not the koto. The curriculum formu-lated by the Ministry of Education overlooks Japanese art in favor of Western art, now an integral part of the curriculum. Visiting Western symphony orchestras pack the concert halls, whereas No drama is performed before tiny audiences. Western rock stars enthrall Japanese youngsters; Michael Jackson is a particular favorite in Japan. And the people who show a serious interest in traditional art and culture are by and large Western scholars of things Japanese. As one such scholar has observed, "I feel that the best in Japan and in Japanese culture is in-deed being destroyed. . . . I think the strongest aesthetic virtue of the Japanese was always based upon *wabi*, on a frugal spirit. . . . This attitude . . . is changing so rapidly in the new age of affluence. . . . To young people a great deal of their culture is no longer understandable to them."[5] The interest in Western culture, however, has resulted in the emergence of internationally famous performers, such as Seiji Ozawa, conductor of the Boston Symphony Orchestra, and the violinist Midori, and many others.

In the intellectual world, professors and intellectuals who had been silenced returned to the podium and their work appeared again in journals and the newspapers. The early Meiji westernizers, the most prominent proponents of enlightenment and civilization, for example, Fukuzawa Yukichi, regained popularity in the intellectual community. So did the Taisho-era proponent of democracy, Yoshino Sakuzo, and the constitutional scholar, Minobe Tatsukichi, who held the emperor to be simply one of the organs of the state, not above the state. While Western liberal, Cartesian scholarship was gaining popularity among certain sectors of academe, Marxism captured a strong following among the intelligentsia. German idealism, which had been prominent in the Japanese field of philosophical contemplation, lost popularity in the academic world. Some critics of the Japanese intellectual circles contend that Japanese intellectuals tend to follow whatever is in ascendancy in the intellectual world in the West. Ideas are like garnishes on a sashimi dish: Western schools of thought are adopted for display. No personal commitment is made, nor is responsibility taken, for an adherent's intellectual discourse. The Japanese intellectuals of this type are like models who adorn themselves with the latest fashion, and when fashions change, they shed the old and don the new.[6]

The random, and seemingly indiscriminate, importation of ideas from the West without fully digesting and assimilating them led an early twentieth-century writer, Natsume Soseki, to conclude that Japan was destined to suffer a nervous breakdown or even perish as a nation.[7] A contemporary intellectual historian, Maruyama Masao, has studied the Japanese propensity to import diverse ideas without any effort to digest and integrate them into a coherent intellectual system. Murayama has concluded that Japan lacks an intellectual tradition that can serve as a nucleus or a frame of reference to link ideas and thoughts of all ages in relation to each other, which would permit all intellectual philosophies, even contradictory ones, to find a historical niche relative to it. In the West, the Christian mode of thinking has provided the framework for judging and correlating ideas. Such a framework is lacking in Japan, so it is possible for contradictory, conflicting intellectual systems to coexist without any interaction among them.[8]

Some see a positive side to this because it does not lead to intellectual intolerance and persecution of people for harboring abstract concepts. In Japan, there has not been religious persecutions of the kind that have prevailed elsewhere. However, one could argue that prewar suppression of Marxists was political persecution rather than intellectual intolerance. Isaiah Ben-Dasan would ascribe the revival of interest in Marxism in the postwar years to the "fashion model" syndrome: Marxsism was popular in the West, so many Japanese intellectuals embraced it. When its popularity began to decline in the West, its appeal among Japanese intellectuals also began to fade.

In the immediate postwar years, the traditional national histories centering on Shinto- and Sun Goddess–based imperial dynastic myths were replaced by positivistic histories, many of them scholarly studies by Marxist historians. The intellectuals' participation in political activism of the sort displayed in the anti–Mutual Security Treaty and anti–Vietnam War movements was motivated largely by procommunist, anti-American sentiments. The heyday of intellectuals taking to the streets began to fade when radical student activists began to storm the academic citadels to crush the "feudalistic" professorial class.

Survival of the Traditional Outlook

It is logical to assume that the defeat in the war and the momentous changes in life wrought by revolutionary political, social, economic, scientific, and technological developments resulted in fundamental changes in Japanese society and its value system. A steady turning away from traditional values, or the seeming lack of any coherent weltanschauung, characterized postwar Japan. One scholar, who had returned to Japan after years in the United States, remarked,

> The most significant change in the past few years has been the emergence of a kind of social and psychological anarchy in Japan. People don't believe in Japanese politics. There are no heroes in Japan. Before World War II my generation had the emperor, but today there is nobody for young Japanese to look up to. There is a lack of spiritual force . . . an absence of purpose and meaning. We are professionals without spirits. And we are still a nation of timid, undaring people.[9]

The shift from traditional values and ways was most prominently visible within the postwar generation. Like young people all over the world, the Japanese youth of the postwar era appeared to be making radical departures from traditional values and institutions. The defeat in the war and the changes introduced in the postwar years have wrought a revolution more far-reaching than has occurred in any other period in Japanese history. The old values and ways were still strongly embedded in the society that emerged immediately after the war because the generation of that era, having been raised and educated in the most authoritarian period of modern Japan, still retained traditional values and attitudes.

The postwar generations, on the other hand, are entirely the product of a new era and have grown up in a completely different intellectual and cultural climate. Today in the 1990s, for the first time, a generation embracing a wholly new attitude and perspective seems to be emerging. The young are no longer as re-spectful and deferential to their elders as Japanese youth once was. Another im-portant barometer of change is the style of speech. The hierarchy of age, sex, and status has historically been reflected in the mode of speech, but that is begin-ning to show signs of erosion. Is the slow decline in the use of honorifics reflec-tive of changes in the hierarchical society? Or are the external signs merely su-perficial, and do the fundamental characteristics of Japan still remain intact? One scholar believes that fundamental changes are occurring: "We've got to con-sider appearances more deeply; we ought to remember what Oscar Wilde said, that it is only superficial people who refuse to judge by appearances. . . . Take, for instance, the family system. It's disintegrating . . . more rapidly in the cities, more slowly in rural areas."[10]

Although the larger framework, the vertical hierarchical structure, has re-mained fundamentally unchanged for centuries, the family system, which is embedded within it, is crumbling, and this may very well have a serious effect on the larger structure. A significant indication of the changing values and attitude of the younger generation is the shift in their conduct in the academic world. In the late 1960s, students turned from protesting the political actions of the gov-ernment to challenging the traditional authority embedded in the citadels of learning, the universities, where formerly the professors were treated with es-teem, if not veneration. Ironically enough, in many ways it has been those pro-fessors who preached democracy, equality, freedom, and justice who have been the ones to retain the most "feudalistic" attitude in their interaction with stu-dents. The traditional master-follower relationship has always been strongly embedded in the academic world. Yet, until recent times, students have been unable to free themselves from their inhibitions and their traditional sense of deference. They were thus inhibited from directing their attacks against the uni-versities and the professors. However, in spring 1968, the cultural restraints were shattered and the "occupation" of the institutions of higher learning took place; then the confrontation between the students and the professors erupted. Students locked up professors and conducted group criticisms. Some of these sessions lasted for days while the students browbeat the professors. True, only a small minority were actually involved in the more radical actions, but when the lines were drawn, many young people in the middle ranks rallied to the support of the extremists.

Many of the radical students were Marxists or Maoists and consequently had a sense of direction and purpose. Among them were anarchists, who considered the destruction of existing institutions to be the first step toward the construc-tion of an ideal society. The majority of Japanese youth, however, did not seem to have the sense of direction or the fixed sense of identity that the radicals or the prewar nationalistic young people had.

The seeming dominance of Marxist ideology in the intellectual world began to abate with the burgeoning of the Japanese economy and the easing of the Cold

War confrontation between the United States and the Soviet Union. As the Marxist intellectual current weakened, pragmatism, rationalism, and positivism began to gain ascendancy in the academic world. In some instances, the reaction against Marxist dogmatism touched off what some regarded as neonationalist thinking. This intellectual trend was not like the militant prewar variety. Instead, its adherents believed that merely emulating Western thinkers and following Western intellectual currents, whether those were liberalism, modernism, or Marxism, might not be the course that Japanese scholars should follow. Japan was to lead Asia to world intellectual leadership "by virtue of its non-Cartesian intellectual orientation and organizational style."[11]

Among the significant conflicts between the traditional and the new value system is the clash between individual versus community interests. In early Japanese society, there were the clans (*uji*), the imperial household, the military chieftains, and the feudal lords, which together formed a social structure that provided people with a sense of community and identity. Throughout Japanese history, there had also always been family and village ties that endowed the individual with a sense of community. Even after the Meiji Restoration, when Japan entered the industrial age, family bonds continued to remain strong. In addition, the revived emperor system and the unfolding of extremely strong nationalistic sentiments gave Japanese people a resolute sense of purpose and identity. In postwar Japan, for the first time in the nation's history, these institutions were seriously challenged.

Legal changes that have been in effect since the end of the war have served to weaken the stem family as the strong foundation unit in the societal order. Liberation of the individual has also contributed to this by loosening family ties. In the prewar era, the eldest son and his wife and children lived with his parents. Today, a large majority of young couples live apart from their families. There may still be some sense of affection for the imperial family in Japan, but no one would die for the emperor any longer. It is probably true that nationalistic sentiments are behind some of the outbursts against American policies, but these do not seem to be akin to the kind of commitment in which the individual submerges the self wholly for the sake of a transcendent ideal.

In reaction to the evident rejection of traditional thought and scholarship and the turn toward Western learning and thought, in the 1980s, some intellectuals began to focus more on things Japanese. A school of thinking that emphasized what it is to be Japanese, called *Nihonjin-ron* (Japanism), emerged. Some observers have been able to detect a reversion to traditional values among the younger generation as well.

Nihonjin-ron thinking centers on the homogeneity of the Japanese people. *Nihonjin-ron* advocates seek to pin down the uniqueness of Japanese culture, language, psychology, national character, and so on. One Japanese social analyst asserts that in contrast to Westerners, the Japanese stress form over substance, actual human experience or pragmatism over abstract principles or laws, flexibility over absolute principles, general sense perception over logic, and conformity and communal harmony over individual thought and action. The Japanese yardstick for proper conduct is based on humanness, not on an omnipotent, omniscient deity. This analyst asserts that the underlying consideration of all Japanese thinking is humanness. All critical judgments about people's behavior are made by asking whether the given behavior is fitting for a human being. This is the law of the Japanese people, which ranks above legalistic prescriptions. Thus, no foreigner can truly understand what Japaneseness (Nihonism) is. Non-Japanese critics regard the concept of Japaneseness as a reversion to the prewar nationalistic mode of thinking and believe that what is regarded as being uniquely Japanese is merely a characteristic common to feudal societies. But the "Japanist" contends that no foreigner can comprehend the essence of Japanism, just as no foreigner can truly master the Japanese language, which is a language beyond the mere mouthing of words or the explicit expression of reasoned thought. Japanese words lack concrete, precise, and logical meaning or real content, unlike Western languages. The Japanese do not communicate by words but do so by the way the language is spoken. Japanists believe that what is important are not words but attitude, deportment, intonation, courtesy—in other words, body language rather than verbal expressions.[12]

Despite the concern that traditional ways and values have been eroded and are vanishing from Japanese culture, some observers contend that traditional values are reviving. A survey conducted in the late 1980s found that the respondents indicated that they value "filial piety and repayment of *on*" (social and personal obligations) over "rights" and "freedom." Eighty percent responded favorably to the concept of filial piety, and only 50 percent responded favorably to freedom as a value.

Robert J. Lifton, after studying the psychology of postwar Japanese youth in the early 1960s, remarked upon "the absence in contemporary Japanese youth of vital and nourishing ties to their own heritage—a break in their sense of connection." The Japanese youths with whom he talked were affected by traditional cultural elements but regarded them as irrelevant and inadequate to meet the demands of the modern world. Five years later, Lifton interviewed the same young Japanese people and found that "they were preoccupied with their cultural and racial heritage—with various aspects of their 'Japaneseness'—to such an extent that I wondered whether [in the essay written in 1961] I had overemphasized the psychological importance of postwar Western influence."[13]

As might be expected, there are those who are critical of the overt pursuit of material things, spurred by the period of rapid economic growth. Some call for a return to the earlier idealization of spiritual over material values. A book urging the Japanese to turn away from rabid consumerism and return to the ideal of the simplicity of old Japan hit the best-seller list in 1993. In this book, *The Concept of Honest Poverty*, the author, Nakano Koji, blames such wild-eyed consumerism on the slavish imitation of American ways. Materialism and consumerism were not prevalent in traditional Japan, he asserts: "For 1,000 years, there was nothing in the Japanese tradition for possessing lots of commodities and personal possessions. Only in the last 30 years has the Japanese lifestyle drastically changed." Nakano believes the Japanese were following an "American production lifestyle."[14] He ignores completely, of course, the fact that idealization of poverty was the result of an impoverished national economy. People did not accept poverty out of choice. The rich at the top, family members of the *zaibatsu*—led a life of luxurious consumerism even before the postwar age of conspicuous consumption.

The shift in the attitude of young people of the 1980s compared to the attitude of radical students of the 1950s, 1960s, and early 1970s, is seen in their reading habits. In the 1970s, the books most widely read by the young generation included Doi Takeo's *Amae* (*The Anatomy of Dependence*), Nobel Prize recipient Oe Kenzaburo's novels, Maruyama Masao's *Between War Years and Postwar Years*, and John Kenneth Galbraith's *The Age of Uncertainty*. This generation, that is, read books that addressed social and political concerns. Among the most popular weekly journals in the 1960s among students was the *Asahi Journal*, which treated serious sociopolitical issues from a leftist perspective. But by the 1990s, its circulation had dropped to about 20 percent of its peak years, and the journal was discontinued in 1992. In the 1980s, college students spent their leisure time watching TV and reading comic books and magazines. The most popular weekly publication was a comic magazine for youth that sold 3.3 million copies a week while the *Asahi Journal* was expiring. Few students read serious works or newspapers. The kind of books they read were light, popular reading.[15] Although this may not reflect a return to traditional values, students certainly seemed no longer bent on transforming the existing society and institutions, or on building an ideal society.

Religion

Religion might be looked upon as a gauge to measure the values and attitudes prevalent in Japanese society, although Japan did not undergo the kind of religious fervor that gripped other societies in the past. However, even though Japan has never experienced that kind of enthusiasm, some critics contend that religious sentiment undergirds Japanese society. In fact, the advocates of Japanism contend that Japanism itself is a religion of a sort.

In the postwar period of confusion and chaos, a large number of new folk religions, like that of the dancing "god," came into existence, but none won a following large enough to become a significant social force. The only truly vigorous religious movement to emerge has been the Soka Gakkai. It was started in the

1920s by an obscure schoolteacher who maintained that within the amorphous flux of human existence the happiness of people could be enhanced by the adoption of proper values. The Soka Gakkai was essentially a faith-healing cult that linked itself to the Buddhist Nichiren sect. In the postwar period, the cult was invigorated by strong, dynamic leadership. The religion became aggressive and proselytizing. It tends to be moralistic and emphasizes the power of positive thinking. This religion has been tremendously appealing to the lower ranks of the working classes, who feel alienated from the rapidly developing bourgeois culture. Consequently, the membership of the Soka Gakkai increased rapidly; it had risen above 14 million by the end of 1968. Nevertheless, it has so far had only limited appeal for the majority of Japanese people; it has not been at all success- ful in converting the more sophisticated and prosperous middle class, and it has yet to capture the imagination of the youth of the nation. In 1964, the Soka Gakkai organized a political party, the Komeito, to further its ideals through the political medium.

For people who are not totally committed to a specific religious faith—and they would constitute a vast majority of the Japanese—religion is a relative thing. Thus, there is tolerance and the willingness to accept a variety of gods and beliefs. People state their religious affiliations if asked, but most people do not have strong commitments to any religious institutions, as do Christians, Jews, and Muslims in other societies.

> It seems safe to say that perceptions of religion differ in Japan and the West. Westerners see religion as something objective that must be acquired through edu- cation or study. The Japanese, by contrast, think of religion as an internal state. It need not have the clear-cut contours of Christian or Buddhist doctrine; it can be sim- ply a nebulous emotional predisposition lying undetected until the individual is made aware of it.[16]

A late 1980s survey indicates that only about 30 percent of those surveyed said they had personal religious faith. Eighty percent responded that they believed a religious attitude to be important. People may profess affiliation with two or three different religions. In 1990, the total number of people that religious orga- nizations claimed as members came to 217 million, twice the size of the popula- tion. Of these, 96.25 million claimed ties with Buddhist institutions, 108.9 mil- lion with Shinto entities, 1.46 million with Christian churches, and 10.5 million with diverse religious sects.[17] Among the major Buddhist sects are those that have emerged and flourished since the Kamakura period (1185–1333), the Zen, Nichiren, Pure Land, and True Pure Land Sects.

As noted later in the chapter, the novelist Noma Hiroshi believes that Buddhism is the only religion or philosophy that has captured the spirit of the Japanese masses. He thus contends that the religious thinking of the Japanese people is basically Buddhist.

During the Occupation, SCAP officials, nurtured in the credo of separation of church and state, banned state affiliation with Shinto and forbade the teaching of Shinto in the schools. For the Japanese populace in general, folk Shinto is an animistic religion in which spiritual forces are perceived as present in nature as well as in all things in the universe. Unlike other religions, in Shinto there is no absolute distinction among the divine, the natural, and the human. Although translated as "god," *kami* is not like God in the Judeo-Christian tradition but is a superior force or being that is present in nature. *Kami* is a charismatic force that can be present in trees, rocks, streams, animals like the fox, or human beings.

Shinto thinking entails abhorrence of defilement and emphasis on purity. Further, paying homage to the charismatic beings may ensure a person's well-being. Shinto deities are not jealous gods who punish sinners. Rather, "Shinto gods seem to be happiest when people are prosperous and enjoying themselves."[18] Thus, people go to pray at Shinto shrines for good fortune or to have evil spirits driven away by the ritual of cleansing (*oharai*) performed by a Shinto priest. Before constructing a building or a house, a company or individual is likely to have a Shinto priest perform the ritual of *oharai* to prevent any misfortune from befalling the house or building. People obtain charms and amulets for good fortune or to exorcise evil spirits.

Zen remains popular as a form of spiritual discipline, and its cultural influence remains strong. Japanese Christians, as in other countries, take their religion more seriously than most Japanese Buddhists.

It is likely that the spiritual drift will continue until a religious or intellectual force that can attract the young people emerges. The form that this will take cannot be foreseen. But if it is true, as has often been asserted, that the Japanese do not like new things (despite the obvious display of attraction to popular fads), then there is still a good chance that today's generation of young people will eventually achieve a sense of wholeness again by reembracing some aspects of traditional Japanese culture, including its religious aspects.

The problems confronting Japan today are not unique. The decline of traditional values and institutions, accompanied by the search for meaning and purpose, continue elsewhere in other industrialized, Westernized societies that have also left their tribal and familial stages far behind. Like other societies, Japan faces such problems as the dislocations and disorientation caused by the exceedingly rapid pace of change that has been brought about by science and technology. The Japanese are confronted with many and diverse modern problems, such as air and water pollution, the desecration of nature, the threat of nuclear destruction, and the population explosion. In addition, they must cope with the undermining of the sense of mystery and awe in life by rationalism and science, the abandonment of the sense of unity with nature and the universe that was at the root of Shinto, and the continued inability of people to stop abusing their fellow humans.

Cultural Developments

With freedom of the press and speech instituted under SCAP, facts about the war that had been kept from the people surfaced in the postwar years. People were now able to criticize their leaders, including even the emperor. Magazines filled with critical, analytical essays dealing with social, economic, political, and cultural issues returned to the bookstores. New left-wing journals attracted a popular readership among the intellectuals and students. The works of popular novelists like Nagai Kafu, Kawabata Yasunari, and Tanizaki Jun'ichiro, of philosophers like Nishida Kitaro, of new writers like Dazai Osamu came to be widely read. Soon, popular weekly magazines began to crowd the bookstores and newsstands.

People could turn to the movies—Japanese as well as Western—for entertainment. Baseball, which had been popular since the late nineteenth century but had been condemned in wartime as a decadent Western sport, made an instant, and popular, comeback. The annual national high-school baseball championship, which had driven the nation into a wild frenzy every August, returned. Baseball mania revived: "This schoolboy tournament is unquestionably the country's single biggest sporting event, a bona-fide national fixation."[19] In June 1951, the state broadcasting network, the NHK, broadcast a professional ball game for the first time, and within a short time, those games began to rival high-school ball games in popularity.

In September 1951, radio broadcasting rights were extended to private companies, and the government monopoly came to an end. From February 1953 on, NHK provided regular television broadcasting. In August of that year, a private television company began broadcasting. By 1958, there were 1 million TV sets in Japanese homes. Coverage of the crown prince's marriage in 1959 caused TV ownership to jump to 6.68 million sets, and it also temporarily diverted public attention from the Kishi government and the security pact revision controversy. In 1989, there were 75 million sets, with 61 units per 100 people. (In the United States the figures were 201 million sets, with 81.4 sets per 100 people.)

The Print Media

The Japanese are avid readers of books, newspapers, and magazines. Even if they do not read as much since the age of television emerged, the number of books, newspapers, and magazines published has continued to increase. In 1991, there were 124 newspapers with a combined circulation of 72.5 million copies. The *Yomiuri Shimbun* had the largest circulation in 1991 with 9.8 million copies followed by the Asahi *Shimbun* with 8.2 million. In contrast, in the United States, with double the population, the *Wall Street Journal* had a circulation of

1.9 million and the *New York Times,* 1.1 million.[20] In 1991, 2,303 monthly magazines and 85 weekly magazines were published; the combined total number of copies came to 4.641 billion. Among these magazines are comic books for adults as well as youngsters. They deal with fiction as well as serious themes, such as politics, economics, and legal affairs.

The number of books published has remained large and is still on the increase. In 1991, 39,996 new books were published, with a total of 339 million copies, which is a significant increase over the 25,421 titles published in 1968, despite the increase in television viewership. The largest number of books were published in the social sciences (10,251 titles) and in literature (8,833 titles). History trailed, with 2,627 titles. The large numbers of books published and purchased by the Japanese people might be explained by the fact that in contrast to the United States, library facilities are limited. There were 1,804 libraries in Japan in 1992, compared to 8,456 in the United States and 10,936 in Germany.

The large number of literary works being published indicates the continued popularity of novelists. In the immediate postwar years, the works of prominent prewar writers like Tanizaki, Kawabata, and Nagai were reissued and widely read. Readers soon discovered the younger writers, for example, Mishima Yukio, Dazai Osamu, and later on, Abe Kobo, Oe Kenjiro, and women writers such as Uno Chiyo, Enchi Fumiko, Miyamoto Yuriko, Tsushima Yuko, and others.

Literature

During the war, writers were compelled to produce novels that inspired the people to work for the glory of the state and the emperor. An author who could not do this was forced to remain silent. Writing about any "unhealthy," immoral, or unpatriotic ideas or behavior was proscribed by the censors. For example, one of the most prolific and prominent writers of prewar Japan, Tanizaki Jun'ichiro (1886–1965) was unable to publish his classic work *The Makioka Sisters* in full. The editors of the magazine in which it was to be serialized justified their decision not to continue its publication because, they contended, it would not be in the national interest. There was nothing "unpatriotic" in the work. However, the theme that the traditional and modern way of life had become inseparably intertwined in the characterization of two sisters, one more traditional, the other more modern, was evidently viewed as unacceptable in the rabidly anti-Western intellectual world of wartime Japan.

In this novel Tanizaki contrasts modern Tokyo with the more traditional Kyoto. One of the sisters "did not really like Tokyo. . . . so lacking in warmth. . . . If this were Kyoto, she could feel at home in a street she was seeing for the first time." An aspiring architect who had been indifferent to Kyoto finds himself turning to it. "He had been drawn to Europe and America, but he had recently begun to feel something like nostalgia for the city of his ancestors. . . . He was beginning to recognize the beauty of old Japanese architecture, and he meant, before he became an architect, to study what was uniquely Japanese, and later to give his designs a strongly Japanese flavor."[21] When the novel was published in the postwar period, it won instant public acclaim, and Tanizaki was invited to dine with the emperor. The novel was translated into English in 1957 and established Tanizaki's reputation in the West. This publication was followed by numerous English translations of his other works.

Tanizaki, whose career had begun at the beginning of the century, continued his work as a writer. He also completed his project of translating the eleventh-century classic, *Tale of Genji.* Tanizaki's prewar writings reveal his interest in the sensuous and the sadomasochistic. He continued to pursue this interest in his postwar best-seller *The Key.* The central personality, a fifty-five year old professor, engages in a maniacal pursuit of sexual fulfillment and dies of overexertion.

Tanizaki believed in evoking mood and atmosphere in his writing rather than describing things too concretely. He told aspiring writers, "Do not try to be too clear. Leave some gaps in the meaning. . . . In the mansion called literature, I would have the eaves deep and the walls dark, I would push back into the shadows the things that come forward too clearly."[22]

Among writers who, like Tanizaki, enjoyed a rebirth of their prewar popularity was Kawabata Yasunari (1899–1972), whose writings were noted for their lyrical quality. E. G. Seidensticker, who translated many of Kawabata's works into English, compares his writing style to that of the haiku masters: "Haiku seeks to convey a sudden awareness of beauty by a mating of opposite or incongruous terms. . . . Similarly Kawabata relies very heavily on a mingling of the senses."[23] Donald Keene points to the evocativeness of Kawabata's style, a style that relies "on the unique possibilities for ambiguous though expressive communication provided by the Japanese language itself."[24] Kawabata worked on his masterpiece, *Snow Country,* from 1934–1947. It was translated into English and published in the United States in 1957. In the postwar years, he continued to publish novels with the lyrical evocativeness that became his trademark. He stated that he planned to write only about "the grief and beauty of Japan. I will live with the mountains and rivers of Japan as my soul."[25] Among Kawabata's postwar creations was *The Sound of the Mountain,* written in the early 1950s, regarded by one Japanese critic as "the very summit of postwar Japanese literature."[26] Although Kawabata was also attuned to Western culture, he maintained a lifelong concern about Japanese tradition and culture. He also held an exalted view of the classics of the East, especially the Buddhist scriptures, which he believed to be "the supreme works of literature of the world."[27]

Thanks to the superb translations of his works, Kawabata's novels became known in the West. Consequently, he was awarded the Nobel Prize in literature in 1968. In his acceptance speech, he spoke of his appreciation of Japanese culture, with its oneness with nature. Speaking of a thirteenth century priest's poems, he noted, "Seeing the moon, he becomes the moon, the moon seen by him becomes him. He sinks into nature, becomes one with nature." He continued this theme, commenting on the Japanese garden: "The Western garden tends to be symmetrical, the Japanese garden asymmetrical, and this is because the asymmetrical has the greater power to symbolize multiplicity and vastness. . . . Nothing is more complicated, varied, attentive to detail, than the Japanese art of landscape gardening." Kawabata's *The Sound of the Mountain* focused on death and premonitions of death. In his Nobel lecture, he also said, "However alienated one may be from the world, suicide is not a form of enlightenment. However admirable he may be, the man who commits suicide is far from the realm of the saint."[28] Yet, ironically, he did commit suicide in 1972 by inhaling gas.

Among the established prewar writers, though unknown to the West until his *Black Rain* was translated into English, is Ibuse Masuji (1898–). Even though this book deals with the city of Hiroshima right after the atomic bomb was dropped, John Bester, the translator, notes that Ibuse "avoids all emotional political considerations, all tendency to blame or to moralize." The novel is based on actual records and interviews. "The author invariably balances the horrors he describes with wry humor. . . . Against the threat of universal destruction, he sets a love for, and sense of wonder at life in all its forms."[29]

The horrors of the aftereffects of the atomic bombing are vividly depicted.

> The people in the street by the shrine grounds were all covered over their heads and shoulders with something resembling dust or ash. There was not one of them who was not bleeding. They bled from the head, from the face, from the hands; those who were naked bled from the chest, from the back, from the thighs, from any place from which it was possible to bleed. . . . The corpses came floating one after the other down the river, and it was a sickening sight to see them butt their heads against the piers of the bridge and swivel round in the water. . . . The corpses lay scattered in every conceivable condition—one with only the upper half of the body burned to the bone, one completely skeletonized save for one arm and one leg, another lying face down, consumed from the knees down, yet another with two legs alone cremated—and an unspeakable stench hanging over all.

The aftereffects of radiation exposure resulted in "lethargy and heaviness of the limbs. After a few days, the hair would come out without any pain, and the teeth would come loose and eventually fall out. Finally, collapse set in and the patient died."[30]

Besides the return of the prewar writers whose works had been under wraps during the war years, a host of talented younger writers, who commenced working from the 1930s through the postwar era, began to emerge as new literary personalities.

Among those whose works have been translated into English is Dazai Osamu (1909–1948), who started his literary career in the 1930s and was among the writers of the literature of despair that flourished in the postwar era. Dazai came to be identified with a group known as the *burai-ha* (the decadents), who turned away from the traditional moral perspective. He firmly asserted, "I am a libertine."[31] In his youth in the 1930s, Dazai was emotionally alienated from society, used drugs, and had a compulsive desire to commit suicide. He got in trouble with the authorities over his ties to the Communist Party, then cut his affiliation with the party under police and family pressure. His early writings were about his driven, intense mental and spiritual anguish. After struggling throughout the 1930s, publishing in small literary magazines, he finally gained national prominence in the postwar years. In his *The Setting Sun* and *No Longer Human,* the heroes, alienated from society and their fellow men, seek consolation in dissipation, which leads ultimately to their destruction.

Dazai relentlessly analyzed in most minute detail the inner thoughts of his heroes, who invariably recognize the essential emptiness of life. Still, the novelist Dazai was not interested solely in making the reader share his sense of futility and anguish; he also sought to make people laugh. Seeing himself in the role of a clown, he injected some humor into his writings and thus saved his work from being irretrievably bleak. Not unlike the heroes of his imagination, Dazai finally succeeded in bringing about his own self-destruction in 1948 by jumping into the Tamagawa Reservoir with a lover. A key personality in *The Setting Sun* writes in his death note,

> I wanted to become coarse, to be strong—no, brutal. . . . I had no choice but to take
> to drugs. I had to forget my family. I had to oppose my father's blood. I had to reject
> my mother's gentleness. I had to be cold to my sister. . . . I cannot think of the slight-
> est reason why I should have to go on living. . . . Just as a man has the right to live, he
> ought also to have the right to die. . . . Somewhere an element is lacking which would
> permit me to continue. I am wanting. It has been all I could do to stay alive up to
> now.[32]

Sakaguchi Ango (1906–1955), whose comment on the state of Japan at the end of the war was noted earlier, also belongs to the *burai-ha.* He asserted that the Japanese must reject the constraints of feudalistic "healthy" moralism and must "degenerate," in order to become real human beings.[33]

As might be expected, writers from the Left made a strong comeback in the postwar era. Among them was Noma Hiroshi (1915–), who had been subjected to oppression by the army because of his political beliefs. Noma, a Communist writer, does not write simple socialist realism novels; he probes the inner struggles of the intellectual seeking self-realization within the masses. He was conscripted in 1941 and served in China and in the Philippines, where he took part in the battles of Corregidor and Bataan. He was sent back to Japan because of malaria but was then detained in an army prison barracks, suspected of harboring "dangerous thought." In his major work, *The Zone of Emptiness,* he depicts the brutalities of Japanese army life. The title is derived from the concept that the army post is a zone of emptiness. Noma writes, "The smell of rice patties grilling on the stove reminded Soda of the world outside, the real world and not the 'zone of emptiness,' as he called the post in his own mind." Noma once explained that this novel was designed "to analyze the responsibilities of the intellectual and revolutionary" elements for Japan's wartime activities. The author's Marxist leaning is reflected in one of the central character's interest in communism: "Soda's mind drifted to the idea of communism. He was not very familiar with its doctrines, though he had always been attracted by its elements of humaneness and generosity. Besides, his heart had always been with the poor and exploited."[34] Noma shows that though the Japanese soldiers had been depicted as men eager to offer their lives for the emperor and the country, many were "terrified of being sent to the front, and spent most of their time in scheming how to avoid danger."[35]

Noma wrote *Dark Pictures* to deliberately create a new style of writing that contrasted with the writings of his predecessors, in whose works "the words simply follow on and on, one after the other." "It is my object," he explained, "to rescue Japanese from its chronic poverty of expression by introducing abstractions or . . . cerebrations, and in this way to come closer to reality."[36] But Noma failed to "revolutionize" the Japanese writing style, and he did not utilize his arcane, contorted style when he later wrote *The Zone of Emptiness*.

Noma had been drawn to Marxism since his college days, and he continued to support Marxist ideals until the 1960s, when Stalin's brutal policies were publicly exposed. In his later years, he turned his attention to the founder of the True Pure Land sect, Shinran, a philosopher of the twelfth century. In 1969, Noma wrote his explication of the *Tan'nisho*, Shinran's teachings as transcribed by his disciple. Shinran believed that salvation was available to everyone, saying in the *Tan'nisho*, "the greater the sin the greater the chance for salvation." Noma noted that Shinran had identified with the masses and had spoken to them, gaining a strong following. Noma thus concluded that Buddhism was the only intellectual force in Japan that captured the mind and spirit of the masses. He reflected that although Marxism may have won over many workers, it had not won over the people as extensively as Buddhism. Despite the influx of the products of Western civilization, Buddhism, he believed, is deeply embedded in the Japanese body.[37] In 1973, the eight-hundredth anniversary of Shinran's birth, Noma wrote a biography of Shinran. In a sense, Noma returned to his roots, because his father was a devotee of Shinran.

Ooka Shohei (1909–1988) won fame with novels that set forth his experiences as a soldier. He had been sent to the Philippines, where he was captured by the Americans and sent to a prisoner of war camp in Leyte. Upon his return to Japan after the war, he wrote about this portion of his life in *A Prisoner's Experience*. In 1952, he published his masterpiece, *Fires on the Plain*. It is a vivid depiction of the plight of a soldier who, reduced to insanity and on the verge of starvation, wanders about in Leyte struggling to survive. Ooka forces the reader to directly confront the horrors of war, and even the horrors of life itself, as he describes rotting corpses and men reduced to cannibalism. The soldiers abandoned in the Philippine forests kill their fellow soldiers to eat their flesh. The central character is told that what he was given to eat was monkey meat, but he realizes that it was in fact human flesh. He comes across the body parts of those who had been killed for food: "Every part of the human anatomy that was gastronomically useless had been amputated and thrown away in this place. Here they lay in a heap—hands, feet, heads—transformed in fullest measure by the baking sun and the saturation of the rain. The great putrid mess that rose before me defies all efforts at description."[38]

The most talented and versatile of the postwar writers was Mishima Yukio (1925–1970). In the estimation of Donald Keene, Mishima was "the most gifted and [had] achieved the most of all the writers who appeared after the war."[39] Mishima was well versed in both Western and traditional Japanese literature. He wrote novels, short stories, poems, as well as Kabuki and No plays. Mishima took for his themes the manners and mores of the postwar generation, the sense of despair and emptiness that faced the young, and the subject of homosexuality. In *The Temple of the Golden Pavilion*, he focuses upon the thematic contrasts of love and hate, reality and illusion, selflessness and self-assertion. The plot of the novel concerns the story of a Buddhist acolyte who, in 1950, burned down the Golden Pavilion (*Kinkakuji*) built by Shogun Ashikaga Yoshimitsu in 1397. The acolyte, who is physically handicapped, is obsessed with a sense of his own inadequacy and sees in the perfect beauty of the Golden Pavilion merely another reminder of his own imperfection: "If beauty really did exist there, it meant that my own existence was a thing estranged from beauty." "Beauty, beautiful things . . . those are my deadly enemies," he believes. He awaits the temple's destruction by American bombers: "It became my secret dream that all Kyoto should be wrapped in flames. . . . Tomorrow the Golden Temple would surely burn down."[40] But the war ends without the anticipated air raid, and the Golden Pavilion still stands. In a desperate act of defiance and self-liberation, the acolyte sets fire to the temple.

In the 1960s, Mishima began addressing himself to the problems of student unrest and the apparent lack of mooring in the younger generation. His solution to this absence of spiritual anchor has a remarkably traditionalist cast. In the early 1960s, he wrote: "To the Japanese whatever is new is desirable. Then, when we are so surrounded by new inventions that we are unable to move—every twenty years, that is—we Japanese suddenly begin to feel that old things are much better after all."[41] He retained the traditional Japanese idealization of the emperor system, believing, "Our society gets broader in space, but it ignores time. We have no bridge to relate us to the future anymore. The Emperor should be our source of glory." He deplored the leftist students for their "unwillingness to recognize the Emperor as the symbolic moral source of loyalty and culture."

Hoping to revive the old samurai spirit, he organized a group of university students into a small private army to teach them patriotism, bodybuilding, and the fine art of combat.

Mishima became increasingly distressed over the disappearance of traditional values among the young. Further, he was profoundly influenced by Wang Yang-ming's teaching that one must act on one's convictions. Acknowledging this tenet, Mishima said, "I have believed that knowing without acting is not sufficiently knowing, and the act itself does not require any effectiveness." He lived up to this dictum and decided to sacrifice himself "for the old, beautiful tradition of Japan, which is disappearing very quickly day by day."[42]

Mishima was obsessed with the idea of death. He was determined not to die in an accident or of old age. Death was to be a positive act. In November 1970, after failing to arouse the members of the Self-Defense Force to follow his philosophy, he committed hara-kiri in classical samurai fashion.

Women writers have traditionally been accorded a prominent place in the Japanese literary world, starting with Lady Murasaki (978–1016?), the creator of the *Tale of Genji*. In the postwar years, Japanese women writers also gained recognition in the West as their writings began to be translated into English and other Western languages. Among these writers is Uno Chiyo (1907–), who began her career as a writer in the early 1920s. In 1933, she wrote a semi-autobiographical novel about thwarted love and passion that was widely acclaimed. After a hiatus, she resumed her career in the postwar period. Unlike many of her contemporaries, such as Miyamoto Yuriko and Sata Ineko, who embraced the Marxist cause, Uno did not concern herself with social issues. Instead, she wrote novels that dealt with the lives of the distinctive personalities whom she had encountered in real life. For example, on one occasion she was impressed by the wooden carving of a puppet, then sought out the wood-carver in Shikoku and wrote a novel based on his life. She also wrote about the love life of a second-hand-book dealer whom she had met on the same trip. The latter story became the basis for her major work, *Ohan* (translated into English as *The Old Woman, the Wife, and the Archer* by Donald Keene). Regarding *Ohan*, a Japanese literary critic said, "The author has created an extraordinarily compelling writing style and, disregarding conventions and time and place, invented a kind of novelistic fantasy world in which the words themselves seem to live by their own strength. This is rare in the contemporary novel, which has abjectly surrendered to facts."[43]

Enchi Fumiko (1905–) is another female writer whose career commenced in the prewar years and reached the peak of productivity in the postwar period. The theme that runs through her stories is the fate of women. In her major work, *Onnazaka* (translated in English as *The Waiting Years*), Enchi depicts the lives of Meiji women who, with nobility and resourcefulness, suffer the oppression of the paternalistic family system. Tomo, the heroine, adheres to the conventional, living the life of a docile, selfless wife: "Toward the Emperor and the authorities she showed the same vaguely submissive attitude as to the feminine ethic that taught her to yield to her husband's wishes in every respect, however unreasonable they might seem." But in her old age, after an unrewarding lifetime spent as the wife of a self-centered, profligate husband, Enchi muses,

> Everything that she had suffered for, worked for, and won within the restricted sphere of a life whose key she had for decades past entrusted to her wayward husband Yukitomo lay within the confines of that unfeeling, hard, and unassailable fortress summed up by the one word 'family.' . . . No doubt, she had held her own in that small world. In a sense, all the strength of her life had gone into doing just that. . . . But . . . she had suddenly seen the futility of that somehow artificial life on which she had lavished so much energy and wisdom.[44]

An old woman in one of Enchi's novels remarks, "Buddhism tells us that human beings are expected to live in a world far superior to that inhabited by cows and horses, but now that I think of it, I can count on my fingers the number of pleasurable moments I've had. And how I've had less free time each day than any cow or horse."[45] Enchi writes semi-autobiographical novels, as well as stories that embody elements of fantasy and mystery.

Hayashi Fumiko (1903–1951), a contemporary of Uno, grew up in poverty, moving from place to place with her itinerant peddler parents. Her early novels were based on her life of poverty, and she eventually published over 270 popular novels. In the 1930s and 1940s, she traveled to the war zones as a "patriotic" supporter of the war effort. In the postwar years, Hayashi published one of the most important of her works, *Bangiku* (Late Chrysanthemum), which deals with a geisha and her former lover. Donald Keene observes, "Of the innumerable stories about geishas, written by both women and men, none rings truer than 'Late Chrysanthemum.'"[46]

Miyamoto Yuriko (1899–1951) was born into a well-off family, but she embraced Marxism after a visit to Russia in 1927 and made it her mission to help bring about a proletarian revolution in Japan. In 1931, she joined the Communist Party. In the following year, she married Miyamoto Kenji (1908–), who became the secretary-general of the Communist Party in the postwar years. Miyamoto Yuriko was sent to prison in the late 1930s but was released for poor health. She published two of her most important works in the postwar years. One of them, *Banshu Heiya* (Banshu Plains), deals with the heroine's visit to Hiroshima after the war. However, rather than describing the devastation of the atomic bombing, Miyamoto depicts the suffering inflicted on the Japanese people by the Japanese army and the hardships endured by the war widows. In general, her works "rise above doctrinal classification and stand as the first impressive rejections of the fifteen-year war and all that it involved."[47]

The other female writer of notable proletarian novels is Sata Ineko (1904–). She had endured a life of poverty since childhood and then experienced an unhappy marriage, which led her to contemplate suicide three times. After she was divorced by her first husband, she married a Marxist and joined the proletarian literary movement. Her early novels are based on her experiences, for example, on her work in a caramel factory as a young girl and on her unhappy marriage with her second husband. Although her stories have a Marxist tinge, the authorities continued to allow her to publish, as she, like Hayashi Fumiko, went on tours of the war zone under military sponsorship. These activities led to her being accused of having been a collaborator of the militarists in the postwar years. Sata justified her travels by saying she had simply wanted to see what was happening. She sought to regain full acceptance in the proletarian circles, played an active role in left-wing women's and literary groups, and in 1955 she was reinstated into the Communist Party. However, she was expelled once again for criticizing the party's policies. Later in life, she became less enthusiastic about the Soviet Union after Stalin's brutal policies were exposed.[48]

Many younger women writers are no longer concerned about women who have endured the traditional social imperatives; instead, they focus on women who chart an independent course. Such a writer is Tsushima Yuko (1949–), Dazai Osamu's daughter. Tsushima believes that as the number of single mothers is increasing, they must learn to deal with the world on their own terms. In particular, they must learn to communicate their true feelings. Communication, the basic theme in her novel *Child of Fortune*, reflects the author's concern with the expression of feelings. Tsushima once remarked that before her own time "writers wrote about women who didn't speak their feelings, who didn't want to be independent. Ever since I was a little girl, I haven't been satisfied with that kind of heroine. Mine are different."[49] Another theme in Tsushima's works is "the stifling nature of family and blood relationships. The families portrayed in her stories are often disjointed and supply neither warmth nor support."[50]

A number of prominent male writers of the postwar generation have concerned themselves with the theme of alienation and the search for meaning and sense of identity in a world in which all the moorings have been destroyed—a world in which "the center does not hold." Among the most radical of these writers is Oe Kenzaburo (1935–), whose work reflects people's lost sense of direction at the end of the war. The values that Oe was taught to live by as a child were shattered, and "the emptiness and enervation" that resulted led him to write about characters who seek meaning in "sex and violence and political fanaticism." His main hero is an "adventurer in quest of peril, which seems to be the only solution to the deadly void."[51] Oe has a close affinity with existentialist writers like Jean-Paul Sartre: "The existentialist view of life, with its principles of autonomous self-governing based on an intuitive understanding of life and death and of freedom with responsibility, informs all of his writings." And since the beginning of his writing career, Oe has emphasized "the importance of imagination in perception, diction, imagery, and style." His most famous work is *A Personal Matter*, published in 1964. It deals with the protagonist's plan to kill his infant son, born with severe brain damage, but the man changes his mind and takes responsibility for his son's well-being. The story is based in part on Oe's own experience, for his son was born with serious brain damage. In 1994, Oe was awarded the Nobel Prize in literature. In awarding the prize to Oe, the Swedish Academy commented on the poetic force of his work, in which he "creates an imagined world where life and myth condense to form a disconcerting picture of the human predicament today."[52]

Abe Kobo (1924–), an avant-garde writer who is often compared to Franz Kafka, focuses on people who are alienated and isolated. In *The Woman in the Dunes,* he mingles fantasy with carefully delineated realities. The hero probes into his inner consciousness and emerges a whole man.

Perhaps the most important recent writer in Japan is Endo Shusaku (1923–), who is a Catholic. He often writes about the struggles of the Christian missionaries, who, when they came to Japan in the sixteenth and seventeenth centuries, were subjected to brutal persecution. In *Silence,* a story of Jesuits being persecuted for not renouncing their faith, the missionaries ask God why he remains silent in the face of all the horrible suffering and pain that the Christian converts are being subjected to. Sebastian Rodrigues, the central figure, hears the Christian peasants moaning as they are being tormented. An apostate missionary tells him that the persecution will not stop unless he steps on the image of Christ. Then he hears Christ tell him to step on the image, and he finally does so. He tells God, "Lord, I resented your silence," and the Lord replies, "I was not silent. I suffered beside you." Finally, a Japanese official informs Rodrigues that Christianity will not survive in Japan in its pristine form because "the teaching has slowly been twisted and changed in the swamp called Japan."[53] An American writer has said of Endo,

> Mr. Endo's art always reminds us that certainties and loyalties are more fluid than we should perhaps like them to be. But in exploring the limits of loyalty he does not forsake it. He remains firmly Catholic in spite of guilt and doubt, and for all his divided feelings about East and West, he remains firmly and mysteriously Japanese. In the end, his most impressive quality as a moralist is his silence.[54]

Despite the creation of superlative works, the literary world seems not to have advanced beyond the search for a new identity following the shattering experience of World War II. The earlier conflict between the "traditional" and the "modern" no longer stirs the passions of the writers. Since the war, no mainstream genre has surfaced—only trends such as existentialism, nihilism, and the search for meaning and identity by turning inward toward fantasy or, in some instances, to the Buddhist concept of *en* (belief in the interdependence of all things). Commentators reflecting upon the literary scene of the early 1980s could only remark that "it has become difficult to grasp the modern age" or that "the novel has entered a difficult period." The search for the "new person" goes on, as symbolized by Oe's 1983 novel, *Atarashii hito yo mezame yo!* (Wake Up, Young People of the New Age!).[55]

In the 1980s a new generation of writers began to emerge with a point of view that departed from that of the earlier writers, who had founded their literary world on traditional Japanese thought, culture, and language. Among the leading writers of this new school is Murakami Haruki, who disagrees with Tanizaki's opinion that the Japanese language is unique and different and, in some ways, superior to Western languages and that its beauty should be preserved. Murakami asserts that he and his contemporaries are trying to reconstruct the Japanese language, create a new Japanese language, and "break through the barrier of isolation so that we can talk to the rest of the world in our own words."[56]

One critic remarks that Murakami's subject matter is different from "the bored esthetes of Yasunari Kawabata, the stiff aristocrats of Jun'ichiro Tanizaki or the tortured young men of Mishima." His protagonists, unlike the young radicals of the 1960s and 1970s who were bent on destroying the system, merely drift along on the fringes of society. Murakami says the writers who have influenced him most were not Japanese writers like Mishima but American writers such as Raymond Chandler and Truman Capote.[57] Thus, he is regarded as "the most international voice" among current Japanese writers. His writing is characterized by "a mixture of magical realism, feckless wandering and stylish writing."[58]

Another young writer who has gained popularity is Yoshimoto Banana, whose novella *Kitchen* has been translated into English. It deals with the orphaned heroine's effort to cope with the death of her grandmother, who had raised her. It is "a lyrical tale about loss and grief and familial love."[59] The novella starts with the following lines: "The place I like best in this world is the kitchen. No matter where it is, no matter what kind, if it's a kitchen, if it's a place where they make food, it's fine with me." When the heroine is invited to move in with a friend, she explores the kitchen: "Mmm, mmm. It was a good kitchen." Thus she feels a sense of rapport with the young man who has invited her to come and live with him and his "mother," who turns out to be a transvestite.[60]

A new genre of novels emerged with the rise of Japan as an economic superpower. These are economic novels in which life in the business world is depicted. Some of these works look into the inner sanctum of the corporate world. This investigation reveals not the idealized harmonious cooperation that is supposed to govern the business world, but rather "a world of back-stabbing, boardroom coups, pressure tactics, cheating and stifling working conditions."[61]

Cinema

In the postwar era, movies as a popular source of entertainment revived almost instantly. But Japanese movies moved beyond being simply a medium of

popular entertainment. An authority on Japanese film comments on the significance of movies in understanding the culture of a nation, as follows:

> The Japanese movie continues to show . . . the most perfect reflection of a people in
> the history of world cinema. . . . If the American film is strongest in action and if the
> European is strongest in character, then the Japanese film is richest in mood or at-
> mosphere, in presenting people in their own context, characters in their own sur-
> roundings. It reflects the oneness with nature which constitutes both the triumph
> and the escape of the Japanese people.[62]

The sudden international fame gained by Japanese films during the postwar
period has made it appear as if the art of the cinema attained instant maturity
after the war. This, of course, is not at all the case; the style and technique had
been evolving since the 1920s. A number of outstanding directors, such as
Mizoguchi Kenji (1898–1956), who produced *Ugetsu*, "the most perfect of all
films," and Kurosawa Akira (1910–), who made *Rashomon* and *The Seven
Samurai*, among many other outstanding films, helped to bring about this tri-
umph of cinema as an important art form.

Mizoguchi, possessing the eye of a painter, excelled in presenting superlative
pictorial scenes. Kurosawa, perhaps the greatest of the Japanese directors, combines an interest in film aesthetics with deep concern about social issues. *The
Seven Samurai*, which embodies all the strong points of Japanese movies, has
been called "the finest Japanese film ever made." Commenting on what he has
been trying to do in his films, Kurosawa has said, "I keep saying the same thing
in different ways. If I look at the pictures I've made, I think they say, 'Why is it
that human beings aren't happy?'" He has continuously experimented and devised new techniques and approaches, endeavoring to make the style fit the
story, the form fit the content. He is a master at producing scenes of striking pictorial beauty. Regarding his film *Rashomon*, he remarked, "I wanted to return to
the simple pictorial values of the silent picture."[63]

Otsu Yasujiro, another movie director active during the same era as Kurosawa,
did not gain a popular following in the United States as Kurosawa did. But Otsu
has had a strong and enduring following among film connoisseurs. He is considered by some film authorities as "the greatest director Japan ever produced and
one of the greatest ever to work in the medium" for his depiction of "emotional
range, character types and sly humor." Otsu's movies frequently deal with "home
drama," with the recurring theme of parents, their grown children, and the dissolution of the family.[64] His career as a filmmaker started in the late 1920s, but he
made widely acclaimed films in the postwar years. His most famous work, *Tokyo
Story*, was produced in 1953. What might turn into "soap opera" becomes "high
art. Reticence, care, fact, and delicacy—those almost archetypal Japanese cultural virtues—combined for sublime aesthetic effects."[65]

After the heyday of the "golden age" of Japanese filmmaking during the two decades following the war, Japanese filmmaking entered a period of lackluster production. One film critic notes

> Japanese cinema entered its golden age in the early postwar years, when filmmakers made a forthright attempt to examine and portray the Japanese experience in a changing world. . . . But cinematic standards began to decline when the economy took off. . . . We have stopped taking an objective look at ourselves. . . . Filmmakers stopped delving into the hearts and minds of the average workers, and the quality of Japanese cinema declined. . . . The studios devoted themselves . . . to churning out light entertainment for the mass teenage audience.[66]

Because of the competition from television and videocassettes, movie theater attendance took a nose dive. In 1960, there were 1 billion moviegoers. This had dropped to 146 million by 1990. In the 1980s, the average family spent a total of 8 hours and 12 minutes per day in front of a television set. Quality movies no longer drew large numbers of viewers. More than one-half of the movies being made in recent years have been pornographic films. Nonetheless, the old masters have continued to push their creative genius to the limit, struggling to achieve aesthetic perfection while probing into the complexities of human existence.

Kurosawa, at age seventy-five, produced in 1985 what critics regard as his crowning achievement, *Ran* (Chaos), an adaptation of *King Lear.* According to an American critic, this work ranks with "the greatest epics of Sergei Eisenstein, D. W. Griffith and Abel Gance." *Ran* is "an original work of cinematic art, a film of primal beauty and grandeur, of great battles, of love and hate and sin and redemption, set in the landscape where even weather is ordered by Fate. It's a movie by a man whose art stands outside time and fashion."[67]

In the 1980s, a younger director, Itami Juzo, gave Japanese filmmaking a shot in the arm with his "hip, jazzy, irreverent films" and blithe, satirical comedies. His movies deal with the "collapse of traditional values since the end of World War Two" and the Japanese devotion to the acquisition of money. "In his films, the Japanese see themselves not as the stoic, tragic victims of fate, which is the way they are usually portrayed in 'serious' films. Instead, they are the comically fallible, heedless guests at an extraordinary party." Recalling his own wartime experience, Itami related,

> We were told that the whole nation would fight to death. But within one month of the end of the war, it was suddenly "Banzai democracy! Banzai MacArthur." The U.S. forces were treated as if they were liberators. Praise was directed toward all things American. . . . It taught me something important. . . . All values are relative. There is no such thing as a war between good and evil. Wars are fought between two "goods"; each side believes itself to be justified.[68]

Perhaps this perspective informs his filmmaking also. In 1984, he produced his first major film, *The Funeral,* in which he parodied the "Japanese way of death" by staging a "hilarious filmic rampage from hospital to crematorium to expose contemporary hypocrisy," with greed masquerading as pietism and ceremony.[69] In *Tampopo,* a comedy with "deadpanned jokes about food and death," a woman sets out to become Tokyo's best noodle maker. A prominent American movie critic observed, "Though Itami's concerns are as deeply rooted in the Japanese culture as the tea ceremony, his methods are as new as the automobiles now being designed for sale in supermarkets."[70] He also produced *A Taxing Woman,* satirizing the Japanese propensity for tax evasion. In 1992, he made *Minbo* (The Gentle Art of Japanese Extortion), parodying the *yakuza* as paper tigers who retreat before determined resistance. This resulted in his being attacked by three *yakuza* gangsters who cut him up with their daggers. This has not deterred him from continuing his goal of getting the Japanese to look at themselves from "outside the confines of nationally prevailing cultural values."[71] He continues to make films as mirrors for the Japanese to see themselves in.

Another sign that Japanese filmmaking was still alive in 1983 was the awarding of the grand prize at the Cannes film festival that year to Imamura Shohei for his *Narayamabushi-ko* (Ballad of Narayama), a film based on the legend that in the feudal years in some regions old people were abandoned to die alone in the mountains. Among Imamura's other films is *Karayuki-san* (Those Sent Abroad) a film about young girls who were sold abroad to serve as prostitutes in various Asian countries in the prewar years.

Art and Architecture

In architecture and design, significant creative works have been produced by contemporary Japanese artists. One American architect, who is a disciple of Frank Lloyd Wright and has spent fifty years in Japan, has asserted that "the Japanese are the best architects in the world today by far."[72]

Tange Kenzo (1913–), the first postwar Japanese architect to win international renown, combines aspects of Charles Le Corbusier's style with such traditional Japanese characteristics as the post-and-lintel configuration. His followers have included a number of outstanding architects, among them Isozaki Arata, whose early work includes the striking *Cluster in the Air,* consisting of short brackets and long supports. Among Isozaki's other architectural projects are the Museum of Contemporary Art in Los Angeles, the Team Disney Building in Orlando, Florida, and the Palau Sant Jordi, the Olympic Hall for the Barcelona Olympics. He, too, retains elements of traditional Japanese architecture in his concepts of space and time. Another leading architect, Maki Fumihiko, combines traditional Japanese elements with modern Western architectural styles. In 1993, Maki was awarded the Pritzker Architecture Prize, considered architecture's equivalent of a Nobel Prize. The award described him as an architect who "uses light in a masterful way, making it as tangible a part of every design as are the walls and roof. In each building, he searches for a way to make transparency, translucency and opacity exist in total harmony."[73] Ando Tadao has become internationally famous for his concrete constructions. Ando never went to college, became a professional boxer after graduating from high school, then turned to architecture on his own. He uses mainly unfinished concrete, bringing "astringent sensibility" to his work and paying "meticulous attention to form, structure, space and geometry," which makes his work appear "reductionist and abstract in the extreme." He fits his architectural structures in with the "spirit of the place," the natural setting.[74] He was awarded the 1995 Pritzker Prize.

Significant creative works have also been produced in other artistic disciplines. Probably the most notable achievements can be seen in the folk arts. For instance, in pottery, Hamada Shoji (1894–1978), among others, has won international recognition. Hamada, wholly without vanity and pretension, lived and worked among village artisans. Considering himself merely a craftsman, not an artist, he did not even sign his work. Hamada studied under the English potter, Bernard Leach, and was influenced by Korean pottery. Nevertheless, he developed an individual style that is characterized by a rugged strength of shape in concert with somber colors. He created spontaneous and striking designs with the freedom of movement displayed by a master calligrapher. Bernard Leach has said of Hamada's work,

> The simple range of natural materials available to him in Mashiko was a self-imposed limitation, considering his profound knowledge of glazes and ceramic chemistry. It is one of the most extraordinary and remarkable things, in my mind, that he has been able to take the ordinary local material without effort and use it so freely that the result becomes extraordinary. . . . His pots articulate like an oak tree, the bones of structure are not concealed, the modulations of form are intuitive, and all his pots stand firm on their feet .. . . The originality is hidden behind the most direct and ordinary and it is born not of theory but from constant practice and close familiarity with his tools and materials, with nature behind it all.[75]

Japanese potters have continued to produce innovative ceramics of diverse style, ranging from roughly glazed pots to shimmering celadon vases. They are "combining sculptural forms with evocative finishes that simulate the look of parched earth, speckled stone, rippled cloth, pitted metal or abstract painting."[76]

There has also been a revival of interest in woodblock printing. A host of artists has continued to work in this medium. The most prominent of them is Munakata Shiko (1903–), who works very rapidly and has produced a prodigious number of prints. Munakata is a Zen Buddhist, and much of his work has to do with religious subjects. Carving dynamic and rough-hewn figures on his woodblocks, Munakata endows his prints with enormous strength of design, movement of line, and dramatic tension. Another woodblock artist who has rivaled Munakata in popularity is Saito Kiyoshi (1907–). His eye-catching style in depicting snowy landscapes and Buddhist temples and gardens won him a popular following.

Artists in woodblock printing have perhaps retained their ties to old Japan more than painters, who have followed the Western artistic tradition. Many contemporary artists have tended to regard traditional Japanese art as folk craft: "They found in the West the excitement of novelty and ideas far removed from their own." But the young generation of artists is looking more to Japan's past artistic tradition, absorbing the thinking and philosophy prevalent since the fourteenth century. One authority on Japanese art states: "It fits into the Zen tradition. . . . Artistically that perception reveals itself in evanescence, in short-lived phenomena that express the harmony between man and nature."[77]

Folk craft as art is seen in simple, everyday things. For example, packaging has developed into an art in Japan. A Japanese graphic designer explains that the highly developed techniques and refined aesthetic sensibilities of the Japanese have taken centuries to develop. Those who developed the art of packaging "were self-conscious craftsmen who endeavored to refine their methods and did so in a spirit of artistry. . . . They were driven by an aesthetic philosophy that said everything could and should be made beautiful." The most distinguishing characteristic of this Japanese approach is the presence of the natural element, which represents the Japanese sense of oneness with nature. An American designer commenting on the Japanese art of packaging remarked, "First one is amazed by the mastery and perfection of all the details: colors and calligraphy, knots and ties, all evolving in some inevitable fashion from the forms or functions contained within and the natural materials used to make them. Finally you stand in awe of the simplicity and clarity of expression."[78]

Popular Culture

In popular culture, pornography and comic books have become the rage. As one authority on Japanese literature and culture has observed, Japan presents a dichotomy of puritanism and the sordid: Cleanliness and dirtiness exist side by side.[79] In Shinto, there is an abhorrence of pollution, but there is also the "muddy goddess of the village, the shamaness who is in touch with the dark mysteries of nature."[80] From this perspective, women are seen as demonic forces that consume men by their passion. Japanese pornographic films and photographs, which are overwhelmingly sadistic, depict brutal abuses of women, thus reflecting, as some believe, a fear of masculine inadequacy. A British woman novelist surmised that pornographic movies and comic books exhibit "a very real fear and hatred of women, maybe even of the female principle. The recurring themes [are] of bondage and mutilation. . . . Men must be very much afraid of women if they want to load them up with so many chains and cut off their breasts and I don't know what."[81] Traditionally, ghost stories entailed the male characters being haunted by terrible hags who come back to avenge the wrong done to them. Thus, the fear of the demonic power of women is not necessarily of recent vintage.

The popularity of comic books among adults may appear to be a reversion to childhood, but the contents are hardly suitable for children given the emphasis on "violence, sex, and scatology." Comic book sales amount to hundreds of millions of copies. One popular weekly comics magazine had a circulation of 6 million in 1991. Their readership includes a wide spectrum of the society, from students and salaried businesspeople to housewives who wish to escape into fantasyland. In the 1970s, Paul Theroux came across a comic book left behind by a reader on a train and was appalled when he picked it up and glanced at it: "The comic strips showed decapitations, cannibalism, people bristling with arrows like Saint Sebastian. . . . and, in general, mayhem."[82]

Boys' comic books deal with stories about sports, adventure, and science fiction. Girls' comic books contain stories of love and romance. Comic books for adults present stories about warriors, gamblers, and gigolos. However, problems at the workplace and human relationships are also treated in a humorous and satirical fashion. A pompous office boss may be lampooned, a henpecked husband ridiculed. Perhaps the pressure to conform, to preserve harmony, and to conform to social proprieties has prompted people to seek outlets in fantasies of violence and sadism. Various critics have charged that comic books are ruining the minds of Japanese youth, but this criticism has had no effect on the ever-growing popularity of the books. Some enterprising journalists have started a comic magazine in English, excerpting and translating selected strips, with the ostensible excuse that the translations are a means to help American readers learn the Japanese language.

8

From Showa to Heisei

The persistence of ethnocentrism, combined with the recovery of self-confidence founded on Japan's phenomenal economic success, some believe, may result in a resurgence of nationalism—not militant nationalism, but rather an inflated sense of "chosen-ness." The habit of being deferential to Americans and Europeans may accordingly undergo a change.

A Revival of Nationalism?

As Jared Taylor has observed, there is a growing sense of smugness: "As Japan overtakes the United States in one area after another, the *gaijin* complex [of deferring to Caucasians] has begun to fade. Those who have long known the Japanese see a new confidence in their foreign and economic policies. . . . Japanese who work in the U.S. will bow and scrape in the presence of whites but as soon as they are alone . . . they wallow in feelings of superiority."[1] A Japanese reporter, who served overseas and returned to Japan in 1983 after a number of years, was surprised at the tone of nationalism in the press: "I realized shortly after I came back that it's intellectually fashionable to criticize the United States."[2]

An indication of this growing willingness to speak up forcefully against U.S. policy was shown in the publication of *The Japan That Can Say No*, a book by a former novelist and leading politician, Ishihara Shintaro. This book aroused an angry response in a certain segment of the American political circle, as it was viewed as an abrasive challenge to the United States. Ishihara certainly overestimated Japan's supremacy in the high-tech area, insofar as he assumed that Japan could tip the balance of power between the United States and the Soviet Union one way or the other (for instance, by selling computer chips to the latter). But his advice to the Japanese leaders makes sense: They should say no when no is what they mean, rather than politely pussyfooting around, or continuing the practice of giving ambiguous responses that could be interpreted to mean yes. In his call for Japan to chart an independent course internationally, Ishihara says,

> There is no need for our country to follow the United States slavishly. . . . I hardly think that possessing ideals of our own means being overconfident or lapsing into an arrogant, dangerous sort of nationalism. . . . We must say 'no' quite firmly when necessary. It is also obvious, however, that we cannot afford suddenly to lose our ties with America. For the sake of the more cooperative and mature relationship that should exist between our two countries, we must say 'yes' equally clearly when that is the appropriate response. At times this will require a determination on the part of our political leaders to say 'no' to the Japanese people.[3]

The resurfacing of Japanese nationalism is not as serious a threat to international peace as some fear, and it is not likely that militant nationalism is on the upsurge. Still, some Japanese leaders are seeking to purge the stain of guilt from Japanese aggression in the 1930s and 1940s and to instill a sense of national pride in the younger generation. For example, the Japanese government does not use the word *haisen* (defeat in the war) but uses *shusen* (end of the war) instead.

From time to time, prominent political leaders play down or deny the aggression and atrocities committed by the Japanese in the great East Asian and Pacific War. As noted earlier, the Ministry of Education insisted that the term "aggression" be changed in the textbook written by Ienaga Saburo. In 1986, the minister of education in the Nakasone cabinet (Fujio Masayuki) said that the Koreans were partly responsible for Japanese colonization of that country. In 1990, Ishihara Shintaro asserted that the Nanjing Massacre was a story made up by the Chinese, and in 1994, the justice minister (Nagano Shigeto) in the Hata cabinet also stated publicly that the Nanjing Massacre was a fabrication.[4]

In May 1994 a right-wing nationalist fired at former prime minister Hosokawa for calling World War II a war of aggression and for apologizing for the conduct of the Japanese troops during the war. In August 1994, a cabinet minister of the Murayama government stated in a news conference that Japanese military action in Asia was launched not for conquest but to liberate the Asian countries from Western colonialism. The benefits of Japanese action are seen in the high literacy rates in East Asia, he asserted.[5] From time to time, prominent government officials pay homage to the war dead at the Shinto Yasukuni Shrine where the war dead are enshrined.

There are other indications that a desire to absolve the Japanese of guilt or responsibility for the war and the atrocities is increasing. Some movies about the war seek to present Japan's role in a favorable light. A 1982 hit movie, *The Imperial Japanese Empire,* depicted Japan as more of a victim than an assailant at Pearl Harbor, because President Franklin D. Roosevelt was plotting to "get the Japanese to attack us."[6] A textbook that was submitted for certification in 1991 stated, in referring to the atrocities committed by the Japanese troops in Nanjing in 1938, "Over 70,000 people were reportedly killed by the Japanese imperial army." Ministry officials suggested that this be changed to: "A large number of Chinese people were killed."[7] The Ministry of Education advised that the national flag be displayed and the national anthem be sung in school ceremonies. And military heroes like Admiral Togo Heihachiro (who defeated the Russian fleet in the Russo-Japanese War of 1904–1905), who had been purged from history books, have been restored in the textbooks.

But concern about the revival of militarism in Japan may be groundless. As noted earlier, writer Mishima Yukio's attempt to arouse nationalistic sentiments in the young men in the Self-Defense force failed to move them. The Japanese populace still remains strongly opposed to building up Japan's defense forces. During the Persian Gulf War of 1991, Japan was subjected to strong criticism by the United States for not providing active military support, but Japanese public opinion staunchly opposed Japanese involvement, except to make financial contributions to the undertaking. The government's decision to send minesweepers to the Gulf region also aroused the opponents of militarism.

There are, however, some members of the Diet who are pushing for a constitutional amendment to change Article 9, the no-war clause, by taking advantage of U.S. criticism of Japan's failure to support the Gulf War effort militarily. Their contention is that the current constitution was imposed on Japan by the United States, so it should be revised to conform to the conditions of Japanese society and culture. As noted earlier, when the new Japanese Constitution was adopted, the Japanese sought to make SCAP's draft version conform as closely as possible to the Meiji Constitution by changing the modality, terminology, and sentence patterns to achieve their objectives.

The general populace, however, seems disinterested in reviving the military forces. Only 10 percent of adults surveyed in 1991 said they were willing to fight for their country.[8] The Asian nations that were victimized by Japanese militarism in the past are extremely sensitive about any indication that Japan might be planning to strengthen its defense forces. When Japan, under pressure from the United States to play a more active role in the Persian Gulf War, agreed to send a squadron of minesweepers to the Gulf region, "it set off alarm bells from Beijing to Burma."[9]

The course of Japan's relations with the rest of the world, particularly the United States, will undoubtedly determine the extent to which militant nationalism can grow. The narrow ethnocentrism and the failure to perceive international affairs from a broad perspective, one Japanese critic believes, could result in xenophobia. Writing in 1987, he remarked,

In the past year or so a certain arrogance—masking, it would seem, a sense of inferiority—has begun to surface, sometimes in combination with reactionary and even xenophobic attitudes. . . . The underlying inferiority feelings are revealed in the defensive, belligerent, even overbearing reaction of the Japanese whenever a sore spot is touched. . . . There is an unfortunate tendency in Japan to see other nations only as markets for Japanese goods rather than as multifaceted societies.

This narrowness of outlook and inability to see how Japanese behavior is perceived abroad, he concludes, "could easily lead to a national conviction of self-righteous martyrdom. It is uncomfortably reminiscent of the conditions that bred paranoia and xenophobia leading to Japan's involvement in World War II."[10]

Ishihara's comments are seen by many Americans as "America-bashing," although there is plenty of "Japan-bashing" occurring in the United States. If, as some believe, the easing of tension between the United States and the Soviet Union results in Japan's replacing the Soviet Union as the major U.S. rival, then there may be a return of the kind of hostile relationship that deteriorated into the outbreak of World War II. For example, this is the thesis of George Friedman and Meredith LeBard in *The Coming War with Japan*. Also Michael Crichton's popular novel, *Rising Sun*, which depicts Japanese business competitors as sinister and Mafia-like, as well as the movie based on that novel, reminds one of the prewar and wartime American perception of Japan.

In 1985, longtime journalist and authority on Asian affairs, T. H. White, published an article in the *New York Times* entitled "The Danger from Japan," in which he discussed the economic threat posed by Japan. He regarded Japanese economic expansion into the world market as a move for domination, and he believed that in penetrating the U.S. economy the Japanese behaved as if they had "the right to press American livelihood to the wall." He compared Japanese economic activity to Japan's prewar military aggression and warned the Japanese that they "might well remember the course that ran from Pearl Harbor to the deck of the USS *Missouri* in Tokyo Bay just 40 years ago." His article revived "the unpleasant memory of prewar 'yellow peril' rhetoric in the minds of the Japanese."[11]

If arguments about trade and economic relations become more acrimonious, a flash point might be reached. That point for the Japanese will have arrived when they feel that it is no longer necessary to preserve *tatemae* (external forms) and that *hon'ne* (true feelings) can be bared. In a sense, what Ishihara is advocating is crossing over the line of *tatemae* to *hon'ne*. In Japanese social relations, the preservation of the former is essential for harmonious relations. Historically, there have been two faces in Japan: the polite, decorum-ridden side of what might be called the face of the Heian aristocracy, and the face of the samurai, who kicks over the traces and, like General Tojo, jumps off the veranda of Kiyomizu Temple to the ravine below (Tojo's analogy to making the decision to attack Pearl Harbor).

The increasing tension over trade is not desperate enough to compel the Japanese to take another leap off the veranda. But if accusations continue concerning Japanese economic imperialism, the Japanese menace, and the Japanese conspiracy to dominate the world industry, as were made in the CIA report, in T. H. White's essay, and in former French Prime Minister Cresson's remarks—or if they become more strident—then the sense of vulnerability and isolation, still embedded in the Japanese psyche, might very well revive the Kiyomizu Temple syndrome.

But most Japanese leaders are aware of the fact that Japan owes its postwar economic success largely to U.S. support and generosity. The United States helped in Japan's economic recovery after the war, assisted the country financially and technologically, and opened up the U.S. market fully to Japanese products to enable the electronics, high-tech, and automobile, and other industries to grow and prosper. Without the U.S. market, Japan would not have been able to develop as one of the world's dominant economic powers. As one observer remarked, "By aligning itself with the U.S. diplomatically, militarily and economically over the past four decades, Japan thrived and prospered. . . . Japan got unimpeded access to the U.S. market."[12]

Of course, Japan deserves credit for achieving its economic success through the hard work and dedication of its people—in short, through the pursuit of excellence that has historically characterized the country. Roger Buckley remarks,

> Who in 1945 would have prophesied that a nation with a lower per capita income than Malaya would later witness an endless procession of overseas politicians and observers intent on observing Japan's progress? When all the qualifications have been made and the reservations noted, the credit ultimately belongs to the Japanese state and the citizens. Fortune and friends have played their part, but they do not account for more than a portion of the result. Pain and national pride have been the real spur. Contemporary Japan has won its way back and more.[13]

The End of the Showa Reign

On January 7, 1989, Emperor Hirohito, now known as Emperor Showa, passed away at age eighty-seven, and Prince Akihito became Japan's one hundred and twenty-fifth emperor (counting mythological ones). Heisei, which means attainment of peace, was adopted as the era name. Emperor Showa had been on the throne for sixty-two years, the longest reign in Japanese history. Prior to becoming emperor on December 25, 1926, he had served as regent to the ailing Emperor Taisho, from November 1921 until the latter's death. Thus, twentieth-century Japan almost perfectly overlaps with Emperor Showa's reign.

Emperor Showa was far from being a charismatic figure or a decisive leader. He constantly had a slightly befuddled look in all of his photographs. The court advisers' efforts to create an aura of mystical majesty never seemed to have been successful. His appearance in prewar days, dressed in military regalia and straddling a white stallion, never made him look like an awesome leader; he remained an unprepossessing figure. And perhaps this was most fitting—because he was not meant to be a ruler but was instead supposed to be a symbol of the nation, just as the SCAP officials defined his position in the postwar constitution. The public was indoctrinated to regard him as a divine figure, the descendant of the Sun Goddess, but his advisers knew better. He was to be their puppet, performing ceremonial duties and endorsing decisions made by government and court officials.

Even though SCAP, in accordance with the U.S. government's decision, excluded him from the list of war criminals to be tried by the International Military Tribunal, some Japanese believed that he should be held responsible for the war. Ideologues from the Left in particular held firmly to this belief, but even moderates believed that he should have taken responsibility and vacated the throne. Among those moderates were Nambara Shigeru (1889–1974), former president of the Imperial University of Tokyo, and constitutional scholar Sasaki Soichi (1879–1965). These men favored retaining the emperor system but felt that the emperor should resign, because even though he may not have been legally responsible for the war, he was morally responsible. Furthermore, his abdication and the subsequent succession of the crown prince would symbolize the change in the status of the emperor, as described in the former Meiji Constitution versus the postwar Japanese Constitution.[14]

Kido Koichi (1889–1977), Emperor Showa's closest adviser at the court as lord keeper of the Privy Seal in the war years, also advised the emperor to abdicate.[15] A survey conducted by the Yomiuri *Shimbun* in August 1948 indicated that 90.3 percent of the population favored preserving the imperial institution, but fewer, 68.5 percent, favored the emperor's remaining on the throne. At that time, 83.1 percent of the National Diet members were against the Emperor's abdication.[16]

It transpired that the emperor had no intention of abdicating. Evidently, he felt that it was his responsibility to carry on the imperial tradition of lifetime occupancy of the throne that had been established by his grandfather, Emperor Meiji. The idea of renouncing his divine status was not his own but was initiated by SCAP officials under the direction of Colonel Ken Dyke, chief of the Civil Information and Education Section. But the draft of the declaration submitted by SCAP was revised by the emperor to include the assertion that the Japanese political system since the Meiji era had been founded on the Charter Oath of Five Principles proclaimed by Emperor Meiji in 1868. He did this to make the point that Japan had been a democracy since the beginning of the Meiji years and that democracy and the imperial institution had coexisted.[17]

The opinion that the nature of the monarchy had not changed since the prewar years was held by scholars like Tsuda Sokichi (1893–1961), who was condemned by prewar ultranationalists for questioning the ancient historical writings that were used to create the imperial myth. But Tsuda was not against the emperor system itself. Rather, he contended that under the Meiji Constitution the imperial role was circumscribed, just as Emperor Showa argued. His role was not to initiate policies but to give sanction to policies decided upon by the government. This accords with the postwar Japanese Constitution, which provides for the emperor to act on the basis of the "advice and approval of the Cabinet."[18]

In 1946, a Communist critic, Masaki Hiroshi (1896–1975), a lawyer who fought for the defense of civil rights, rejected the imperial court's pronouncement that the emperor ended the war, ignoring his own safety in order to end the suffering of the people. Masaki contended that everything the emperor did, he did for his own interest: When he declared war, he was thinking of his own well-being, and he ended the war for the same reason. Masaki argued that if he really had been interested in the welfare of the people, he would have ended the war sooner; the imperial clan had been nothing more than a parasitic entity throughout history.[19]

Some social critics continued to idealize the emperor. Among them was Kamei Katsuichiro (1907–1966), one of the romantic literati. He penned "A Missive to His Majesty," in which he stated, "I am one of those who in my youth as a Communist rebelled against Your Majesty." But he professed that he realized that his opposition was based on ignorance. By reading the Japanese classics like the *Man'yoshu* and visiting the ancient temples in Nara and Kyoto, Kamei awoke to the reality that "the Emperor is the loftiest embodiment of the human tragedy of the Japanese people. . . . The concept of the emperor is not something that can be taught, it is not some entity that is to be paid homage to pro forma. It is an idea that must be discovered at the penultimate point of one's spiritual craving." Kamei asserts that out of love for his people the emperor had saved them from death and destruction by ending the war. The Communists, who had been saved by his benevolent act, were insulting him by demonstrating before the imperial palace. Kamei concludes that "the Emperor prevailed as the foundation of the people's beauty and faith, as the source of their spiritual hope. . . . The Emperor is the embodiment of art. The preservation of the Emperor as art—this is where the essence of the national polity resides."[20]

The members of the imperial court, and the emperor himself, propagated the story that the emperor made the difficult decision to end the war for the good of the people. A poem Emperor Showa wrote expresses this: "Thinking of the people dying endlessly in the air raid, I ended the war, having no thought of my own fate."[21]

Both the condemnation and idealization of the emperor system that surfaced in the postwar years continues into the present, in the 1990s. Some people favor abolishing the emperor system, whereas others see a mystical ideal in the system. A Marxist, Takakura Teru (1891–), expressed the opinion in 1946 that "the emperor system is nothing more than a form of shamanistic domination made possible by the serflike existence of the Japanese people." He believed that if the living conditions of the people improved the people would no longer hold the imperial family in religious awe and the institution would fade away.[22]

Justification of the institution still persists among those who find a nonlegalistic, nonrational, nonpragmatic, and nonpolitical aspect in the emperor system, which has enabled it to survive over the ages, and they foresee its survival into the future. They equate the system with nondoctrinaire Shinto, the Japanese language, the national flag. In sum, it is a given, like air: "The emperor doesn't have a position in the secular world. He simply exists, but that very existence is vital, like the air we breathe."[23]

The imperial court set out to transform the image of the emperor from that of a sacred being residing high above the clouds to a physical being close to the people. Thus from early 1946 on, the emperor traveled to out-of-the-way villages, factories, schools, and hospitals and visited those who had suffered from the war. In the first few years after the war, he covered nearly one-half of the country, traveling by train and sleeping in simple inns.

The idea for the tour was initiated by Colonel Dyke of SCAP. He wanted the emperor to mingle with the people and boost their morale and their conscience, to inspire them to help their neighbors cope with the food shortages and curb the flourishing black market profiteers. The other aim of SCAP was to make use of the proimperial public sentiment to check the left-wing activists, who were staging strikes and challenging the General Headquarters. The warm reception the emperor was receiving from the public led officials of the Soviet Union, China, and Australia to conclude that the emperor was attempting to exert pressure to influence the outcome of the war crimes trials that were being conducted then. SCAP therefore advised the emperor to curtail his travels temporarily. After the military tribunal had handed down its verdict, the emperor resumed his tour. By the time the peace treaty was signed in 1951, he had traveled to virtually all the prefectures.[24]

The emperor, who was theoretically to remain removed from the political world, was worried about the rising tide of left-wing movements. He expressed his concern about the growing number of strikes and "third party elements seeking to further their own interests by taking advantage of the poor conditions in the country." He visited General MacArthur eleven times to discuss the state of affairs. MacArthur reassured the emperor that the respect and affection the Japanese people showed for the emperor was proof that they would not turn to destructive, leftist extremism. And he encouraged the emperor to resume his travels.[25]

Emperor Showa did not abstain from giving political advice to SCAP or to government officials. One controversial example is when he sent a message to SCAP in 1947 expressing his desire to have the United States continue its occupation of Okinawa for the defense of Japan against the possible threat from the Soviet Union. He suggested that this be done by concluding a long-term lease (twenty-five to fifty years) to enable the United States to continue its military occupation of Okinawa.[26] When this information became public in 1979, the Okinawans were understandably upset that the emperor regarded them as mere political pawns and ignored the huge sacrifices they had made during the U.S. invasion of their island.

The emperor continued to express political opinions to his close advisers but evidently ceased doing so after the conclusion of the 1951 San Francisco peace treaty. Perhaps he did not consider the postwar constitution, which made him merely a symbol of the state, to be fully operative while Japan was under U.S. occupation. He therefore would not be violating the constitution with his political activities until after the Occupation had ended. Furthermore, he may have been responding to the advice of his close advisers, such as Kido Koichi. After the peace treaty was signed, Kido, who had been convicted as a war criminal and was imprisoned in Sugamo, advised the emperor that he should now resign, taking responsibility for the war and the defeat.[27]

The policy of cultivating the image of an accessible emperor, as well as creating the image of the imperial family as a social rather than a political elite, was enhanced by the marriage of Crown Prince Akihito to a "commoner" in 1959. In 1975, Emperor Showa visited the United States, where his reception was surprisingly cordial. The American public did not manifest the kind of hostility that was displayed by the British and the Europeans when he visited Europe in 1971. The Emperor began to play a more visible role as the head of the state, at least ceremonially, as he received a number of past and present political leaders, including Queen Elizabeth of England, Presidents Ford and Carter from the United States, and Deng Xiaoping of China.

Despite the effort to create the image of an imperial court that was close to the people, the court attendants kept close guard over imperial family members to keep their personal lives as private as possible. Although the staff of the Imperial Household Agency was reduced substantially, from 6,211 to 1,452, by the Socialist government of Katayama in 1947, a large number of attendants committed to preserving the mystique of the imperial family remained at the court. Thus, the people's hope for a more open imperial court was curtailed by the protocol-minded palace guard. In 1993, when Crown Prince Naruhito married Owada Masako, a Harvard-educated foreign ministry official, some people hoped that she would become involved in public affairs; this was especially desired by women, who hoped she would serve as a role model for Japanese women. But palace guards seemingly succeeded in placing her behind the imperial curtain as well. The strain of adhering to a narrowly prescribed way of life seems to have caused the empress to suffer a nervous depression, which for a short while affected her ability to speak.

In April 1987, Emperor Showa become ill with cancer and, after a brief respite, entered the critical stage in September. Upon receiving this news, the public went into a period of prayerful waiting. Finally, on January 7, 1989, he passed away. Crown Prince Akihito then succeeded him and the Heisei era, a new era for the Japanese people, began. The passing of Emperor Showa in a way signifies a final cleansing of the slate. As long as he was on the throne, the memory of the war and the atrocities committed by the Japanese could not help but remain firmly embedded in the minds of those living in the nations that had been victimized by Japanese militarism and imperialism.

Regardless of Emperor Showa's personal role during his reign, there is little question that his reign was as momentous, or even more so, than Emperor Meiji's. The Showa era saw the years of parliamentary government of the 1920s, the rise of ultranationalism and radical militarism in the 1930s, the invasion of Manchuria and China, the Pacific War, the devastating defeat, the occupation years, and recovery.

The reforms introduced by SCAP involved the introduction of a new constitution and the establishment of parliamentary government. The concepts of democracy, freedom, individual rights, and equality were fostered, and though these concepts were never realized to perfection, they have nonetheless, been firmly implanted in Japan. The early Meiji proponents' dream of introducing "enlightenment and civilization" to the country may have failed, but it could be argued that the effort was given a second chance in the postwar years. Certainly no society can achieve perfection or undergo a complete transformation, and many social problems—social and gender discrimination, an aging population, narrow parochialism, environmental problems, and so on—remain, but the old and new ideals and practices have intermeshed to produce a society radically different from that of prewar Japan.

In many ways, Japan remains a closed society with the island mentality still present, but even so, advocates of internationalism have become more vocal, challenging those who cling to the myth of Japanese uniqueness. Culturally and intellectually, one might argue that the best of old Japan has been retained, that the best from the outside world is being adopted by many writers and artists to produce intellectual and cultural works that are imaginative and creative.

The most spectacular developments have unfolded in the economic arena, in which Japan rose from the ruins—like an Eastern Phoenix—to become a major economic force in the world. And despite the problems that accompany rapid industrial and technological changes, the lifestyle of the Japanese people, especially among the young generation, and the standard of living have changed dramatically. If, as Marx believed, economic factors determine the nature of all other aspects of life—political, social, cultural, intellectual—it is likely that the future of Japan will be determined by the course of economic developments.

Given this perception, then essentially Emperor Showa was merely a figurehead, and the successes and failures, the adversities and triumphs, the oppression and freedom, the fortune and misfortune were not of his making. But in the minds of the Japanese people, many of these developments emanated from the court. Thus, the end of the Showa era could mean, in a sense, a cleansing of the stains that the militaristic, imperialistic years had left on the Japanese soul—and the chance for a truly new beginning for Japan. Regardless of the actual role he played, as long as Emperor Showa was on the throne, Japan was still the old semifeudal land, with its legacy of militarism, "fascism," and imperialism.

What, then, will the Heisei era bring to the Japan of the 1990s and the twenty-first century? Will the reign of the new emperor—who has never ridden astride a white horse in military regalia—portend a truly liberal, democratic era? Will he elicit the kind of popular fanaticism that led to an attack on the mayor of Nagasaki for having said that Emperor Showa must bear some responsibility for the misfortune wrought by the war? Emperor Akihito is unstained with even symbolic guilt for the ravages of totalitarianism and war, unlike his predecessor, thus it is possible that the Japanese psyche will be freed of the mystique of the emperor system and the *kokutai* (the unique national polity), which lingered in the soul of the generation identified with Emperor Showa. Emperor Akihito's formative years occurred at a time when Japanese imperialism and militarism had been crushed and discredited. Democracy, openness, internationalism, and liberalism were ideals that had filled the air for forty-five postwar years before he mounted the throne. Perhaps these ideals—as a symbol of the nation—will come to be more closely identified with the Heisei era than the Showa era.

Appendix: Prime Ministers Since 1945, with Dates of Term Changeovers

Suzuki Kantaro (April 7, 1945)
Prince Higashikuni (August 17, 1945)
Shidehara Kijuro (October 9, 1945)
Yoshida Shigeru (May 22, 1946)
Katayama Tetsu (May 24, 1947)
Ashida Hitoshi (March 10, 1948)
Yoshida Shigeru (October 15, 1948)
Hatoyama Ichiro (December 10, 1954)
Ishibashi Tanzan (December 23, 1956)
Kishi Shinsuke (Feburary 25, 1957)
Ikeda Hayato (July 19, 1960)
Sato Eisaku (November 9, 1964)
Tanaka Kakuei (July 7, 1972)
Miki Takeo (December 9, 1974)
Fukuda Takeo (December 24, 1976)
Ohira Masayoshi (December 7, 1978)
Suzuki Zenko (June 17, 1980)
Nakasone Yasuhiro (November 27, 1982)
Takeshita Noboru (November 6, 1987)
Uno Sousuke (June 3, 1989)
Kaifu Toshiki (August 9, 1989)
Miyazawa Kiichi (November 6, 1991)
Hosokawa Morihiro (July 29, 1993)
Hata Tsutomu (April 28, 1994)
Murayama Tomiichi (June 29, 1994)

Notes

CHAPTER 1

1. See John Dower, *War Without Mercy* (New York: Pantheon Books, 1986), pp. 295–301 for casualty figures in the Asian war. Statistics and accounts of the immediate postwar conditions and developments are based primarily on: Russell Brines, *MacArthur's Japan* (Philadelphia: Lippincott, 1948), p. 39, pp. 144–145; Jerome B. Cohen, *Japan's Economy in War and Reconstruction* (Minneapolis: University of Minnesota Press, 1949), pp. 417ff., and *Japan's Postwar Economy* (Bloomington: Indiana University Press, 1960), pp. 11 ff.; Kazuo Kawai, *Japan's American Interlude* (Chicago: University of Chicago Press, 1960), pp. 135–139; Fujihara Akira, *Sekai no naka no Nihon* (Japan in the World Community), vol. 15 of *Nihon no Rekishi* (History of Japan) (Tokyo: Shogakukan, 1980), pp. 23–29; *Iwanami Koza Nihon no Rekishi* (History of Japan, Iwanami Lecture Series) (Tokyo: Iwanami Shoten, 1977), vol. 22, pp. 224–229; Oe Shinobu, *Sengo Henkaku* (Postwar Changes), vol. 31 of *Nihon no Rekishi* (History of Japan) (Tokyo: Shogakukan, 1976), pp. 56–65. See also *Statistical Handbook of Japan* (Bureau of Statistics, Office of the Prime Minister), several editions; *Nippon, A Charted Survey of Japan* (Tokyo: Kokuseisha), several editions from 1970 to 1994.

2. Theodore Cohen, *Remaking Japan* (New York: Free Press, 1987), pp. 189–190.

3. Quoted in Tsurumi Shunsuke et al., eds., *Nihon no Hyakunen* (Hundred Years of Japan), 10 vols. (Tokyo: Chikuma Shobo, 1961–1964), vol. 2, pp. 301–302.

4. Kawai, op. cit., pp. 137–138.

5. "Report of Government Section, Supreme Commander for the Allied Powers" *Political Reorientation of Japan*, 2 vols. (Grosse Pointe, Mich.: Scholarly Press, 1968), p. 427.

6. Douglas MacArthur, *Reminiscences* (New York: McGraw-Hill, 1964), pp. 282–283.

7. *Political Reorientation of Japan*, op. cit., pp. 423 ff. See also Edwin M. Martin, *The Allied Occupation of Japan* (Westport, Conn.: Greenwood Press, 1972), p. 117 for directives sent to SCAP.

8. Donald Keene, *Dawn to the West: Japanese Literature of the Modern Era* (New York: Holt, 1984), pp. 1075–1076.

9. Oe, op. cit., p. 193.

10. Victor Minear, *Victor's Justice: The Tokyo War Crimes Trial* (Princeton: Princeton University Press, 1971), p. 7.

11. Ibid., pp. 71–72.

12. Tsurumi, op. cit., p. 66.

13. Minear, op. cit., p. 133.

14. Ibid., pp. 32–33.

15. MacArthur, op. cit. p. 288.

16. Shigeru Yoshida, *The Yoshida Memoirs* (Cambridge, Mass.: Riverside Press, 1962), p. 51.

17. Edward Behr, *Hirohito, Behind the Myth* (New York: Villard Books, 1989), pp. 253–254; Daikichi Irokawa, *The Age of Hirohito: In Search of Modern Japan*, translated by Mikiso Hane and John K. Urda (New York: Free Press, 1995), p. 80.

18. MacArthur, op. cit., p. 288.

19. Matsuo Takayoshi, *Kokusai Kokka e no Shuppatsu* (Beginning of an International Nation-State), vol. 21 of *Nihon no Rekishi* (Tokyo: Shueisha, 1993), p. 20.

20. Robert J. C. Butow, *Tojo and the Coming of the War* (Stanford: Stanford University Press, 1961), p. 495.

21. Minear, op. cit., note 83, pp. 114–115.

22. *Emperor Hirohito and His Chief Aide de Camp: the Honjo Diary, 1933–1936*, trans. Mikiso Hane (Tokyo: University of Tokyo Press, 1982), p. 134.

23. Irokawa, op. cit., pp. 82–83.

24. Japanese records indicate that 937 were executed, 358 received life sentences, and 4,121 received fixed-term sentences. Oe, op. cit., p. 226.

25. Ibid., pp. 227–228.

26. Fujiwara, op. cit., pp. 61–62.

27. Nakamura Takafusa, *Showashi* (Showa History), 2 vols. (Tokyo: Toyo Keizai Shimposha, 1993), pp. 388–389; Kawai, op. cit., pp. 91–96.

28. *Political Reorientation of Japan*, op. cit., p. 741.

29. Toshio Nishi, *Unconditional Diplomacy, Education and Politics in Occupied Japan, 1945–1952* (Stanford: Hoover Institution Press, 1982), p. 59.

30. *Political Reorientation of Japan*, op. cit., p. 470.

31. Ibid., p. 467; Tsurumi, op. cit., p. 243.

32. Ibid., p. 423.

33. Nishi, op. cit., p. 87.

34. *Political Reorientation of Japan*, op. cit., p. 460.

35. Nishi, op. cit., p. 88.

36. Ibid., pp. 105–106; Kawai, op. cit., pp. 214–215.

37. Michael Schaller, *The American Occupation of Japan* (London: Oxford University Press, 1985), pp. 33–36.

38. Ibid., p. 35; Jerome Cohen, *Japan's Postwar Economy*, p. 165.

39. *Political Reorientation of Japan*, op. cit., p. 425.

40. Ibid., p. 435.

41. Theodore Cohen, op. cit., pp. 354, 359.

42. Eleanor M. Hadley, *Antitrust in Japan* (Princeton: Princeton University Press, 1970), p. 26.

43. Theodore Cohen, op. cit., pp. 353–377; Kawai, op. cit., pp. 142–149.

44. The zaibatsu banks were not dissolved but they were banned from using the old zaibatsu names. Thus Mitsubishi Bank became Chiyoda Bank, Yasuda Bank became Fuji Bank, Sumitomo Bank became Osaka Bank. The Mitsui family bank had been renamed Teikoku Bank during the war so a name change was not required. Nakamura, op. cit., p. 397.

45. *Political Reorientation of Japan*, op. cit., p. 575. Statistics for the rest of the section on land reform are from Kawai, op. cit., pp. 171–174; Robert A. Feary, *The Occupation of*

Japan: Second Phase, 1948–1950 (New York: Macmillan, 1950), pp. 87–98; Ronald Dore, *Land Reform in Japan* (London: Oxford University Press, 1958), pp. 174ff.

46. Labor reform statistics come from Sheldon Garon, *The State and Labor in Modern Japan* (Berkeley: University of California Press, 1987), p. 236; Kawai, op. cit., pp. 160–170; Feary, op. cit., pp. 75–78; Royama Masamichi, *Yomigaeru Nihon* (Japan's Resurrection) (Tokyo: Chuokoron-sha, 1967), pp. 75–78, 108–114.

47. Nishi, op. cit., pp. 148, 165.

48. On educational reforms, see ibid., pp. 160 ff.; Kawai, op. cit., pp. 183–201; Feary, op. cit., pp. 33–46; John W. Hall and Richard K. Beardsley, *Twelve Doors to Japan* (New York: McGraw-Hill, 1965), pp. 419–426.

49. Yoshida, op. cit., p. 131.

50. Kyoko Inoue, *MacArthur's Japanese Constitution* (Chicago: University of Chicago Press, 1991), p. 16.

51. Ibid., pp. 33–34, 69.

52. Ibid., pp. 221, 240, 265.

53. Fujiwara, op. cit., p. 60.

54. Yoshida, op. cit., p. 75. The statistics for the 1946 election are from Fujiwara, op. cit., pp. 52–54, for the 1947 election, p. 71, and for the 1949 election, pp. 95–96.

55. Yoshida, op. cit., p. 92.

56. MacArthur, *Reminiscences*, op. cit., p. 323.

57. Disagreement between President Truman and General MacArthur intensified when the general supported pursuing an aggressive campaign against China to settle the Korean War. When MacArthur realized that President Truman was moving to end the war with a truce, he indicated his disapproval of this policy and went public in a letter to Congressman Joseph W. Martin, indicating that he favored using Chinese nationalist troops in Formosa against the mainland Chinese forces. MacArthur was challenging the president's policymaking prerogatives, so Truman decided the General had to be removed from his position. William Manchester, *American Caesar: Douglas MacArthur, 1880–1964.* (Boston: Little, Brown and Co., 1978), pp. 629ff.

CHAPTER 2

1. Shigeru Yoshida, *The Yoshida Memoirs* (Cambridge, Mass.: Houghton Mifflin, Riverside Press, 1962), p. 172. The political data in this chapter are derived primarily from Eguchi Bokuro, *Gendai no Nihon* (Contemporary Japan), vol. 32 of *Nihon no Rekishi* (Tokyo: Shogakukan, 1989); Fujiwara Akira, *Sekai no Naka no Nihon* (Tokyo: Shogakukan, 1989); Irokawa Daikichi, *Showashi to Tenno* (Tokyo: Iwanami Shoten, 1991); Matsuo Takayoshi, *Kokusai Kokka e no Shuppatsu* (Tokyo: Shueisha, 1993); Morita Minoru, *Seikai Dairan* (Turmoil in the Political World) (Tokyo: Toyo Keizai Simposha, 1993); Nakamura Takafusa, *Showashi*, vol. 2 (Tokyo: Toyo Keizai Shimposha, 1993); Oe Shinobu, *Sengo Henkaku* (Tokyo: Shogakukan, 1989); Royama Masamichi, *Yomigaeru Nihon* (Japan's Resurrection), vol. 26 of *Nihon no Rekishi* (Tokyo: Chuokoron-sha, 1968).

2. Yoshida, op. cit., p. 191.

3. The Progressive Party won 85 seats; the right-wing Socialists, 57; left-wing Socialists, 54. The Communist Party failed to gain any seats.

4. The Progressive Party won 76 seats; Hatoyama's Japan Liberal Party, 35; the left-wing Socialists, 72; the right-wing Socialists, 66; and Communists, 1.

5. This was Ishibashi Tanzan (1884–1973).

6. Charles F. Gallagher, in Ronald Bell, *The Japanese Experience* (New York: Weatherhill, 1973), p. 186.

7. In the February 1967 election the LDP dropped from 283 seats to 277, despite the increase in the number of Diet seats by 19. The Socialist Party lost 4 seats. In the February 1970 election the LDP won 288 seats; the Socialist Party dropped to 90 seats from its previous 140. The Komeito won 47 seats; the Democratic Socialist Party, 31; and the Communists, 14.

8. *New York Times,* December 17, 1993.

9. The New Liberal Party, formed by those who defected from the LDP following the Lockheed scandal, won 17 seats; the Socialists gained 5 seats to hold 123; the Democratic Socialists won 29; and the Komeito rose from 29 to 55. The Communists dropped from 38 to 17 seats.

10. The Socialists won 104; the Komeito, 57; and the Communists, 39.

11. The Socialists' total remained the same, at 107. The Komeito dropped from 57 to 33; the Democratic Socialists dropped from 35 to 32; and the Communists went from 39 to 29 seats.

12. Nakamura, op. cit., p. 648.

13. The Socialists retained the same number of seats as before, 112; the Komeito and Democratic Socialist Party increased their seats to 58 and 38, respectively. The Communist Party dropped from 29 to 8.

14. Fujiwara, op. cit., p. 265.

15. The Komeito dropped from 58 to 56 seats, and the Democratic Socialist Party dropped from 38 to 26. However, the Communists rose from 8 to 26.

16. Morita, op. cit., pp. 65–66.

17. *Japan Echo* (pub. by Japan Echo, Inc., Tokyo), Autumn 1989, p. 38.

18. The Socialist Party also made a comeback from its downturn in the past several elections and increased its 83 seats to 136. The Communist Party won only 16 seats, less than the number of seats required to propose legislation in the Diet.

19. Takeshita and Kanemaru had received $172,000 a year from construction companies. These companies rated politicians according to the political influence they could buy. Takeshita and Kanemaru were rated Super A. Miyazawa was rated A, and Kaifu, B. *New York Times,* March 28, 1993.

20. The Socialist Party also suffered at the hands of voters, winning only 70 seats compared to the 136 it had won in 1990. The Japan New Party (Hosokawa Morihiro's party) won 35 seats; the Japan Renewal Party, 55; the Harbinger Party, 13. The Komeito won 6 seats more than in the previous election, capturing 51 seats. The Communists and the Democratic Socialist Party remained more or less the same at 15 each. (In 1990 they had won 16 and 14 respectively.)

21. Previously, in the 1952 election, the right-wing Socialists had increased their seats from 30 to 57, and the left wing had risen from 16 to 54. In the 1953 election the left wing won 72 seats, and the right wing, 66. In the 1955 election the left-wing Socialists won 89 seats; the right wing won 67.

22. Allan B. Cole, George O. Totten, and Cecil H. Uyehara, *Socialist Parties in Postwar Japan* (New Haven: Yale University Press, 1966), p. 92.

23. In the 1969 election the number of Socialist Diet seats dropped from 134 to 90. In the elections held in the 1970s and 1980s the Socialists managed to win only slightly more than 100 seats. Their representation dropped to a low of 85 in 1986, and then, as political scandals beset the LDP, the Socialists won 136 seats, but they were unable to sustain their position.

24. *Japan Times Weekly,* April 25–May 1, 1994.

25. In 1976 they won only 17 seats, then went up to 39 in 1979, and then moved downward, with 29 in 1980, 26 in 1983, 26 in 1986, 16 in 1990, and 15 in 1993.

26. *Japan Times Weekly,* April 25–May 1, 1994.

27. James W. White, "Dynamics of Political Opposition," in *Postwar Japan as History,* ed. Andrew Gordon (Berkeley: University of California Press, 1993), p. 426.

28. Iwao Hoshii in Ronald Bell, *The Japanese Experience* (New York: Weatherhill, 1973), p. 75.

29. *Far Eastern Economic Review,* November 11, 1993, p. 30.

30. Murakami Hyoe and Johannes Hirschmeier, eds., *Politics and Economics in Contemporary Japan* (New York: Kodansha, 1983), p. 81.

31. *New York Times,* July 30, 1993; *Far Eastern Economic Review,* November 11, 1993, p. 30.

32. Karl van Wolferen, *The Enigma of Japanese Power* (New York: Alfred A. Knopf, 1989), p. 44.

33. *Chicago Tribune,* February 6, 1994.

34. *New York Times,* November 4, 1991.

35. Ibid.

36. *New York Times,* May 15, 1994.

37. Japan Foundation Newsletter, May 1991.

38. Wolferen, op. cit., p. 45.

CHAPTER 3

1. However, if services are included in calculating the balance of economic relations between Japan and the United States, the balance in 1993 is estimated to have been $15 billion in favor of the United States. This calculation includes payments for services in the areas of travel, transport (e.g., airline travel), information services, movies, royalties, banking, education, fees for managing construction projects, telecommunications, insurance, financial transactions, legal services, etc., according to *Intersect,* July 1994, p. 28. In 1993 Japanese tourists spent $13.7 billion in the United States, 18 percent of all foreign tourist expenditures in the United States. *New York Times,* September 11 1994. Statistics in this chapter are based primarily on *Japan, An International Comparison* (Tokyo: Keizai Koho Center), several editions; *Nippon, A Charted Survey of Japan* (Kokuseisha), editions from 1971 to 1994; *Facts and Figures of Japan* (Tokyo: Foreign Press Center), editions from 1982 to 1992; *Statistical Handbook of Japan* (Bureau of Statistics, Office of the Prime Minister), editions from 1969 to 1994; *Statistical Survey of Japan's Economy* (Tokyo: Economic and Foreign Affairs Research Association), editions from the 1980s to 1994; *White Paper on International Trade, Japan 1990* (Tokyo: Japan External Trade Association); the *New York Times, Japan Times Weekly, Far Eastern Economic Review,* and other newspapers and journals.

2. *Japan Times Weekly,* June 6–12, 1994.

3. *New York Times,* January 5 and July 7, 1994.

4. Murray Sayle, "Japan Victorious," in *New York Review of Books,* March 28, 1985, p. 36.

5. *Japan 1992: An International Comparison* (Tokyo: Keizai Koho Center, 1993), pp. 19, 55.

6. *Nippon: A Charted Survey of Japan, 1993–1994* (Tokyo: Kokuseisha, 1993), p. 332.

7. *New York Times,* June 20 and 23, 1991.

8. Robert C. Christopher. *The Japanese Mind* (New York: Linden Press, 1983), p. 174.

9. *Japan 1992: An International Comparison,* op. cit., pp. 39, 55.

10. Matsuo Takayoshi, *Kokusai Kokka e no Shuppatsu* (Tokyo: Shueisha, 1993), p. 289 ff.

11. *Japan 1992,* op. cit., p. 65.

12. *Far Eastern Economic Review,* February 28, 1991, p. 60.

13. Hugo M. Enomiya-LaSalle, in Ronald Bell, *The Japanese Experience* (New York: Weatherhill, 1973), p. 96.

14. *New York Times,* March 11, 1985.

15. *New York Times,* August 6, 1988.

16. *Nippon: A Charted Survey of Japan, 1993–1994,* op. cit., p. 93.

17. *Newsweek,* June 24, 1991.

18. *Japan 1992,* op. cit., p. 57.

CHAPTER 4

1. Nakamura Takafusa, *Showashi,* 2 vols. (Tokyo: Toyo Keizai Shimpo-sha, 1993), pp. 424–430; Theodore Cohen, *Remaking Japan* (New York: Free Press, 1987), pp. 425–428. Statistics in this chapter are derived primiarly from *Japan Almanac, 1993* (Asahi Shimbun); *Japan 1992: An International Comparison* (Tokyo: Keizai Koho Center, 1993); *Facts and Figures of Japan,* 1993 edition (Tokyo: Foreign Press Center, 1993); *Japan: A Pocket Guide, 1992* (Tokyo: Foreign Press Center, 1992); *Nippon: A Charted Survey of Japan, 1993–94* and earlier editions (Tokyo: Kokuseisha; *Statistical Handbook of Japan,* several editions, (Bureau of Statistics, Office of the Prime Minister); *White Papers of Japan, 1988–89* (Japan Institute of International Affairs); *A Key to Japan's Recovery* (Tokyo: Japan Resources Association, 1986); *Japan Statistical Yearbook, 1990* (Tokyo: Japan Statistical Association).

2. Nakamura, op. cit., p. 440.

3. Kozo Yamamura, "Behind the Made in Japan Label," in *Politics and Economics in Contemporary Japan,* ed. Murakami Hyoe and Johannes Hirschmeir (Tokyo: Kodansha, 1979), pp. 138–140.

4. An American shipbuilder, Elmer Hann, played a key role in Japan's success in rebuilding and expanding its shipbuilding industry by teaching the Japanese U.S. construction methods that were instrumental in the production of Liberty and Victory ships during the war. *New York Times,* March 16, 1990.

5. *Nippon: A Charted Survey of Japan, 1971,* pp. 58ff, 82ff.

6. Fujiwara Akira, *Sekai no Naka no Nihon* (Tokyo: Shogakukan, 1989), p. 231.

7. *Nippon: A Charted Survey, 1993,* p. 55.

8. *Japan Times Weekly,* April 4–10, 1994; *Chicago Tribune,* November 29, 1993.

9. *Nippon, A Charted Survey, 1993–94,* p. 179ff; *Japan Almanac, 1993,* p. 132.

10. *Nippon: A Charted Survey, 1993–94,* pp. 195–198.

11. See *Newsweek,* December 13, 1993 for the U.S. comeback in the computer industry. See also James Fallows, *Looking at the Sun* (New York: Pantheon Books, 1994), pp. 34–35, 48 ff., 449–450 for a discussion of the rise of the Japanese semiconductor business and the role the Japanese government played in its success. Fallows also discusses the role the U.S. government played in the ascendancy of the U.S. chip makers through its signing of the 1986 Semiconductor Trade Agreement, which called for 20 percent of the semiconductors bought in Japan to be supplied by U.S. companies by 1991. Fallows attributes U.S. success to the interaction between market forces and state intervention in the semiconductor industry.

12. The ASEAN nations include Thailand, Singapore, Malaysia, Brunei, the Philippines, and Indonesia. The NIE nations are the Republic of Korea, Taiwan, Hong Kong, and Singapore.

13. *Far Eastern Economic Review,* November 2, 1989, p. 46; *New York Times,* February 27, 1994.

14. *Intersect,* June, 1990, p. 9.

15. *Far Eastern Economic Review,* November 2, 1989, p. 46.

16. Lester Thurow sees this as being among the differences in approaches used by U.S., Japanese, and German management. Lester Thurow, *Head to Head* (New York: William Morrow, 1992), pp. 118, 149.

17. At the same time the *sokaiya* engage in blackmail and extort money from company executives by threatening to expose wrongdoings by the company or personal misconduct of executives. In recent years payoffs have been made by famous trading companies, department stores, camera companies, securities companies, and insurance companies with payoffs ranging as high as $200,000. A law was passed in 1982 to make payoffs to *sokaiya* gangs illegal by the end of 1992. Between 1982 and 1992, officials of twenty-two companies were charged with making illegal payments. *New York Times,* December 6, 1992.

18. In 1991 it was 100 to 1. Salaries for corporate heads were $18.3 million for United Air Lines; Apple Computer, $16.7 million; for Reebok International, $14.8 million. In 1993, the chairman of Chrysler Coporation received $6.79 million in salary, bonus, and stock options. He exercised stock options in the company for another $4.47 million. *New York Times,* March 18, 1994.

19. Ronald Dore in Satoshi Kamata, *Japan in the Passing Lane* (New York: Pantheon Books, 1982), p. xii.

20. *Nippon: A Charted Survey, 1993–94,* p. 63.

21. Jared Taylor, *Shadows of the Rising Sun* (New York: Quill, 1983), p. 305.

22. *Japan Times Weekly,* February 28–March 6, 1994; *New York Times,* March 3, 1993.

23. Omae Kenichi, "Zero senkei kokka" (Zero Fighter-type State), in Bungei Shunju, March 1994, p. 124.

24. Talyor, op. cit., p. 171.

25. Charles F. Gallagher, in Ronald Bell, *The Japanese Experience* (New York: Weatherhill, 1973), p. 183.

26. Frank Gibney, *Miracle by Design* (New York: Times Books, 1982), p. 161.

27. *Political Reorientation of Japan,* SCAP Government Section (Grosse Pointe, Mich.: Scholarly Press, 1968), p. 435.

28. Sheldon Garon, *The State and Labor in Modern Japan* (Berkeley: University of California Press, 1987), pp. 236–237, p. 332.

29. Fujiwara Akira, *Sekai no Naka no Nihon* (Tokyo: Shogakukan, 1989), p. 44.

30. Theodore Cohen, *Remaking Japan* (New York: Free Press, 1987), pp. 267–268.

31. Ibid., p. 271.

32. Ibid., p. 278.

33. Matsuo Takayoshi, *Kokusai Kokka e no Shuppatsu* (Tokyo: Shueisha, 1993), pp. 102–104.

34. Garon, op. cit., p. 237, p. 240; Matsuo, op. cit., p. 136.

35. Matsuo, op. cit., pp. 136–137.

36. Garon, op. cit., p. 241.

37. Andrew Gordon, "Contests for the Workplace," in Andrew Gordon, ed., *Postwar Japan as History* (Berkeley: University of California Press, 1993), p. 381.

38. *Nakamura*, op. cit., pp. 498–499.

39. Ibid., pp. 498–499.

40. Fujiwara, op. cit., p. 196.

41. On the establishment of quality control groups, see Kumazawa, *Nihon no Rodoshazo* (Images of Japanese Workers) (Tokyo: Chikuma Shobo, 1993). Translation to be published by Westview Press.

42. Fujiwara, op. cit., p. 307.

43. *Japan Almanac 1993* (Asahi Shimbun), p. 87.

44. The statistics on agriculture are primarily from *Nippon: A Charted Survey, 1993–94*, pp. 116 ff.

45. Robert J. Samuelson, in *Newsweek,* December 6, 1993.

46. *Far Eastern Economic Review,* November 26, 1992, p. 56.

47. *New York Times,* June 1, 1994.

48. Fallows, op. cit., p. 13.

CHAPTER 5

1. Statistics used in this chapter are based mainly on the sources cited in footnote 1 in Chapter 2, as well as on data published in newspapers and journals such the *New York Times,* the *Chicago Tribune,* the *Japan Times Weekly, Intersect,* the *Far Eastern Economic Review, Focus Japan* (JETRO), and *Japan Report* (Japan Information Center).

2. *Japan Times Weekly,* June 15–21, 1990.

3. National income is national product minus capital depreciation, indirect taxes, government subsidies, etc.

4. *New York Times,* May 23, 1992.

5. *Chicago Tribune,* February 6, 1994.

6. Roger Buckley, *Japan Today* (Cambridge: Cambridge University Press 1985), p. 59.

7. See Mikiso Hane, *Peasants, Rebels, and Outcastes* (New York: Pantheon Books, 1982), pp. 262–265.

8. *Japan Report,* December 1992.

9. *Intersect,* July 1989, pp. 37–38.

10. *New York Times,* December 28, 1992.

11. *Nippon: A Charted Survey of Japan, 1993–94* (Tokyo: Kokuseisha), pp. 306–307, 312.

12. *Facts and Figures of Japan,* p. 77.

13. Noda Masaaki, "Why Are Middle-Aged Men Killing Themselves," in *Japan Echo,* vol. 15, 1988, p. 25.

14. *Japan Almanac,* p. 208; Mark Schreiber, "A Nation Without Guns," *Intersect,* November 1993, pp. 10 ff.

15. *Far Eastern Economic Review,* October 14, 1993.

16. Uli Schmetzer, in the *Chicago Tribune,* November 17 and 20, 1991.

17. *New York Times,* June 15, 1992.

18. See David E. Kaplan and Alec Dubro, *Yakuza* (New York: Macmillan, 1986). See also *Intersect,* July 1987, pp. 12–13.

19. *Japan Times Weekly,* July 8–14, 1991.

20. *Far Eastern Economic Review,* December 3, 1992, p. 18.

21. Kaplan and Dubro, op. cit., pp. 78, 82, 101 ff., 116–117.

22. *New York Times,* June 15, 1992.

23. Antonin Raymond, in Ronald Bell, *The Japanese Experience* (New York: Weatherhill, 1973), p. 166.

24. Karel van Wolferen, *The Enigma of Japanese Power* (New York: Knopf, 1989), pp. 430–431.

25. Jared Taylor, *Shadows of the Rising Sun* (New York: Quill, 1983), p. 32.

26. Ibid., p. 33.

27. *Intersect,* Sept. 1987, p. 10.

28. *New York Times,* October 24, 1989.

29. 29 Miyachi Soshichi, "The Dangerous Tide of 'Soap Nationalism'," *Japan Echo,* spring 1987, p. 53.

30. Hugo M. Enomiya-LaSalle, in Bell, *The Japanese Experience,* pp. 96–97.

31. Fosco Maraini, in Bell, *The Japan Experience,* pp. 10–11.

32. *Far Eastern Economic Review,* February 18, 1993, p. 32 ff.

33. *New York Times,* August 8, 1992.

34. *Japan Times Weekly,* August 3–9, 1992, August 1–7, 1994; *Far Eastern Economic Review,* February 18, 1993, p. 32 ff.; *New York Times,* August 31, 1994. An early account of this practice was presented by Kim Il-meon in his *Tenno no Guntai to Chosenjin Ianfu* (The Emperor's Army and Korean Comfort Women) (Tokyo: San'ichi Shobo, 1976).

35. *New York Times,* October 3, 1983; *Japan Times,* July 6, 1990.

36. *New York Times,* May 2, 1990; January 11, 1991; and May 21, 1992.

37. *Japan Times Weekly,* June 3–9, 1991.

38. Donald Richie, in Bell, *The Japanese Experience,* p. 60. See also *Hiroshima and Nagasaki,* published by The Committee for the Compilation of Materials on the Damage Caused by the Atomic Bombs in Hiroshima and Nagasaki, trans. Eisei Ishikawa and David L. Swain (New York: Basic Books, 1981), pp. 462–475.

39. *New York Times,* November 5, 1986.

40. *New York Times,* April 12, 1991.

41. *Chicago Tribune,* November 17, 1991.

42. *New York Times,* April 12, 1991.

43. *Japan Times Weekly,* April 6–12, 1992.

44. David Kaplan and Alex Durbo, *Yakuza,* op. cit., p. 22.

45. Mikiso Hane, *Peasants, Rebels, and Outcastes,* op. cit., p. 153.

46. "The Reality of Buraku Discrimination in Japan" (Osaka: Buraku Kaiho Kenkyusho, 1991), p. 2.

47. *Chicago Tribune,* May 16, 1992.

48. *Buraku Liberation News,* op. cit., May 1994.

49. *Intersect,* May 1991, pp. 25–26.

50. Buraku Kaiho Kenkyusho Report, p. 9.

51. Robert Guest, "A Tale of Two Sisters," in *Far Eastern Economic Review,* July 9, 1992, p. 29.

52. *Japan Times,* July 8, 1990.

53. *Intersect,* June 1994, pp. 30–31. Much of the information on San'ya here is based on Edward B. Fowler's "San'ya: Scenes from Life at the Margins of Japanese Society," *Transactions of the Asiatic Society of Japan,* 4th series, vol. 6, 1991. See also Brett de Bary's "Sanya: Japan's Internal Colony," in Patricia Tsurumi, ed., *The Other Japan: Postwar Realities* (Armonk, N.Y.: M. E. Sharpe, 1988).

54. *Intersect,* June 1944, p. 32.

55. *New York Times,* October 11, 1990.

56. *Japan: A Pocket Guide,* 1992 edition, p. 133, and *Japan Times Weekly,* February 22, 1993.

57. Taylor, op cit., p. 198.

58. *Chicago Tribune,* May 5, 1991.

59. *Whole Earth Review,* 1990, p. 78.

60. Jane Condon, *A Half Step Behind* (New York: Dodd Mead and Co., 1985), p. 194.

61. *Intersect,* August 1989, p. 12.

62. For various estimates of the number of women in administrative positions see *Intersect,* November 1993, p. 28; *Japan Times Weekly,* December 6–12, 1993; *New York Times,* December 4, 1988. See also Susan Pharr, *Losing Face: Status Politics in Japan* (Berkeley: University of California Press, 1990), p. 62; *Facts and Figures of Japan, 1993,* p. 55.

63. Statistics in this paragraph are from *New York Times,* May 27, 1994; *Chicago Tribune,* April 2, 1993; *New York Times,* December 1, 1992; *Japan Times Weekly,* May 23–29, 1994.

64. *New York Times,* February 24, 1985.

65. *Japan Almanac,* 1993, p. 82.

66. Kumazawa Makoto, *Nihon no Rodoshazo* (Tokyo: Chikuma Shobo, 1993), pp. 232, 261–262.

67. *Japan Almanac,* 1993, p. 84, and *Japan Times Weekly,* June 6–12, 1994.

68. *New York Times,* May 27, 1994.

69. *Japan Times Weekly,* June 6–12, 1994; *Japan Almanac,* 1993, p. 84.

70. *Japan Times Weekly,* June 6–12, 1994.

71. Taylor, op. cit., p. 166.

72. *New York Times,* July 4, 1988.

73. *Chicago Tribune,* June 16, 1991.

74. *Chicago Tribune,* June 10, 1991.

75. Condon, op. cit., p. 183; *Japan: A Pocket Guide, 1992,* p. 133; *Newsweek,* January 22, 1990.

76. *PHP* (Tokyo: PHP Institute), December 1981, p. 7.

77. Toshimi Kayahi Antram, "The Programmed Path," in *Whole Earth Review,* winter 1990, pp. 78–79.

78. *Japan Report,* April 1991; *Focus Japan,* July 1992.

79. *Nichibei Times,* San Francisco, April 20, 1980.

80. Louise de Rosari, "The Perfect Woman," in *Far Eastern Economic Review,* February 10, 1994, p. 62.

81. *Chicago Tribune,* January 18, 1989.

82. *Japan Almanac,* 1993, p. 38.

83. *Nippon: A Charted Survey of Japan,* 1993–94, p. 37.

CHAPTER 6

1. From Harry Wray's (Yokohama National University) study on Japanese education (forthcoming).

2. Imamura Taketoshi, *Kyoiku Gyosei* (Educational Administration) quoted by Wray.

3. *Intersect,* May 1988, p. 11.

4. Benjamin C. Duke, *The Japanese School: Lessons for Industrial America* (New York: Praeger, 1986), pp. 165, 211.

5. *New York Times,* November 3, 1991.

6. *Japan Times Weekly,* November 1–7, 1993.

7. Matsuo Takayoshi, *Kokusai Kokka e no Shuppatsu* (Tokyo: Shueisha, 1993), pp. 276–277.

8. *Nippon: A Charted Survey of Japan, 1993–94* (Tokyo: Kokuseisha), pp. 300–304.

9. *Facts and Figures of Japan,* p. 90.

10. Ibid.; *Japan Report,* March 1989 (New York: Japan Information Center Consulate General).

11. Jared Taylor, *Shadows of the Rising Sun* (New York: Quill, 1983), p. 97.

12. See *New York Times,* April 27, 1992, for information on *jukus.*

13. A Japanese teacher, Mr. Endo, wrote on May 25, 1991, in a letter to this author, "Strangely enough, nearly half of the students in the class are asleep with their faces on the top of desks because to them school may not be where they study and discipline themselves"; Duke, op. cit., pp. 223–227.

14. *New York Times,* July 13, 1983.

15. Taylor, op. cit., p. 95.

16. Duke, op. cit., pp. 200–201.

17. Letter from Endo, May 25, 1991.

18. *New York Times,* July 11, 1983.

19. David Halberstam, "Can We Rise to the Japanese Challenge?" *Parade Magazine,* October 9, 1983. Another scientist who was frustrated in his pursuit of original research is Nishizawa Jun'ichi, who made significant discoveries in optical telecommunication but did not gain recognition in Japan until the Japanese found verification of his theories in an American science magazine. In 1983 he was awarded the Jack A. Morton Prize, regarded as the Nobel Prize in electronics. *Intersect,* March 1986, p. 15.

20. *New York Times,* May 4, 1994.

21. *Bungei Shunju,* March 1994, p. 123.

22. Robert Cutts and David Thornbrugh, "Teachers in the Firing Line," in *Intersect,* May 1988, p. 12.

23. Duke, op. cit., p. 20ff.

24. *Japan: A Pocket Guide,* pp. 125–126.

25. Jonathan Friedland, "Disconnected," in *Far Eastern Economic Review,* June 30, 1994, p. 47.

26. *Japan Times Weekly,* February 10–16, 1992.

27. *New York Times,* August 4, 1991.

28. Wray manuscript, op. cit.

29. *Japan Almanac,* p. 226.

30. *New York Times,* June 29, 1988.

31. *New York Times,* June 24, 1983.

32. Taylor, op. cit., p. 98.

33. *Far Eastern Economic Review,* June 30, 1994, p. 50.

34. *New York Times,* June 29, 1988.

35. Cutts and Thornbrugh, op. cit., p. 10.

36. Robert Scalapino, *The Japanese Communist Movement, 1920–1966* (Berkeley: University of California Press, 1967), pp. 109–111.

37. Nakamura Takafusa, *Showashi,* vol. 2 (Tokyo: Toyo Keizai Shimpo-sha, 1993), pp. 563–568; Fujiwara Akira, *Nihon no Rekishi* (Tokyo: Shogakukan, 1989), vol. 15, pp. 215–218.

CHAPTER 7

1. Nakamura Takafusa, *Showashi,* vol. 2 (Tokyo: Toyo Keizai Shimposha, 1993), pp. 415–416. Statistics in this chapter are based on *Nippon, A Charted Survey,* 1990–1991 and 1993–1994 (Tokyo: Kokuseisha); the *New York Times*; *Japan Times Weekly*; and *Far Eastern Economic Review.*

2. *New York Times,* Book Review Section, September 27, 1992, p. 28.

3. Ichiro Kawasaki, *Japan Unmasked* (Rutland, Vt.: Charles E. Tuttle, 1969), p. 21.

4. Jared Taylor, *Shadows of the Rising Sun* (New York: Quill, 1983), p. 229.

5. Donald Richie, in Ronald Bell, *The Japanese Experience* (New York: Weatherhill, 1973), p. 39.

6. Isaiah Ben-Dasan, *The Japanese and the Jews* (Tokyo: Weatherhill, 1972), pp. 180–182. The author, Yamamoto Shichihei, is actually Japanese.

7. *Kaikoku Hyakunen Kinen Bunka* (Hundredth Anniversary of the Opening of the Country), ed., *Meiji Bunka-shi* (Meiji Cultural History), 10 vols. (Tokyo: Obunsha, 1955–1958), vol. 4, pp. 433–437.

8. Maruyama Masao, *Nihon no Shiso* (Japanese Thought) (Tokyo: Iwanami Shoten, 1961), pp. 2 ff, 128 ff.

9. *Chicago Tribune,* June 16, 1991.

10. June Silla, in Ronald Bell, *The Japanese Experience,* p. 142.

11. Victor J. Koschmann, "Intellectuals and Politics," in Andrew Gordon, ed., *Postwar Japan as History* (Berkeley: University of California Press, 1993), p. 423.

12. Isaiah Ben-Dasan, op. cit., pp. 112–113, 185–188. On *Nihonjin-ron*, see Peter N. Dale, *The Myth of Japanese Uniqueness* (New York: St. Martin's Press, 1986). See also Ian Buruma, "New Japanese Nationalism," *New York Times*, April 12, 1987, p. 23 ff; Clyde Haberman, "Presumed Uniqueness of Japan," *New York Times Magazine*, August 28, 1988, pp. 39 ff.

13. Robert Jay Lifton, *History and Human Survival* (New York: Random House, 1970), pp. 26, 29–30.

14. *Chicago Tribune*, October 10, 1993.

15. *Far Eastern Economic Review*, May 7, 1992, p. 29; Nakamura, *Showashi*, op. cit., pp. 658–661.

16. Hayashi Chikio, "The National Character in Transition," in *Japan Echo*, 1988, vol. 15, pp. 8–9.

17. *Japan Almanac*, 1993, p. 240.

18. Taylor, op. cit., p. 136.

19. *American Way*, August 1, 1994, p. 60.

20. Statistics in this section are based primarily on *Facts and Figures of Japan*; *Japan, A Pocket Guide*; *Nippon: A Charted Survey, 1993–94*; and *Japan Almanac*, 1993.

21. Junichiro Tanizaki, *The Makioka Sisters*, trans. by Edward G. Seidensticker (Tokyo: Charles E. Tuttle Co., 1957), p. 216–217, p. 489.

22. Junichiro Tanizaki, "In Praise of Shadows," in *Perspective of Japan, Atlantic Monthly* supplement (New York, 1954), pp. 47–48.

23. *Japan Report*, New York Consulate General of Japan, 1968, vol. 14, nos. 20, 22.

24. Donald Keene, *Dawn to the West: Japanese Literature in the Modern Era* (New York: Henry Holt, 1984), pp. 818–819.

25. *Japan Report*, op. cit.

26. Keene, op. cit., p. 832.

27. Ibid., p. 807.

28. *Japan Report*, op. cit., January 31, 1969.

29. Masuji Ibuse, *Black Rain*, trans. by John Bester (New York: Bantam Books, 1985), introduction, p. 2.

30. Ibid. In order of quotes cited, p. 44, p. 108, p. 14 .

31. Keene, op. cit., p. 1024.

32. Osamu Dazai, *The Setting Sun*, trans. by Donald Keene (New York: New Directions, 1956), pp. 165–166.

33. Keene, op. cit., p. 1077.

34. Hiroshi Noma, *Zone of Emptiness*, trans. from the French by Bernard Frechtman (New York: World Publishing Company, 1956), pp. 47, 252.

35. Keene, op. cit., pp. 980–981.

36. Ibid., p. 978.

37. Hiroshi Noma, *Tan'nisho* (Lamenting the Deviations) (Tokyo: Chikuma Shobo, 1973), pp. 6–17.

38. Shohei Ooka, *Fires on the Plain*, trans. by Ivan Morris (London: Secker and Warburg, 1957), p. 187.

39. Keene, op. cit., p. 1216.

40. Yukio Mishima, *The Temple of the Golden Pavilion*, trans. by Ivan Morris (Rutland, Vt.: Charles E. Tuttle Co., 1959). Quotes are from p. 21, p. 47, p. 217.

41. Yukio Mishima. "Party of One: Japan, the Cherished Myths," in *Holiday,* October 1961, p. 13.

42. *New Yorker,* December 12, 1970, pp. 40–41.

43. Keene, op. cit., p. 1136.

44. Fumiko Enchi, *Waiting Years,* trans. by John Bestor (Tokyo: Kodansha International, 1971), pp. 43, 189–190.

45. Christine Chapman, "Women Writers: Three Portraits," *PHP,* November 1984, p. 40.

46. Keene, op. cit., p. 1144.

47. Ibid., p. 1150.

48. Ibid., pp. 1151–1159.

49. Chapman, op. cit., p. 44.

50. *This Kind of Woman,* ed. Yukiko Tanaka and Elizabeth Hanson (New York: Perigee Books, 1982), p. 226.

51. Translator's note in Kenzaburo Oe, *A Personal Matter,* trans. by John Nathan (New York: Grove Press, 1969), pp. viii–ix.

52. Yoshiko Yokochi Samuel, *The Life and Works of Oe Kenzaburo* (Ann Arbor, Mich.: University Microfilms International, 1981), p. 10. See also *New York Times,* October 14, 1994 on Oe's Nobel Prize award.

53. Shusaku Endo, *Silence* (New York: Taplinger, 1980), pp. 259, 281, 285.

54. A. N. Wilson, "Firmly Catholic and Firmly Japanese," *New York Times,* Book Review, July 21, 1985, p. 21.

55. Masaaki Kawanishi, "A Survey of Literature in 1983," in *Japanese Literature Today* (Japan P.E.N. Club, March, 1984), p. 1.

56. *New York Times,* Book Review section, September 27, 1992, p. 29.

57. Ibid., p. 28.

58. *New York Times,* May 12, 1993.

59. Reviewed by Michiko Kakutani, *New York Times,* January 13, 1993.

60. Banana Yoshimoto, *Kitchen,* translated by Megan Backus (New York: Washington Square Press, 1993), pp. 3, 10.

61. *New York Times,* May 17, 1993.

62. Donald Richie, *Japanese Movies* (Tokyo: Japan Travel Bureau, 1961), p. vii.

63. Ibid., p. 161.

64. *New York Times,* April 3, 1994.

65. Michael Wilmington, in *Chicago Tribune,* August 14, 1994.

66. Nagasaka Toshihisa, in *Japan Echo,* autumn, 1991, p. 87.

67. *New York Times,* December 15 and 29, 1985.

68. Quoted in Vincent Canby, "What's So Funny About Japan," *New York Times Magazine,* June 18, 1989, pp. 26 ff.

69. Nick Bornoff, "The Gentle Art of Savage Satire," in *Intersect,* July 1988, p. 29.

70. Vincent Canby, op. cit.

71. Nick Bornoff, op. cit., p. 29.

72. Antonin Raymond, in Bell, *The Japanese Experience,* p. 169.

73. *Chicago Tribune,* April 26, 1993.

74. Peter McGill, "Boxing Ando," in *Intersect,* November 1993, pp. 34–40.

75. Bernard Leach, *Hamada, Potter* (Tokyo: Kodansha International, 1975), pp. 103, 125.

76. *New York Times,* January 2, 1994.

77. *New York Times,* May 19, 1985.

78. Hideyuki Oka, *How to Wrap Five More Eggs* (New York: Weatherhill, 1975), pp. 7–13.

79. Edward Seidensticker, *This Country Japan* (Tokyo: Kodansha, 1984), p. 52.

80. Ian Buruma, *Behind the Mask* (New York: Pantheon Books, 1984), p. 36.

81. Angela Carter, in Bell, *The Japanese Experience,* p. 29.

82. Frederick L. Schodt, "Reading the Comics," *Wilson Quarterly,* summer 1985, p. 57.

CHAPTER 8

1. Jared Taylor, *Shadows of the Rising Sun* (New York: Quill, 1983), p. 58.

2. *Intersect,* February 1985, p. 9.

3. *Japan Echo,* spring 1990, p. 35.

4. *Japan Times Weekly,* May 25–29, 1994.

5. *New York Times,* May 31, 1994; August 15, 1994.

6. James Bailey, "At the Movies," *Wilson Quarterly,* summer 1985, p. 70.

7. *Japan Times Weekly,* July 8–14, 1991.

8. *Newsweek,* July 6, 1991.

9. *Chicago Tribune,* June 17, 1991.

10. Miyachi Soshichi, "The Dangerous Tide of 'Soap Nationalism'," in *Japan Echo,* spring 1987, pp. 51–54.

11. Theodore H. White, "The Danger from Japan," *New York Times Magazine,* July 28, 1985, p. 38 ff.; Ishikawa Yoshimi, in *Japan Echo,* November 1, 1987, p. 47. On Japan bashing, see John C. Campbell, "Japan Bashing: A New McCarthyism?" in *Japan Foundation Newsletter,* March, 1991.

12. Ronald E. Yates, in the *Chicago Tribune,* June 18, 1991.

13. Roger Buckley, *Japan of Today* (Cambridge: Cambridge University Press, 1985), p. 133.

14. Matsuo Takayoshi, *Kokusai Kokka e no Shuppatsu* (Tokyo: Shueisha, 1993), p. 117.

15. James Fallows, *Looking at the Sun* (New York: Pantheon Books, 1994), p. 159.

16. Matsuo, op. cit., pp. 119, 121.

17. Ibid., p. 20, 41.

18. *Japan Echo,* summer 1989, p. 11.

19. Irokawa Daikichi, *Aru Showashi* (A Showa History) (Tokyo: Chuokoron-sha, 1975), pp. 348–350.

20. Ibid., pp. 352–353.

21. Daikichi Irokawa, *The Age of Hiroshito: In Search of Modern Japan,* trans. M. Hane and John K. Urda (New York: Free Press, 1995), p. 97.

22. *Japan Echo,* summer 1989, p. 10.

23. *Bungei Shunju,* July 1993, p. 116 ff; *Japan Echo,* summer 1989, p. 14.

24. Irokawa, *Age of Hirohito,* pp. 101ff.

25. Ibid., p. 105.

26. Ibid., pp. 99–101.

27. Matsuo, op. cit., pp. 170–171.

Bibliography

GENERAL

Bell, Ronald. *The Japanese Experience.* New York: Weatherhill, 1971.

Buckley, Roger. *Japan of Today.* Cambridge: Cambridge University Press, 1990.

Cambridge Encyclopedia of Japan. Edited by Richard Bowring and Peter Konicki. Cambridge: University of Cambridge Press, 1993.

Dowers, John W. *Japan in War and Peace: Selected Essays.* New York: New Press, 1993.

———. *Empire and Aftermath: U.S. and Japanese Experience, 1978–1954.* Cambridge: Harvard University Press, 1979.

Duus, Peter, ed. *The Cambridge History of Japan, Vol. 6: The Twentieth Century.* New York: Cambridge University Press, 1988.

Fallows, James. *More Like Us.* Boston: Houghton Mifflin, 1989.

Field, Norma. *In the Realm of a Dying Emperor: A Portait of Japan at Century's End.* New York: Pantheon Books, 1991.

Gibney, Frank. *Japan: The Fragile Superpower.* New York: Norton, 1975.

Gluck, Carol, and Stephen R. Grambard, eds. *Showa, the Japan of Hirohito.* New York: Norton, 1992.

Gordon, Andrew, ed. *Postwar Japan as History.* Berkeley: University of California Press, 1993.

Grossberg, Kenneth A., ed. *Japan Today.* Philadelphia: Institute for the Study of Human Issues, 1981.

Halberstam, David. *The Reckoning.* New York: William Morrow, 1986.

Halloran, Richard. *Japan: Images and Realities.* New York: Knopf, 1969.

Hidaka, Rokuro. *The Price of Affluence: Dilemma of Contemporary Japan.* Tokyo: Kodansha, 1984.

Horsley, William. *Nippon: New Superpower Since 1945.* London: BBC Books, 1992.

Irokawa, Daikichi. *The Age of Hirohito: In Search of Modern Japan.* Translated by Mikiso Hane and John K. Urda. New York: Free Press, 1995.

Kawahara, Toshiaki. *Hirohito and His Times: A Japanese Perspective.* Tokyo: Kodansha, 1990.

Livingston, Jon, Joe Moore, and Felicia Oldfather, eds. *The Japan Reader 2: Postwar Japan, 1945 to Present.* New York: Pantheon Books, 1973.

Pyle, Kenneth B. *The Japanese Question: Power and Purpose in a New Era.* Washington, DC: AEI Press, 1992.

Reischauer, Edwin O., and Marius B. Jansen. *The Japanese Today.* Cambridge: Harvard University Press, 1995.

Seidensticker, Edward. *This Country Japan.* Tokyo: Kodansha, 1984.

Taylor, Jared. *Shadows of the Rising Sun.* New York: Quill, 1983.

Tsurumi, Shunsuke. *A Cultural History of Postwar Japan: 1945–1980.* London: Kegan Paul, 1987.

Vogel, Ezra. *Japan as Number One.* Cambridge: Harvard University Press, 1979.

Wilson, Dick. *The Sun at Noon: An Anatomy of Modern Japan.* London: Hamish Hamilton, 1986.

Wolferen, Karl Van. *The Enigma of Japanese Power.* New York: Knopf, 1989.

THE OCCUPATION YEARS

Baerwald, Hans H. *The Purge of Japanese Leaders Under the Occupation.* Berkeley: University of California Press, 1959.

Brackman, Arnold. *The Other Nuremberg: The Untold Story of the Tokyo War Crimes Trials.* New York: Morrow, 1987.

Brines, Russell. *MacArthur's Japan.* Philadelphia: Lippincott, 1948.

Buckley, Roger. *Occupation Diplomacy: Britain, the United States, and Japan, 1945–1952.* Cambridge: Cambridge University Press, 1982.

Cohen, Theodore. *Remaking Japan.* New York: Free Press, 1987.

Dore, Ronald P. *Land Reform in Japan.* London: Oxford University Press, 1959.

Fearey, Robert A. *The Occupation of Japan: Second Phase, 1948–50.* New York: Macmillan, 1950.

Feis, Herbert. *Contest Over Japan.* New York: Norton, 1967.

Gayn, Mark. *Japan Diary.* New York: W. Sloane Associates, 1948.

Hadley, Eleanor H. *Antitrust in Japan.* Princeton: Princeton University Press, 1970.

Harries, Meiron, and Susie Harries. *Sheathing the Sword: The Demilitarization of Japan.* London: Hamish Hamilton, 1987.

Harris, Sheldon H. *Factories of Death: Japan's Secret Biological Warfare Projects in Manchuria and China, 1932–45.* London: Routledge, 1994.

Hosoya, Chihiro et al., eds. *The Tokyo War Crimes Trial.* Tokyo: Kodansha International, 1986.

Inoue, Kyoko. *MacArthur's Japanese Constitution.* Chicago: University of Chicago Press, 1991.

Kawai, Kazuo. *Japan's American Interlude.* Chicago: University of Chicago Press, 1960.

MacArthur, Douglas. *Reminiscences.* New York: McGraw-Hill, 1964.

Manchester, William. *American Caesar: Douglas MacArthur.* Boston: Little, Brown, 1978.

Martin, Edwin M. *The Allied Occupation of Japan.* New York: Institute of Pacific Relations, 1948.

Minear, Richard H. *Victor's Justice: The Tokyo War Crimes Trial.* Princeton: Princeton University Press, 1971.

Nishi, Toshio. *Unconditional Democracy: Education and Politics in Occupied Japan, 1945–1952.* Stanford: Hoover Institution Press, 1982.

Perry, John Curtis. *Beneath the Eagle's Wings: Americans in Occupied Japan.* New York: Dodd Mead and Co., 1980.

Record of Proceedings of the International Military Tribunal for the Far East. Washington, DC: Library of Congress. Microfilm.

Schaller, Michael. *The American Occupation of Japan.* London: Oxford University Press, 1985.

———. *Douglas MacArthur, Far Eastern General.* London: Oxford University Press, 1989.

Schoenberger, Howard B. *Aftermath of War: Americans and Remaking of Japan, 1945–1952.* Kent, OH: Kent State University Press, 1989.

Sebald, William. *With MacArthur in Japan.* New York: Norton, 1965.

"Supreme Commander for the Allied Powers: Government Section." *Political Reorientation of Japan, Sept. 1945 to Sept. 1948: Report.* 2 vols. Westport, CN: Greenwood, 1968.

Textor, Robert B. *Failure in Japan.* Westport, CT: Greenwood, 1951.

Tsuchimochi, Gary Houichi. *Education Reform in Postwar Japan: The 1946 U.S. Education Mission.* Tokyo: University of Tokyo Press, 1993.

Ward, Robert. *Democratizing Japan: The Allied Occupation.* Honolulu: University of Hawaii Press, 1987.

Williams, Justin Sr. *Japan's Political Revolution Under MacArthur: A Participant's Account.* Tokyo: University of Tokyo Press, 1979.

FOREIGN RELATIONS

Buckley, Roger. *Occupation Diplomacy: Britain, the United States, and Japan, 1945–1952.* Cambridge: Cambridge University Press, 1982.

———. *US-Japan Alliance Diplomacy, 1945–1990.* London: Cambridge University Press, 1992.

Cheong, Sung-hwa. *The Politics of Anti-Japanese Sentiments in Korea: Japanese–South Korean Relations Under American Occupation, 1945–1952.* Westport, CT: Greenwood, 1991.

Cronin, Richard P. *Japan, the United States, and Prospects for the Asia-Pacific Century: Three Scenarios for the Future.* New York: St. Martin's Press, 1993.

Curtis, Gerald L., ed. *Japanese-American Relations in the 1970s.* New York: Columbia Books, 1970.

———, ed. *Japan's Foreign Policy After the Cold War: Coping with Change.* Armonk, NY: M. E. Sharpe, 1993.

Friedman, George, and Meredith LeBard. *The Coming War with Japan.* New York: St. Martin's Press, 1991.

Gibney, Frank. *The Pacific Century: America & Asia in a Changing World.* New York: Scribner's Sons, 1992.

Hellmann, Donald. *Japanese Foreign Policy and Domestic Politics.* Berkeley: University of California Press, 1969.

Holland, Harrison M. *Japan Challenges America: Managing an Alliance in Crisis.* Boulder: Westview Press, 1992.

Iriye, Akira. *China and Japan in the Global Setting.* Cambridge: Harvard University Press, 1992.

Jansen, Marius. *Japan and China: From War to Peace, 1894–1972.* Chicago: Rand McNally, 1975.

Johnson, Sheila K. *American Attitudes Toward Japan, 1941–1975.* Stanford: Stanford University Press, 1975.

———. *The Japanese Through American Eyes.* Stanford: Stanford University Press, 1988.

Morley, James W., ed. *Forecast for Japan: Security in the 1970s.* Princeton.: Princeton University Press, 1972.

Olson, Lawrence. *Japan in Postwar Asia.* New York: Praeger, 1970.

Passin, Herbert, ed. *The United States and Japan.* Englewood Cliffs, NJ: Prentice Hall, 1966.

ECONOMIC AND BUSINESS AFFAIRS

Bennett, John W., and Iwao Ishino. *Paternalism in the Japanese Economy: Anthropological Studies of Oyabun-Kobun Patterns.* Minneapolis: University of Minnesota Press, 1963.

Calder, Kent E. *Strategic Capitalism: Private Business and Public Purpose in Japan.* Princeton: Princeton University Press, 1993.

Caves, Richard E., and Masu Uekusa. *Industrial Organization in Japan.* Washington, DC: Brookings Institution, 1976.

Choate, Pat. *Agents of Influence.* New York: Knopf, 1990.

Christopher, Robert C. *Second to None: American Companies in Japan.* New York: Crown, 1986.

Clark, Rodney. *The Japanese Company.* New Haven: Yale University Press, 1979.

Cohen, Jerome B. *Japan's Economy in War and Reconstruction.* Minneapolis: University of Minnesota Press, 1949.

———. *Japan's Postwar Economy.* Bloomington: Indiana University Press, 1958.

Denison, Edward E., and William K. Chung. *How Japan's Economy Grew So Fast.* Washington, DC: Brookings Institution, 1976.

Dore, Ronald. *British Factory—Japanese Factory.* Berkeley: University of California Press, 1973.

———. *Taking Japan Seriously.* Stanford: Stanford University Press, 1987.

Emmott, Bill. *The Sun Also Sets: Why Japan Will Not Be Number One.* London: Simon and Schuster, 1989.

Fallows, James. *Looking at the Sun: The Rise of the New East Asian Economic System and Political System.* New York: Pantheon Books, 1994.

Farley, Miriam S. *Aspects of Japan's Labor Problems.* New York: Day, 1950.

Fingleton, Eamonn. *Blindside: Why Japan Is Still on Track to Overtake the U.S. by 2000.* New York: Houghton Mifflin, 1995.

Fucini, Joseph, and Suzy Fucini. *Working for the Japanese: Inside Mazda's American Auto Plant.* New York: Free Press, 1992.

Gerlach, Michael L. *Alliance Capitalism: The Social Organization of Japanese Business.* Berkeley: University of California Press, 1992.

Gibney, Frank. *Miracle by Design: The Real Reasons Behind Japan's Economic Success.* New York: Times Books, 1982.

Gordon, Andrew. *The Evolution of Labor Relations in Japan's Heavy Industry, 1853–1955.* Cambridge: Harvard University Press, 1985.

Halliday, Jon. *A Political History of Japanese Capitalism.* New York: Pantheon Books, 1975.

Hirschmeier, Johannes, et al. *Politics and Economics in Contemporary Japan.* Tokyo: Kodansha, 1979.

Hirschmeier, Johannes, and Tsunehiko Yui. *The Development of Japanese Business, 1600–1973.* Cambridge: Harvard University Press, 1975.

Johnson, Chalmers. *MITI and the Japanese Miracle: The Growth of Industrial Policy 1925–1975.* Stanford: Stanford University Press, 1985.

Kamata, Satoshi. *Japan in the Passing Lane.* New York: Pantheon Books, 1982.

Klein, Lawrence, and Kazushi Ohkawa. *Economic Growth: The Japanese Experience Since the Meiji Era.* Homewood, IL: R. D. Irwin, 1968.

Levine, Solomon B., and Hiroshi Kawada. *Human Resources in Japanese Industrial Development.* Princeton: Princeton University Press, 1980.

Lockwood, William W., ed. *The State and Economic Enterprise in Japan.* Princeton: Princeton University Press, 1965.

Marsh, Robert, and Hiroshi Mannari. *Modernization and the Japanese Factory.* Princeton: Princeton University Press, 1976.

Morishima, Michio. *Why Has Japan "Succeeded"? Western Technology and the Japanese Ethos.* London: Cambridge University Press, 1982.

Murakami, H., and J. Hirschmeier. *Politics and Economics in Contemporary Japan.* Tokyo: Kodansha, 1983.

Nishiguchi, Toshihiro. *Strategic Industrial Sourcing: The Japanese Advantage.* London: Oxford University Press, 1993.

Ohkawa, Kazushi, and Henry Rosovsky. *Japanese Economic Growth.* Stanford: Stanford University Press, 1973.

Okimoto, Daniel I. *Japan's Economy: Coping with Change in the International Environment.* Boulder: Westview Press, 1982.

Okimoto, Daniel I., and Thomas P. Rohlen, eds. *Inside the Japanese System: Readings on Contemporary Society and Political Economy.* Stanford: Stanford University Press, 1988.

Okita, Saburo. *The Developing Economies of Japan.* Tokyo: University of Tokyo Press, 1981.

Ouchi, William G. *Theory Z: How American Business Can Meet the Japanese Challenge.* Reading, MA: Addison-Wesley, 1981.

Ozaki, Robert. *The Control of Imports and Foreign Capital in Japan.* New York: Praeger, 1972.

Pascale, Richard T., and Anthony C. Athos. *The Art of Japanese Management.* New York: Simon and Schuster, 1981.

Patrick, Hugh, ed. *Japanese Industrialization and Its Social Consequences.* Berkeley: University of California Press, 1976.

Patrick, Hugh, and Henry Rosovsky, eds. *Asia's New Giant: How the Japanese Economy Works.* Washington, D. C.: Brookings Institution, 1976.

Prestowitz, Clyde V., Jr. *Trading Places: How We Are Giving Our Future to Japan and How to Reclaim it.* New York: Basic Books, 1990.

Reading, Brian. *Japan: The Coming Collapse.* New York: Harper Business, 1992.

Richardson, Bradley M., and Taizo Ueda, eds. *Business and Society in Japan: Fundamentals for Businessmen.* New York: Praeger, 1981.

Taira, Koji. *Economic Development and the Labor Market in Japan.* New York: Columbia University Press, 1970.

Thurow, Lester C. *Head to Head: The Coming Economic Battle Among Japan, Europe, and America.* New York: William Morrow, 1992.

———. *The Management Challenge: The Japanese View.* Cambridge: MIT Press, 1987.

Wood, Christopher. *The Bubble Economy.* New York: Atlantic Monthly, 1992.

Woronoff, Jon. *Inside Japan, Inc.* Rutland, VT: Tuttle, 1982.

————. *The Japanese Business Mystique: The Reality Behind the Myth.* Chicago: Probus Publishing, 1992.

————. *Japan's Commercial Empire.* New York: M. E. Sharpe, 1984.

Yamamura, Kozo. *Economic Policy in Postwar Japan.* Berkeley: University of California Press, 1967.

————, ed. *Japan's Economic Structure: Should It Change?* Seattle: Society for Japanese Studies, 1990.

Yoshino, Michael. *Japan's Management System.* Cambridge: MIT Press, 1968.

Ziemba, William T., and Sandra L. Schwartz. *Power Japan: How and Why the Japanese Economy Works.* Chicago: Probus, 1992.

POLITICAL AFFAIRS

Allinson, Gary, and Yasunori Sone, eds. *Political Dynamics in Contemporary Japan.* Ithaca: Cornell University Press, 1993.

Apter, David E., and Nagayo Sawa. *Against the State.* Cambridge: Harvard University Press, 1984.

Baerwald, Hans H. *Japan's Parliament: An Introduction.* London: Cambridge University Press, 1974.

Behr, Edward. *Hirohito: Behind the Myth.* New York: Villard Books, 1989.

Boyer, Paul. *By the Bomb's Early Light.* New York: Pantheon Books, 1985.

Braw, Monica. *The Atomic Bomb Suppressed: American Censorship in Occupied Japan.* Armonk, NY: M. E. Sharpe, 1991.

Burks, Ardath. *Japan: A Postindustrial Power.* Boulder: Westview Press, 1991.

Butow, Robert J. C. *Japan's Decision to Surrender.* Stanford: Stanford University Press, 1954.

Campbell, John Creighton. *How Policies Change: The Japanese Government and the Aging Society.* Princeton: Princeton University Press, 1992.

Colbert, Evelyn S. *Left Wing in Japanese Politics.* New York: Institute of Pacific Relations, 1952.

Craig, William. *The Fall of Japan.* New York: Dial, 1967.

Crump, Thomas. *The Death of an Emperor.* New York: Oxford University Press, 1989.

Curtis, Gerald L. *Election Campaign Japanese Style.* New York: Columbia University Press, 1971.

————. *The Japanese Way of Politics.* New York: Columbia University Press, 1988.

Dower, John W. *Empire and Aftermath: Yoshida Shigeru and the Japanese Experience, 1878–1954.* Cambridge: Harvard University Press, 1979.

Feis, Herbert. *Japan Subdued: The Atomic Bomb and the End of the War in the Pacific.* Princeton: Princeton University Press, 1961.

Finn, Richard B. *Winners in Peace: MacArthur, Yoshida, and Postwar Japan.* Berkeley: University of California Press, 1992.

Hardacre, Helen. *Shinto and the State, 1869–1988.* Princeton: Princeton University Press, 1989.

Henderson, Dan Fenno, ed. *The Constitution of Japan: Its First Twenty Years, 1947–1967.* Seattle: University of Washington, 1968.

Hersey, John. *Hiroshima.* New York: Knopf, 1946.

Hoyt, Edwin P. *Hirohito: The Emperor and the Man.* New York: Praeger, 1992.

Inoguchi, Takeshi, and Daniel I. Okimoto, eds. *The Political Economy of Japan, Volume 2: The Changing International Context.* Stanford: Stanford University Press, 1988.

Johnson, Chalmers. *Conspiracy at Matsukawa.* Berkeley: University of California Press, 1972.

Kanda, Mikio, ed. *Widows of Hiroshima: The Life Stories of Nineteen Peasant Wives.* New York: St. Martin's Press, 1980.

Kataoka, Tetsuya, ed. *Creating Single-Party Democracy: Japan's Postwar Political System.* Stanford: Hoover Institution, 1990.

Kersten, Rikki. *Democracy in Postwar Japan: Maruyama Masao and the Search for Autonomy.* London: Routledge, 1995.

Koh, B. C. *Japan's Administrative Elite.* Berkeley: University of California Press, 1989.

Kubota, Akira. *Higher Civil Servants in Postwar Japan: Their Social Origins, Educational Backgrounds, and Career Patterns.* Princeton: Princeton University Press, 1970.

Kumon, Shumpei, and Henry Rosovsky, eds. *The Political Economy of Japan, Volume 3: Cultural and Social Dynamics.* Stanford: Stanford University Press, 1992.

Langer, Paul F. *Communism in Japan: A Case of Political Naturalization.* Stanford: Hoover Institution, 1972.

Large, Stephen. *Emperor Hirohito and Showa Japan: A Political Biography.* London: Routledge, 1992.

Mainichi Daily News Staff. *Fifty Years of Light and Dark: The Hirohito Era.* Tokyo: Mainichi Newspaper, 1975.

Masumi, Junnosuke. *Contemporary Politics in Japan.* Translated by Lonny E. Carlile. Berkeley: University of California Press, 1995.

Nakamura, Masanori. *The Japanese Monarchy: Ambassador Joseph Grew and the Making of the "Symbol Emperor System."* Translated by Herbert P. Bix et al. Armonk, NY: M. E. Sharpe, 1992.

Pempel, J. T. *Policy and Politics in Japan: Creative Conservatism.* Philadelphia: Temple University Press, 1982.

Pharr, Susan J. *Losing Face: Status Politics in Japan.* Berkeley: University of California Press, 1990.

Richardson, Bradley M. *Political Culture of Japan.* Berkeley: University of California Press, 1974.

Scalapino, Robert A. *The Japanese Communist Movement, 1920–1966.* Berkeley: University of California Press, 1967.

Scalapino, Robert A., and Junnosuke Masumi. *Parties and Politics in Contemporary Japan.* Berkeley: University of California Press, 1962.

Shiroyama, Saburo. *War Criminal: The Life and Death of Hirota Koki.* Translated by John Bester. Tokyo: Kodansha, 1977.

Steiner, Kurt. *Local Government in Japan.* Stanford: Stanford University Press, 1965.

Stockwin, James Arthur A. *The Japanese Socialist Party and Neutralism.* London: Cambridge University Press, 1968.

Takeda, Kyoko. *The Dual Image of the Japanese Emperor.* New York: New York University Press, 1989.

Thayer, Nathaniel B. *How the Conservatives Rule Japan.* Princeton: Princeton University Press, 1969.

Thurston, Donald R. *Teachers and Politics in Japan.* New York: Columbia University Press, 1973.

Upham, Frank K. *Law and Social Change in Postwar Japan.* Cambridge: Harvard University Press, 1987.

Vogel, Ezra F., ed. *Modern Japanese Organization and Decision Making.* Berkeley: University of California Press, 1975.

Weinstein, Martin E. *Japan's Postwar Defense Policy, 1947–1968.* New York: Columbia University Press, 1971.

Wyden, Peter. *Day One: Before Hiroshima and After.* New York: Simon and Schuster, 1984.

Yamamura, Kozo, and Yasukichi Yasuba, eds. *The Political Economy of Japan, Volume I: The Domestic Transformation.* Stanford: Stanford University Press, 1987.

Yanaga, Chitoshi. *Big Business in Japanese Politics.* New Haven: Yale University Press, 1968.

Yoshida, Shigeru. *The Yoshida Memoirs.* Translated by Kenichi Yoshida. Boston: Houghton Mifflin, 1962.

STATUS OF WOMEN

Bernstein, Gail. *Haruko's World: A Japanese Farm Woman and Her Community.* Stanford: Stanford University Press, 1983.

Brinton, Mary C. *Women and the Economic Miracle: Gender and Work in Postwar Japan.* Berkeley: University of California Press, 1992.

Condon, Jane. *Japanese Women in the Eighties: Half a Step Behind.* New York: Dodd Mead, 1985.

Cook, Alice, and Haruko Hayashi. *Women in Japan: Discrimination, Resistance and Reform.* Ithaca: Cornell University Press, 1980.

Fujioka, Wake A., comp. and trans. *Women's Movement in Postwar Japan.* Honolulu: East-West Center, 1968.

Hunter, Janet, ed. *Japanese Women Working.* London: Routledge, 1993.

Iwao, Sumiko. *The Japanese Woman: Traditional Image and Changing Reality.* New York: Free Press, 1993.

Lam, Alice C. L. *Women and Japanese Management: Discrimination and Reform.* London: Routledge, 1992.

Lebra, Joyce, et al. *Women in Changing Japan.* Stanford: Stanford University Press, 1976.

Lebra, Takie Sugiyama. *Japanese Women: Constraint and Fulfillment.* Honolulu: University Press of Hawaii, 1984.

———. *Above the Clouds: Status Culture of the Modern Japanese Nobility.* Berkeley: University of California Press, 1993.

Morley, John David. *Pictures from the Water Trade.* New York: Harper and Row, 1985.

Pharr, Susan. *Political Women in Japan.* Berkeley: University of California Press, 1981.

Robins-Mowry, Dorothy. *The Hidden Sun: Women of Modern Japan.* Boulder: Westview Press, 1983.

Sievers, Sharon. *Flowers in Salt: The Beginning of Feminine Consciousness in Modern Japan.* Stanford: Stanford University Press, 1983.

Smith, R. J., and E. L. Wiswell. *Women of Suye-Mura.* Chicago: University of Chicago Press, 1982.

Trager, James. *Letters from Sachiko: A Japanese Woman's View of Life in the Land of Economic Miracle.* New York: Atheneum, 1982.

SOCIAL ISSUES

Allinson, Gary. *Suburban Tokyo*. Berkeley: University of California Press, 1979.

Bailey, Jackson H. *Ordinary People, Extraordinary Lives: Political and Economic Change in a Tohoku Village*. Honolulu: University Press of Hawaii, 1991.

Barker, Rodney. *Hiroshima Maidens: A Study of Courage, Compassion, and Survival*. New York: Viking, 1985.

Beardsley, Richard K., John W. Hall, and Robert Ward. *Village Japan*. Chicago: University of Chicago Press, 1959.

Boronoff, Michael. *Pink Samurai: Love, Marriage, and Sex in Contemporary Japan*. New York: Pocket Books, 1991.

Buruma, Ian. *Behind the Mask*. New York: Pantheon Books, 1984.

Cole, Robert C. *Japanese Blue Collar*. Berkeley: University of California Press, 1971.

DeVos, George. *Social Cohesion and Alienation: Minorities in the United States and Japan*. Boulder: Westview Press, 1992.

———. *Socialization for Achievement: The Cultural Psychology of the Japanese*. Berkeley: University of California Press, 1972.

DeVos, George, and Hiroshi Wagatsuma. *Japan's Invisible Race: Caste in Culture and Personality*. Berkeley: University of California Press, 1966.

DeVos, George, and William Witherall. *Japan's Minorities: Burakumin, Koreans, Ainus, and Okinawans*. Claremont, NY: Minority Rights Group, 1983.

Doi, Takeo. *Amae, the Anatomy of Dependence*. Tokyo: Kodansha, 1974.

Dore, Ronald P., ed. *Aspects of Social Change in Modern Japan*. Princeton: Princeton University Press, 1967.

———. *City Life in Japan: A Study of a Tokyo Ward*. Berkeley: University of California Press, 1958.

———. *Shinohata: A Portrait of a Japanese Village*. London: Allen Lane, 1978.

Fukutake, Tadashi. *Japanese Rural Society*. Translated by R. P. Dore. London: Oxford University Press, 1967.

Garon, Sheldon. *The State and Labor in Modern Japan*. Berkeley: University of California Press, 1987.

Hachiya, Michihiko. *Hiroshima Diary*. Translated and edited by Warner Wells. Chapel Hill: University of North Carolina Press, 1955.

Hilger, M. Inez. *Together with the Ainu: A Vanishing People*. Norman: University of Oklahoma Press, 1971.

Ishida, Takeshi. *Japanese Society*. New York: Random House, 1971.

Kaplan, David, and Alex Dubro. *Yakuza*. New York: Macmillan, 1986.

Kayano, Shigeru. *Our Land Was a Forest: An Ainu Memoir*. Translated by Kyoko Selden and Lili Selden. Boulder: Westview Press, 1994.

Kosaka, Masataka. *100 Million Japanese: The Postwar Experience*. Tokyo: Kodansha, 1972.

Koschmann, J. Victor, ed. *Authority and the Individual in Japan*. Tokyo: University of Tokyo Press, 1978.

Krauss, Ellis, Thomas Rolen, and Patricia Steinhoff, eds. *Conflict in Japan*. Honolulu: University Press of Hawaii, 1984.

Lebra, Takie Sugiyama. *Japanese Patterns of Behavior*. Honolulu: University Press of Hawaii, 1976.

——, ed. *Japanese Social Organization*. Honolulu: University Press of Hawaii, 1992.

Lee, Changsoo, and George DeVos. *Koreans in Japan: Ethnic Conflict and Accommodation*. Berkeley: University of California Press, 1982.

Lifton, Robert Jay. *Death in Life: Survivors of Hiroshima*. New York: Random House, 1967.

Maraini, Fosco. *Japan: Patterns of Continuity*. Tokyo: Kodansha, 1971.

——. *Meeting with Japan*. New York: Viking, 1959.

Minear, Richard, ed. and trans. *Hiroshima: Three Witnesses*. Princeton: Princeton University Press, 1990.

——, ed. *Through Japanese Eyes*. New York: Praeger, 1974.

Mishima, Akio. *Bitter Sea: The Human Cost of Minamata Disease*. Tokyo: Kosei Publishing Co., 1992.

Mitchell, Richard M. *The Korean Minority in Japan*. Berkeley: University of California Press, 1967.

Moeran, Brian. *Okubo Diary: Portrait of a Japanese Valley*. Stanford: Stanford University Press, 1985.

Moore, Charles A., ed. *The Japanese Mind: Essentials of Japanese Philosophy and Culture*. Honolulu: University Press of Hawaii, 1967.

Nagai, Takashi. *The Bells of Nagasaki*. Translated by William Johnston. Tokyo: Kodansha, 1974.

Nakane, Chie. *Japanese Society*. Berkeley: University of California Press, 1970.

Ohnuki-Tierney, Emiko. *Illness and Culture in Contemporary Japan: An Anthropological View*. London: Cambridge University Press, 1984.

Plath, David W. *Long Engagement: Maturity in Modern Japan*. Stanford: Stanford University Press, 1980.

——, ed. *Work and Life Course in Japan*. Albany, NY: State University of New York Press, 1983.

Robertson, Jennifer. *Native and Newcomer: Making and Remaking a Japanese City*. Berkeley: University of California Press, 1991.

Rohlen, Thomas O. *For Harmony and Strength: Japanese White-Collar Organization in Anthropological Perspective*. Berkeley: University of California Press, 1974.

Singer, Kurt. *Mirror, Sword, and Jewel*. Tokyo: Kodansha, 1981.

Smith, Robert J. *Kurusu, A Japanese Village, 1951–1975*. Stanford: Stanford University Press, 1978.

——. *Japanese Society*. London: Cambridge University Press, 1983.

Sumii, Sue. *The River with No Bridge*. Translated by Susan Wilkinson. Rutland, VT: Tuttle, 1990.

Tanaka, Stefan. *Japan's Orient: Rendering Pasts into History*. Berkeley: University of California Press, 1993.

Tobin, Joseph J. *Re-Made in Japan: Everyday Life and Consumer Taste in a Changing Society*. New Haven: Yale University Press, 1992.

Tsurumi, Kazuko. *Social Change and the Individual: Japan Before and After Defeat in World War II*. Princeton: Princeton University Press, 1970.

Tsurumi, Patricia, ed. *The Other Japan: Postwar Realities*. Armonk, NY: M. E. Sharpe, 1988.

Vogel, Ezra F. *Japan's New Middle Class: The Salary Man and His Family in a Tokyo Suburb*. Berkeley: University of California Press, 1963.

White, James W. *The Sokagakkai and Mass Society.* Stanford: Stanford University Press, 1970.

INTELLECTUAL AND CULTURAL ISSUES

Anderson, Joseph L., and Donald Richie. *The Japanese Film: Art and Industry.* Princeton: Princeton University Press, 1982.

Aoki, Michiko Y., and Margaret B. Dardess, eds. *As the Japanese See It.* Honolulu: University of Hawaii Press, 1981.

Bailey, Jackson, ed. *Listening to Japan.* Berkeley: University of California Press, 1988.

Ben-Dasan, Isaiah. *The Japanese and the Jews.* New York: Weatherhill, 1972.

Benedict, Ruth. *The Chrysanthemum and the Sword: Patterns of Japanese Culture.* Boston: Houghton Mifflin, 1946.

Christopher, Robert C. *The Japanese Mind: The Goliath Explained.* New York: Linden Press, 1983.

Craig, Albert M. *Japan: A Comparative View.* Princeton: Princeton University Press, 1979.

Cummings, William A. *Education and Equality in Japan.* Princeton: Princeton University Press, 1980.

Dale, Peter N. *The Myth of Japanese Uniqueness.* New York: St. Martin's Press, 1986.

Duke, Benjamin C. *Education and Leadership for the Twenty-first Century: Japan, America, and Britain.* New York: Praeger, 1991.

———. *Japanese Schools: Lessons for Industrial America.* New York: Praeger, 1986.

———. *Japan's Militant Teachers: A History of the Left-Wing Teachers' Movement.* Honolulu: University Press of Hawaii, 1973.

Havens, Thomas R. H. *Artists and Patrons in Postwar Japan: Dance, Music, Theatre, and the Visual Arts, 1955–1980.* Princeton: Princeton University Press, 1982.

Hirano, Kyoko. *Mr. Smith Goes to Tokyo: Japanese Cinema Under the American Occupation, 1945–1952.* Washington, D. C.: Smithsonian Press, 1992.

Iriye, Akira. *The Chinese and Japanese.* Princeton: Princeton University Press, 1980.

Leach, Bernard. *Hamada, Potter.* Tokyo: Kodansha, 1975.

Maruyama, Masao. *Thought and Behaviour in Modern Japanese Politics.* Edited by Ivan Morris. London: Oxford University Press, 1963.

Miyoshi, Masao. *Off Center: Power and Culture Relations Between Japan and the United States.* Cambridge: Harvard University Press, 1991.

Nolletti, Arthur Jr., and David Desser. *Reframing Japanese Cinema: Authorship, Genre, History.* Bloomington: Indiana University Press, 1992.

Piovesana, Gino K. *Recent Japanese Philosophical Thought, 1862–1962.* Tokyo: Enderle, 1963.

Richie, Donald. *The Film of Akira Kurosawa.* Berkeley: University of California Press, 1984.

———. *Japanese Movies.* Tokyo: Japan Travel Bureau, 1961.

White, Merry. *The Japanese Educational Challenge.* New York: Free Press, 1986.

———. *The Japanese Overseas: Can They Go Home Again?* New York: Free Press, 1988.

———. *The Material Child: Coming of Age in Japan and America.* Berkeley: University of California Press, 1994.

Yoshino, Kosaku. *Cultural Nationalism in Contemporary Japan: A Sociological Inquiry.* London: Routledge, 1992.

LITERATURE

Copeland, Rebecca L. *The Sound of the Wind: The Life and Works of Uno Chiyo.* Honolulu: University Press of Hawaii, 1992.

Keene, Donald. *Dawn to the West: Japanese Literature in the Modern Era.* Fiction. New York: Henry Holt, 1984.

———. *Dawn to the West: Japanese Literature in the Modern Era. Poetry, Drama, Criticism.* New York: Henry Holt, 1984.

———. *Landscapes and Portraits: Appreciation of Japanese Culture.* Tokyo: Kodansha, 1971.

Lyons, Phyllis I. *The Saga of Dazai Osamu.* Stanford: Stanford University Press, 1985.

Miyoshi, Masao. *Accomplices of Silence: The Modern Japanese Novel.* Berkeley : University of California Press, 1974.

Nakamura, Mitsuo. *Contemporary Japanese Fiction, 1926–1968.* Tokyo: Kokusai Bunka Shinkosha, 1969.

Nathan, John. *Mishima: A Biography.* New York: Little, Brown, 1974.

Rimer, J. Thomas. *A Reader's Guide to Japanese Literature from the Eighth Century to the Present.* Tokyo: Kodansha, 1988.

Scott-Stokes, Henry. *The Life and Death of Yukio Mishima.* New York: Ballantine, 1985.

Seidensticker, Edward G. *Kafu the Scribbler.* Stanford: Stanford University Press, 1965.

Ueda, Makoto. *Modern Japanese Poets and the Nature of Literature.* Stanford: Stanford University Press, 1983.

———. *Modern Japanese Writers and the Nature of Literature.* Stanford: Stanford University Press, 1976.

Zebroski, Claire. *Japanese Women Writers in English Translation: An Annotated Bibliography.* New York: Garland, 1989.

MODERN JAPANESE FICTION TRANSLATED INTO ENGLISH

Abe, Kobo. *The Box Man.* Translated by E. Dale Saunders. New York: Putnam Perigee, 1981.

———. *Friends.* Translated by Donald Keene. New York: Grove, 1969.

———. *Secret Rendezvous.* Translated by Juliet W. Carpenter. New York: Knopf, 1979.

———. *Three Plays by Abe Kobo.* Translated by Donald Keene. New York: Columbia University Press, 1993.

———. *Woman in the Dunes.* Translated by E. Dale Saunders. New York: Knopf, 1964.

Akutagawa, Ryunosuke. *Japanese Short Stories.* Translated by Takashi Kojima. New York: Liveright, 1961.

———. *Rashomon and Other Stories.* Translated by Takashi Kojima. New York: Liveright, 1952.

Arai, Shinya. *Shoshaman: A Tale of Corporate Japan.* Translated by Chieko Mulhern. Berkeley: University of California Press, 1991.

Arishima, Takeo. *A Certain Woman.* Translated by Kenneth Strong. Tokyo: Tokyo University Press, 1978.

Ariyoshi, Sawako. *The Doctor's Wife.* Translated by Wakako Hironaka and Ann Siller Kostant. Tokyo: Kodansha, 1978.

———. *The River Ki.* Translated by Mildred Tahara. Tokyo: Kodansha, 1982.

———. *The Twilight Years.* Translated by Mildred Tahara. Tokyo: Kodansha, 1984.

Dazai, Osamu. *No Longer Human.* Translated by Donald Keene. New York: New Directions, 1958.

———. *The Setting Sun.* Translated by Donald Keene. New York: New Directions, 1956.

Enchi, Fumiko. *Mask.* Translated by Juliet Winters Carpenter. New York: Random House, 1983.

———. *The Waiting Years.* Translated by John Bester. Tokyo: Kodansha, 1981.

Endo, Shusaku. *The Samurai.* Translated by Van C. Gessel. New York: Harper and Row, 1980.

———. *Silence.* Translated by William Johnston. New York: Taplinger Publishing Co., 1980.

———. *Stained Glass Elegies.* Translated by Van C. Gessel. New York: Dodd, Mead, and Co., 1984.

———. *Wonderful Fool.* Translated by Francis Mathy. New York: Harper and Row, 1974.

Gessel, Van C., and Tomone Matsumoto, eds. *The Showa Anthology: Modern Japanese Short Stories.* New York: Kodansha, 1985.

Ibuse, Masuji. *Black Rain.* Translated by John Bester. Tokyo: Kodansha, 1980.

Kawabata, Yasunari. *The Old Capital.* Translated by J. Martin Hofman. Berkeley: North Point Press, 1987.

———. *Snow Country.* Translated by Edward G. Seidensticker. New York: Knopf, 1956.

———. *The Sound of the Mountain.* Translated by Edward G. Seidensticker. New York: Berkeley Publishing Corp., 1970.

———. *Thousand Cranes.* Translated by Edward G. Seidensticker. New York: Knopf, 1958.

Keene, Donald, ed. and trans. *Modern Japanese Literature from 1868 to the Present Day.* New York: Grove, 1956.

———, ed. and trans. *The Old Woman, the Wife, and the Archer: Three Modern Japanese Short Novels.* New York: Viking, 1961.

Lippit, Noriko M., and Kyoko Seldon, eds. and trans. *Stories by Contemporary Japanese Women Writers.* New York: M. E. Sharpe, 1982.

Mishima Yukio. *After the Banquet.* Translated by Donald Keene. New York: Knopf, 1963.

———. *Confessions of a Mask.* Translated by Meredith Weatherby. New York: New Directions, 1958.

———. *Five Modern No Plays.* Translated by Donald Keene. New York: Knopf, 1957.

———. *The Sound of Waves.* Translated by Meredith Weatherby. New York: Knopf, 1956.

———. *Sun and Steel.* Translated by John Bester. Tokyo: Kodansha, 1970.

———. *The Temple of the Golden Pavilion.* Translated by Ivan Morris. New York: Knopf, 1959.

Mori, Ogai. *The Wild Geese.* Translated by Kingo Ochiai and Sanford Goldstein. Rutland, VT.: Tuttle, 1959.

Morris Ivan, ed. *Modern Japanese Stories: An Anthology.* Tokyo and Rutland, VT: Tuttle, 1962.

Murakami, Haruki. *Dance, Dance, Dance.* Translated by Alfred Birnbaum. Tokyo: Kodansha, 1994.

———. *The Elephant Vanishes.* Translated by Alfred Birnbaum. New York: Knopf, 1993.

———. *The Hard-Boiled Wonderland and the End of the World.* Translated by Alfred Birnbaum. Tokyo: Kodansha, 1991.

———. *A Wild Sheep.* Translated by Alfred Birnbaum. Tokyo: Kodansha, 1989.

Nagatsuka, Takashi. *The Soil.* Translated by Ann Waswo. London: Routledge, 1989.

Natsume, Soseki. *Grass on the Wayside.* Translated by Edwin McClellan. Chicago: University of Chicago Press, 1969.

———. *Kokoro.* Translated by Edwin McClellan. Chicago: Regnery, 1967.

———. *Light and Darkness.* Translated by V. H. Viglielmo. Honolulu: University of Hawaii Press, 1970.

———. *Wayfarer.* Translated by Beong-cheon Yu. Detroit: Wayne State University Press, 1967.

Noma, Hiroshi. *Zone of Emptiness.* Translated by Bernard Frechtman. Cleveland: World, 1956.

Oe, Kenzaburo. *A Personal Matter.* Translated by John Nathan. New York: Grove, 1968.

———. *The Pinch Runner Memorandum.* Translated by Michiko N. Wilson and Michael K. Wilson. Armonk, NY: M. E. Sharpe, 1993.

———. *The Silent Cry.* Translated by John Bester. Tokyo: Kodansha, 1981.

———. *Teach Us to Outgrow Our Madness.* Translated by John Bester. New York: Grove, 1977.

Ooka, Shohei. *Fires on the Plain.* Translated by Ivan Morris. New York: Knopf, 1957.

Osaragi, Jiro. *Homecoming.* Translated by Brewster Horowitz. New York: Knopf, 1955.

Rabbits, Crabs, Etc.: Stories by Japanese Women Writers. Translated by Phyllis Biernbaum. Honolulu: University of Hawaii Press, 1989.

Shimazaki, Toson. *Broken Commandment.* Translated by Kenneth Strong. Tokyo: University of Tokyo Press, 1974.

Tanaka, Yukiko, and Elizabeth Hanson, trans. *This Kind of Woman: Ten Stories by Japanese Women Writers, 1960–1976.* Stanford: Stanford University Press, 1982.

Tanizaki, Junichiro. *The Key.* Translated by Howard Hibbett. New York: Knopf, 1971.

———. *The Makioka Sisters.* Translated by Edward G. Seidensticker. New York: Knopf, 1957.

———. *Seven Japanese Tales.* Translated by Howard Hibbett. New York: Knopf, 1963.

———. *Some Prefer Nettles.* Translated by Edward G. Seidensticker. New York: Knopf, 1955.

Tsushima, Yuko. *Child of Fortune.* Translated by Geraldine Harcourt. Tokyo: Kodansha, 1983.

———. *The Shooting Gallery.* Translated by Geraldine Harcourt. New York: Pantheon Books, 1988.

Ueda, Makoto, ed. *The Mother of Dreams and Other Short Stories: Portrayals of Women in Modern Japanese Fiction.* Tokyo: Kodansha International, 1986.

Yamasaki, Toyoko. *Bonchi.* Translated by Harue and Travis Summersgill. Honolulu: University of Hawaii Press, 1982.

Yoshimoto, Banana. *Kitchen.* Translated by Megan Backus. New York: Washington Square Press, 1993.

———. *Lizard.* Translated by Ann Sherif. New York: Grove Press, 1994.

———. *NP.* Translated by Ann Sherif. New York: Grove Press, 1993.

About the Book and Author

It has been fifty years since Japan admitted defeat and accepted the terms of the Potsdam Declaration following World War II. At the time, Japan was in a shambles, its imperial dream shattered, and its people reduced to scrounging for sufficient food to stay alive. Yet over the last half century, Japan has remade itself and emerged as one of the leading economic powers in the world. How did Japan achieve this success, and what has this remarkable rebirth meant for the Japanese people?

In *Eastern Phoenix*, Mikiso Hane closely examines historical factors that have contributed to Japan's postwar development politically, economically, socially, and culturally. Beginning with the occupation by U.S. forces under General Douglas MacArthur, Hane shows how American reforms and initiatives combined with the political actions of subsequent Japanese leaders to create a country able to forge ahead economically while retaining many traditional aspects of prewar Japanese society.

In addition to presenting a narrative overview of important events since 1945, *Eastern Phoenix* provides insight into the evolution of Japan's foreign relations, internal effects of prosperity on Japanese society, and problems that remain despite extraordinary progress. The book critically examines such media-hot topics as education, environmental degradation, organized crime, racial and class discrimination, the Japanese work ethic, and the role of women in society. To provide useful context for student readers, Hane frequently punctuates his discussion by contrasting Japanese statistics with those of the United States. The book also excels in examining how artists and writers have grappled with Japan's rapidly evolving contemporary history, and Hane points the reader toward books and films that can shed additional light on Japanese perceptions of the past fifty years.

Mikiso Hane is professor of history at Knox College and is author of *Pre-Modern Japan* (Westview, 1991) and *Modern Japan* (Westview, 1992).

Index